CREATIVE COOKING
POULTRY

TABLE OF CONTENTS

INTRODUCTION

Poultry is one of the most versatile cooking ingredients and can be used to create an endless variety of delicious dishes. In addition to being a tasty part of many meals, poultry is a great source of protein, B vitamins, and other valuable nutrients. **Creative Cooking** contains hundreds of recipes for everything from soup to main courses and this section contains some hints that make preparing and storing poultry easy.

◆ Fresh chicken and game should be refrigerated at home for no more than two days after it is purchased. Fresh turkey can be refrigerated a little longer, but should be kept no longer than one week. The poultry should be tightly wrapped and stored in the coldest part of the refrigerator. If fresh poultry will not be used within two days, it is best to either cook or freeze it.

◆ Cooked poultry can be stored in the refrigerator a little bit longer than uncooked poultry. Another advantage to cooking poultry before using it is that it can easily be stored and reheated in a sauce or combined into a recipe.

◆ Uncooked poultry can be stored for a longer period of time if it is frozen instead of refrigerated. To freeze, wrap uncooked poultry tightly in aluminum foil or moisture-proof paper. When properly wrapped, whole chickens and turkeys can be frozen for up to one year, while whole ducks and geese can be stored frozen for up to six months. However, cut-up pieces and parts of poultry cannot be stored as long as whole birds. They can only be frozen for up to six months, whereas giblets should be frozen for no more than three months.

◆ Keep poultry cold when thawing and never thaw at room temperature. For best results, place poultry on a dish and thaw in the refrigerator. For quicker thawing, defrost in a microwave oven or leave poultry in its storage bag and place in very cold water until thawed. However, be sure to change the cold water every thirty minutes if using this thawing method.

◆ All whole turkeys and chickens contain a packet of giblets carefully tucked into the body cavity. The giblets are actually the heart, liver, and gizzards, and the packet should be removed before proceeding with any recipe. Some recipes call for them as ingredients, but if not, giblets may be used to make soups, stuffings, or gravies. Whole birds, after giblets are removed, and poultry parts should always be rinsed thoroughly before cooking.

◆ For many people, stuffing is the best part of a poultry meal. There are a number of ways to make stuffing, and certainly any stuffing recipe can be personalized by adding or changing ingredients.

- Bread crumbs are a key ingredient in any stuffing recipe. Packaged bread crumbs can be purchased quite easily and are available seasoned or unseasoned. Certain recipes specify fresh bread crumbs as a stuffing ingredient. It's easy to make fresh bread crumbs, but remember, it's best to start with slightly hardened bread rather than fresh bread.

- When a recipe calls for the stuffing to be cooked inside the bird, add the stuffing just before the bird will be cooked. Remember, don't stuff the poultry cavity more than two-thirds full since the stuffing will expand as it cooks. Additionally, by leaving a little room, the tail end of the bird will be easier to close after it has been stuffed.

- The nutritional value of poultry can be increased by simply removing any skin before cooking. The skin contains a lot of fat and prepared without skin, chicken and turkey have less fat than do beef, pork, or lamb.

- The flavor of poultry can easily be enhanced through seasonings. After washing the bird, dry the flesh and rub seasonings all over outside and inside of it. Try experimenting with favorite herbs and spices to create a new twist to a great recipe or an exciting new dish.

- Another way to enhance flavor and maintain moisture is to marinate, or soak, the poultry in a seasoned liquid. It is very important, however, that the poultry is refrigerated while it soaks in the marinade.

    – Do not reuse the marinade. Be sure it is discarded after the poultry has soaked in it.

- Be sure that the poultry is cooked thoroughly, making sure that all the pink is gone from the meat. Take care to wash all surfaces and utensils, including hands, that may have come in contact with the uncooked meat in hot, soapy water.

The recipes in this book are designed to be easy-to-follow and simple-to-prepare and should provide many hours of eating enjoyment. So go ahead. Enjoy!

GREAT STARTERS: APPETIZERS AND SOUPS

Baked Chicken Wings

Serves 8 to 12

1 (10-ounce) bottle soy sauce
2 teaspoons freshly grated ginger
  or 1 teaspoon powdered ginger
2 cloves garlic, peeled and minced
1/3 cup brown sugar
1 teaspoon dark mustard
24 whole chicken wings
Garlic powder

1. Mix soy sauce, ginger, minced garlic, brown sugar, and mustard together. Blend well. Marinate chicken wings in this mixture for at least 2 hours. Drain wings, reserving marinade.
2. Preheat oven to 350 degrees.
3. Place wings in baking dish and bake 1 1/2 hours, turning and basting with marinade frequently. Discard any leftover marinade.
4. Sprinkle with garlic powder and broil wings for 1 or 2 minutes, until crispy. Remove from heat, and serve.

Chicken Wings in Oyster Sauce

Serves 4

3 tablespoons peanut oil
2 cloves garlic, peeled and halved
8 chicken wings
2 tablespoons soy sauce
3 tablespoons oyster sauce
1 tablespoon sugar
1/2 cup water

1. Preheat wok or frying pan; coat bottom and sides with oil. Rub bottom and sides of pan with garlic, then discard garlic.

2. Disjoint wings into 3 pieces. Add middles and tips of wings to pan and brown on both sides. Add rest of wing pieces and brown also.
3. Mix soy and oyster sauces together and add to chicken wings. Stir in sugar and water. Cover pan and cook over medium-low heat for 15 minutes. Transfer to serving dish, and serve.

Nutty Chicken Wings

Serves 4

1 cup finely chopped dry roasted,
  skinless peanuts
1/2 cup fine dry bread crumbs
1 1/4 teaspoons salt
1/2 teaspoon poultry seasoning
Freshly ground black pepper
8 chicken wings
1/4 cup chicken broth

1. Preheat oven to 400 degrees.
2. Mix peanuts, bread crumbs, and seasonings together.
3. Dip chicken wings in broth, then in peanut mixture until coated all over.
4. Place in single layer on foil-lined pan. Bake for 40 minutes, or until tender. Do not turn chicken during baking. Remove from oven, and serve.

Lemon-Flavored Chicken Wings

Serves 4

12 to 16 chicken wings
2 cups lemon juice
1 teaspoon salt
1/2 teaspoon black pepper
4 tablespoons butter or margarine

1. Cut off wing tips and freeze to use at a later time for soup. Combine

lemon juice, salt, and pepper. Pour over wings and marinate for 4 hours, stirring occasionally to ensure that wings are well coated on all sides.
2. Drain wings on paper towels. Place on foil-lined broiler pan and rub each piece liberally with butter. Broil for 15 to 20 minutes, or until crisp; or, place in 500 degree F oven for 30 to 45 minutes. Place in serving dish, and serve.

Crusty Chicken Wings

Serves 10 to 12

18 to 24 chicken wings
1/4 cup vegetable oil
1 cup bread crumbs
1/2 teaspoon salt
1/4 teaspoon pepper
1/4 teaspoon oregano
2 teaspoons curry powder

1. Disjoint chicken wings into 3 pieces. Freeze wing tips to use at a later time for soup. Brush remaining wing pieces with oil.
2. Combine bread crumbs, salt, pepper, oregano, and curry powder in plastic bag. Add 6 wing pieces at a time; shake well to coat evenly. Repeat process until all wing pieces are well coated.
3. Preheat oven to 400 degrees.
4. Place chicken in large baking dish. Bake 35 minutes, or until chicken is crusty outside and tender inside. Serve hot.

Sweet and Sour Chicken Wings

Serves 10 to 12

18 to 24 whole chicken wings
¹/₂ teaspoon salt
¹/₂ teaspoon freshly ground black
** pepper**
¹/₄ teaspoon garlic powder
¹/₂ cup ketchup
¹/₂ cup vinegar
¹/₂ cup sugar
¹/₂ cup water

1. Preheat oven to 350 degrees.
2. Season wings with salt, pepper, and garlic powder. Place in shallow baking dish and bake for 15 minutes.
3. In small saucepan, combine ketchup, vinegar, sugar, and water. Heat, stirring, until well blended.
4. Brush sauce over wings and continue to bake for 20 to 30 minutes, or until wings are tender. Remove from oven, and serve.

Wings in Sesame Sauce

Serves 6 to 8

12 to 16 chicken wings
¹/₂ cup vegetable oil
¹/₂ cup sherry
4 tablespoons soy sauce
4 tablespoons lemon juice
2 cloves garlic, peeled and minced
3 tablespoons toasted sesame
** seeds**

1. Disjoint wings into 3 pieces. Freeze wing tips to use at a later time for soup. Place wings in large bowl or dish.
2. Place remaining ingredients in food processor or blender and process until smooth. Pour mixture over wings and marinate, refrigerated, for 1 hour. Turn wings after 30 minutes.
3. Preheat broiler. Line broiler pan with foil. Place wings on pan and broil 5 inches from heat for 7 minutes on each side; baste each side once with marinade. Discard remaining marinade. Place wings in serving dish, and serve.

Fried Chicken Balls

Serves 4

¹/₂ large onion, chopped
1 cup water
1 cup finely chopped uncooked
** chicken**
1 tablespoon sugar
1¹/₂ tablespoons sweet rice wine
** (or 1 tablespoon sherry mixed**
** with ¹/₂ tablespoon sugar)**
2 tablespoons soy sauce
1 egg
2 tablespoons oil
3¹/₂ tablespoons water
1¹/₂ tablespoons sherry

1. Soak chopped onion in water for 10 minutes; squeeze out moisture.
2. Combine onion, chicken, sugar, rice wine, 1 tablespoon soy sauce, and egg. Stir until thoroughly mixed. Roll into bite-size balls.
3. Heat oil in pan. Add chicken balls and brown on all sides.
4. Combine water, sherry, and remaining soy sauce. Pour over chicken balls and cook until liquid is almost evaporated. Remove from heat, and serve.

Chicken Kebabs

Serves 6

³/₄ pound boneless chicken
** breasts, skinned**
2 teaspoons lemon juice
1 teaspoon curry powder
¹/₈ teaspoon chili powder or
** cayenne pepper**
¹/₄ teaspoon salt
Oil for deep-frying
Lemon wedges

Batter
1 cup flour
1 cup water
¹/₂ teaspoon salt
1 teaspoon baking powder
¹/₂ teaspoon curry powder
¹/₂ cup dry bread crumbs

1. Rub chicken breasts with a mixture of lemon juice, curry powder, chili powder or cayenne, and salt. Place on a plate, cover, and set aside at room temperature for 10 minutes.

2. Cut chicken meat into 12 strips and thread each strip onto a bamboo or metal skewer.
3. Mix all batter ingredients except bread crumbs together in a bowl. Spread bread crumbs on a plate.
4. Heat deep oil to moderately hot in wok or large frying pan. Dip chicken into batter, then coat with bread crumbs. Deep-fry kebabs about 2¹/₂ minutes, or until cooked through and golden brown.
5. Serve hot with lemon wedges.

Chicken Hedgehogs

Serves 8 to 10

¹/₂ pound boneless chicken
** breasts, cubed**
1 egg
3 tablespoons flour
2 teaspoons sugar
2 teaspoons light soy sauce
2 teaspoons dry sherry
¹/₄ teaspoon salt
1¹/₄ cups rice vermicelli

1. Place chicken cubes in food processor container. Add egg, flour, sugar, soy sauce, sherry, and salt. Process until smooth paste forms, then transfer mixture to bowl. Cover with plastic wrap and chill for 20 minutes.
2. Form mixture into 18 balls. Finely crush vermicelli. Roll each ball in vermicelli until well coated.
3. Heat about 1 inch of cooking oil in wok or frying pan. Fry 6 chicken balls at a time for 3 minutes, or until golden and thoroughly cooked. Drain well and serve warm with soy sauce or sweet chili sauce.

Salted Chicken

Serves 12

1¹/₂ tablespoons plus ¹/₄ teaspoon
** salt**
1 tablespoon rice wine
2 small slices fresh ginger or
** ¹/₄ teaspoon ginger powder**
2 scallions, cut into 1-inch pieces
1 (2¹/₂- to 3- pound) chicken
Cold water
1 cup chicken broth
1 tablespoon sesame oil

1. Mix 1½ tablespoons salt, wine, ginger, and scallions together. Rub chicken with mixture and let stand 30 minutes.

2. Place chicken in stock pot. Cover with cold water and bring to a boil. Reduce heat and simmer for 40 minutes. Remove chicken from pot and refrigerate until chilled.

3. Remove skin from chicken. Cut chicken meat into pieces approximately 2 inches long and 1 inch wide.

4. Mix broth, ¼ teaspoon salt, and sesame oil together. Pour over chicken. Garnish with additional scallions, if desired.

Chicken-Liver Paté

Makes 1¼ cups

2 tablespoons butter
½ pound chicken livers
2 hard-boiled eggs, peeled
1 (3-ounce) package cream cheese, softened
1 tablespoon finely chopped parsley
¾ teaspoon salt
⅛ teaspoon pepper
1 tablespoon cognac

1. Melt butter in medium frying pan. Add chicken livers and cook over medium heat for 3 to 5 minutes, stirring occasionally. Drain.

2. Chop livers and eggs in food grinder or food processor.

3. With wooden spoon, stir cream cheese until light and fluffy. Mix cheese into liver mixture along with remaining ingredients. Refrigerate for several hours.

4. Serve with hot toast or crackers.

Oriental Chicken Livers

Serves 4

8 ounces chicken livers, halved
⅓ cup soy sauce
½ cup flour
2 tablespoons oil
1 small onion, sliced

1. Marinate chicken livers overnight in soy sauce.

2. Remove livers from marinade and dredge in flour; discard marinade. Heat oil in frying pan. Add livers and onion slices; saute until tender and brown. Transfer to serving dish, and serve hot.

Chicken Livers Wrapped in Bacon

Serves 4

8 slices bacon, halved
1 pound chicken livers, halved
1 (6-ounce) can whole water chestnuts, drained and sliced
2 tablespoons oil

1. Lay bacon slices flat. Place chicken livers and water chestnuts on top of bacon. Roll up and secure with toothpicks.

2. Heat oil in frying pan or wok. Add chicken liver roll-ups and cook until bacon is browned. Remove from pan, and serve.

Chicken Liver Teriyaki

Serves 4

1 pound chicken livers
½ cup soy sauce
½ cup sugar
½ cup water
Soy sauce or mustard for dipping

1. Marinate livers in mixture of soy sauce, sugar, and water for at least 2 hours.

2. Place livers on skewers. Cook on hibachi or charcoal grill until done.

3. Serve livers with soy sauce or mustard for dipping.

Turkey-Oyster Balls

Makes 3 dozen

¼ cup oysters
½ cup cooked turkey
½ teaspoon ground mace
¼ teaspoon pepper

¼ teaspoon celery salt
2 tablespoons heavy whipping cream
¼ cup blanched almonds, finely chopped
¼ cup dry bread crumbs
Oil for deep-frying

1. Heat oysters in a small quantity of water for 3 minutes. Remove oysters from pan and reserve 1 tablespoon of liquid.

2. Grind oysters and turkey in food grinder or food processor.

3. Add mace, pepper, celery salt, reserved oyster liquid, cream, and egg yolks to ground oysters and turkey. Stir until well blended. Spoon into jar with lid or covered bowl and chill for 24 hours.

4. Form turkey mixture into small balls. Combine almonds and bread crumbs, then roll balls in this mixture until well coated.

5. Deep-fry balls in oil until golden brown. Serve hot on toothpicks.

Curried Turkey Canapés

Makes 3 dozen

1 cup finely chopped cooked turkey
¼ cup mayonnaise
1 tablespoon finely chopped chutney
1 tablespoon chutney juice
1 teaspoon curry powder
Square, round, and triangular crackers
Hard-boiled egg slices
Shredded coconut
Chopped peanuts

1. Blend turkey, mayonnaise, chutney and juice, and curry powder together well. Spread on different kinds of crackers.

2. Top some crackers with egg slices, some with shredded coconut, and some with chopped peanuts. Arrange on a platter, and serve.

Chicken Stock

Makes 2 quarts

1 cooked chicken carcass, chopped into pieces
Chicken giblets, if available
1 onion, sliced
2 carrots, peeled and sliced
2 stalks celery
1 bay leaf
1 sprig thyme or ¼ teaspoon dried thyme
6 sprigs parsley
6 black peppercorns
Salt to taste
water

1. Place chopped chicken carcass and bones into stock pot with giblets, if available. Add vegetables, herbs, and seasonings. Add enough water to completely cover carcass. Slowly bring to a boil, then simmer for 3 hours, or until well flavored.
2. Strain and cool. If not using at once, pour into ice-cube trays and freeze. Remove from trays, wrap individually, then return to freezer and use as needed in other recipes.

Curried Chicken Soup

Serves 4

2 tablespoons butter or margarine
2 teaspoons curry powder
1½ tablespoons flour
3 cups chicken stock
Paprika to taste
Salt to taste
1 egg yolk
¼ cup milk
½ cup chopped cooked chicken
Chopped chives, for garnish

1. Melt butter or margarine in saucepan. Add curry power and flour, whisking constantly over low heat for 3 minutes. Gradually add stock, whisking until boiling. Reduce heat. Season with paprika and salt.
2. Combine egg yolk with milk. Add to soup, whisking constantly until soup is slightly thickened.
3. Add chicken and simmer until thoroughly heated. Serve sprinkled with chopped chives.

Egg Drop Soup

Serves 4 to 6

4 scallions
5 cups chicken stock
6 small mushrooms, finely sliced
2 cups shredded cooked chicken
2 eggs
Salt and pepper to taste
2 teaspoons soy sauce

1. Finely slice scallions and reserve green part for garnish. Heat chicken stock until boiling. Add mushrooms and scallions; cook for 2 to 3 minutes. Add chicken to soup.
2. Beat eggs slightly with a little salt and pepper.
3. Stir soup well. Pour beaten eggs slowly and steadily into soup, stirring constantly, so that eggs remain in shreds. Cook for 1 or 2 minutes, until egg is set. Add soy sauce and serve in soup bowls, sprinkled with reserved green slices of scallions.

Chicken Noodle Soup

Serves 4 to 6

6 cups chicken stock
¼ cup thin egg noodles
Salt and pepper to taste
2 tablespoons finely chopped parsley

1. Bring stock to boil in large saucepan. Add noodles, stirring constantly. Boil noodles following package directions. Stir frequently to prevent noodles from sticking to pan. Add salt and pepper.
2. Serve hot in soup mugs, liberally sprinkled with finely chopped parsley.

Chicken Giblet Soup

Serves 4 to 6

2 packages chicken giblets, thawed if frozen
1 large onion, sliced
2 carrots, sliced
2 stalks celery, sliced
Chicken carcass (if available)
5 cups water
4 sprigs parsley, 1 sprig thyme, and 1 bay leaf, tied together
6 black peppercorns
Salt to taste
1 chicken bouillon cube, optional
2 tablespoons butter
1½ tablespoons flour

Garnish
1 tablespoon butter
2 chicken livers
2 tablespoons chopped parsley

1. Wash chicken giblets, removing livers. Set livers aside for garnish.
2. Place giblets, onion, carrots, celery, and carcass if available into large saucepan. Add water, herbs, peppercorns, and a little salt. Bring slowly to a boil, skimming as needed. Reduce heat and simmer for 1 to 1½ hours, or until vegetables are tender and giblets well cooked. Add bouillon cube if needed for flavoring.
3. Remove carcass from soup. Strain soup into another saucepan.
4. Melt butter in small saucepan and whisk in flour. Add a few tablespoons hot chicken stock, whisking constantly until smooth; then whisk mixture into remaining stock. Bring to a boil, stirring constantly. Simmer for 3 to 4 minutes.
5. Melt 1 tablespoon butter in frying pan and saute chicken livers for 5 to 8 minutes, depending on their size. Chop livers roughly and divide among soup bowls before pouring on hot soup. Sprinkle with chopped parsley.

Chicken Gumbo

Serves 4 to 6

2 tablespoons butter
1 large onion, chopped
1½ cups canned tomatoes,
    chopped
½ green pepper, seeded and
    chopped
¾ cup canned okra
½ cup rice
5 cups chicken stock
Salt and pepper to taste
2 cups chopped cooked chicken
1 tablespoon chopped parsley
1 teaspoon tarragon
½ cup cooked corn, optional

1. Melt butter in large saucepan. Saute onion for 5 to 6 minutes, or until tender but not brown. Add tomatoes, green pepper, okra, and rice. Pour in stock, mixing thoroughly. Season with salt and pepper. Bring to a boil, cover, and simmer for 20 minutes, or until rice is cooked.
2. Add chicken, herbs, and corn if desired. Reheat and serve hot.

Cock-a-Leekie Soup

Serves 6

1 small stewing chicken
1 onion
4 carrots, 2 whole, 2 sliced
1 stalk celery
8 cups water
6 peppercorns
1 bay leaf
1 sprig thyme or ¼ teaspoon dried
    thyme
6 sprigs parsley
1 sprig tarragon or ¼ teaspoon
    dried tarragon
Salt to taste
4 leeks, white part only
2 tablespoons rice
1 tablespoon chopped parsley

1. Place chicken, onion, 2 whole carrots, celery, and water in stock pot. Add peppercorns, herbs, and salt. Simmer for 1½ to 2 hours, or until chicken is very tender. Remove chicken and strain stock. Cut chicken meat off bones and refrigerate until ready to use.

2. Slice white part of leeks and soak in salted water for 5 minutes to remove grit. Drain well. Place leeks and sliced carrots in large saucepan and add 6 cups strained chicken stock. Bring to a boil, then cover and simmer for 10 minutes. Add rice and continue simmering for 15 minutes.
3. Add parsley and some cooked chicken meat to soup. Simmer until heated through. Serve soup hot with whole-wheat bread. The remaining chicken meat can be used for another dish.

Chicken
and Ham Soup

Serves 4 to 6

4 to 5 cups clear chicken stock
    or consomme
½ cup white wine
2 slices mild cooked ham, fat
    removed and shredded
½ cup lightly cooked fresh peas
1 tablespoon chopped fresh
    tarragon or ½ teaspoon
    dried tarragon
1 tablespoon chopped parsley

1. Heat chicken stock in large saucepan. When stock is hot, add wine, ham, peas, and tarragon.
2. Sprinkle with parsley, and serve.

Chicken Chowder

Serves 5 to 6

1 chicken carcass and giblets
7½ cups cold water
1 onion, sliced
3 stalks celery with leaves,
    chopped
1 carrot, diced
1¼ teaspoons salt
1 pound cream-style corn
1 hard-boiled egg, finely
    chopped
1 cup flour
1 egg, beaten

1. Break up chicken carcass and place in large kettle with giblets. Add water, onion, celery, carrot, and 1 teaspoon salt. Cover and simmer for 1½ hours, skimming soup as needed.
2. Remove carcass pieces and giblets from pot. Cut off all chicken meat and return it to pot.
3. Add corn and simmer for 10 minutes. Add chopped hard-boiled egg. Adjust seasoning.
4. Sift flour and ¼ teaspoon salt together. Stir in beaten egg with a fork until mixture resembles cornmeal. Drop by spoonfuls into soup a few minutes before serving.

Country-Style
Chicken Soup

Serves 6

1 small stewing chicken or
    6 backs and necks
8 cups water
1 cup chopped celery
1 cup sliced carrots
1 medium onion, sliced
1 small bay leaf or ½ teaspoon
    dill seeds
1 large potato, diced
2 teaspoons salt
¼ teaspoon pepper

1. Place chicken and water in large pot; simmer for 1 to 1½ hours.
2. Add celery, carrots, onion, and bay leaf or dill; simmer 30 minutes longer. Remove chicken meat from carcass. Refrigerate chicken and vegetables in broth overnight.
3. Skim off excess fat. Add potato, salt, and pepper to soup. Simmer 30 minutes, and serve.
4. You can use leftover chicken to make this soup and omit refrigerating overnight.

Hungarian Chicken Soup

Serves 4

1 (2¹/₄-pound) chicken,
  cut into serving pieces
6¹/₄ cups water
1 bunch parsley
1 teaspoon salt
2 cups cooking apples,
  peeled and thinly sliced
1 teaspoon honey
1 tablespoon uncooked oats
¹/₂ cup sour cream
1 egg yolk, optional

1. Place chicken and 6 cups water in large pot. Bring to a boil, then reduce heat. Simmer 30 minutes, skimming soup as needed.
2. Chop parsley leaves and set aside. Add parsley stalks and salt to broth. Simmer for 50 minutes more.
3. Place apples, remaining ¹/₄ cup water, and honey in covered saucepan and cook gently until apples are just soft.
4. Remove parsley stalks and chicken pieces from broth. Remove skin and bones; dice chicken meat.
5. Toast oats on baking sheet in 400 degree oven until light brown. Stir oatmeal into sour cream, then add mixture to soup. Simmer for 5 minutes. Add diced chicken and apple slices to soup and simmer just until chicken and apple slices are heated through. Remove from heat.
6. If desired, beat egg yolk with 2 tablespoons of hot soup. Stir mixture into soup until soup thickens. Sprinkle with chopped parsley, and serve.

Spicy Chicken Soup

Serves 4

1 pound chicken giblets
6 cups water
1 teaspoon salt
1 (10-ounce) package frozen
  soup vegetables, such as
  carrots, peas, and corn
1 tablespoon butter
1 onion, finely chopped
¹/₂ pound boneless chicken
  breasts, cut into thin
  strips
¹/₂ cup sliced mushrooms
1 tablespoon curry powder
¹/₈ teaspoon cayenne pepper
Finely chopped chives for
  garnish

1. Place giblets in large saucepan, cover with water, and bring to a boil. Simmer for 30 minutes, skimming soup as needed. Add salt and soup vegetables. Simmer for 30 minutes more.
2. Melt butter in heavy frying pan. Saute onion and chicken gently, stirring frequently, until both are tender. Add mushrooms and saute 1 minute longer. Stir in curry powder and cayenne pepper.
3. Strain chicken broth over chicken strips and vegetables; discard giblets. Garnish with chopped chives.

Sapporo Chicken Soup

Serves 4

1¹/₄ pounds boneless chicken
  breasts, cubed
2 tablespoons coconut oil
1 small white radish, cut into
  julienne strips
1 small carrot, cut into julienne
  strips
1 cup potatoes, cut into julienne
  strips
1 leek, white part only, cut into
  julienne strips
1 cup green beans, cut into
  julienne strips
4 cups chicken bouillon
5 tablespoons soy sauce
2 teaspoons honey

¹/₈ teaspoon salt
1 teaspoon green peppercorns
¹/₄ pound cooked, shelled and
  deveined shrimp

1. Saute chicken cubes in hot coconut oil until tender. Add vegetable strips and saute a few minutes longer, stirring constantly.
2. Heat chicken bouillon and pour onto vegetables. Cover pan and simmer for 15 minutes. Season with soy sauce, honey, salt, and green peppercorns.
3. Add shrimp and reheat over low heat for 1 minute. Remove from heat, and serve.

Chicken Consommé with Tiny Dumplings

Serves 4

1 pound boneless chicken breasts,
  skin removed
2 shallots, peeled and finely
  chopped
1 teaspoon salt
¹/₈ teaspoon white pepper
¹/₈ teaspoon thyme
²/₃ cup fine bread crumbs
1 tablespoon chopped parsley
1 egg
¹/₄ cup light cream
4 cups chicken bouillon
1¹/₄ cups frozen peas

1. Grind chicken meat in meat grinder or food processor. Mix ground chicken with shallots, salt, pepper, thyme, bread crumbs, parsley, and egg. Add just enough cream to make a workable, not too stiff mixture.
2. Place bouillon and peas in large saucepan. Bring to a boil, then reduce heat and simmer gently.
3. Shape chicken mixture into little dumplings, using 2 teaspoons dipped in cold water. Put dumplings into simmering bouillon; cook gently for 10 minutes.
4. Serve soup immediately.

Chicken and Rice Soup

Serves 4

2 tablespoons butter or margarine
2 carrots, sliced
2 stalks celery, sliced
1/2 cup chopped green pepper
1 small onion, chopped
4 cups chicken broth or stock,
  preferably homemade
1/4 cup uncooked long-grain rice
1 1/2 cups chopped cooked chicken
1 large tomato, skinned and
  chopped
Salt and pepper to taste
1/2 cup frozen peas

1. Melt butter in large saucepan. Add carrots, celery, green pepper, and onion. Saute 6 minutes, stirring occasionally.
2. Add chicken broth, rice, chicken, tomato, salt, and pepper. Simmer for 20 minutes. Add peas, stirring well. Simmer for 5 minutes longer, or until heated through. Remove from heat and serve piping hot.

Balnamoon Skink

Serves 6

1 (3-pound) chicken
6 cups water
2 teaspoons salt
1/2 teaspoon pepper
1 celery root, cubed
1 leek, sliced
1 large carrot, sliced
2 tablespoons chopped parsley
1 1/4 cups frozen peas
1/4 teaspoon ground mace
2 egg yolks
1/2 cup heavy whipping cream
2 cups shredded leaf lettuce or
  outer leaves of an iceberg
  lettuce

1. Place chicken, water, salt, and pepper in Dutch oven. Cover and bring to a boil over moderate heat. Skim as needed. Reduce heat and simmer for 1 hour.
2. Add celery root, leek, and carrot to soup; simmer for 15 minutes longer.
3. Remove chicken from broth and cool slightly. Remove skin and bones,

then dice chicken meat. Return diced chicken to soup. Add parsley, peas, and mace; simmer for 8 to 10 minutes.
4. Beat egg yolks and cream together well in small bowl. Add 2 tablespoons hot soup to cream mixture, stirring constantly. Slowly add cream mixture to soup. Stirring constantly, cook over very low heat for 3 minutes.
5. Ladle soup into serving bowls. Sprinkle each bowl with shredded lettuce.

Lemon-Curry Chicken Soup

Serves 4 to 6

6 tablespoons rice
8 cups chicken stock
4 eggs
1/4 cup lemon juice
1/2 teaspoon curry powder
1 tablespoon parsley

1. Bring rice and chicken stock to a boil in large pot. Reduce heat and simmer for 20 minutes, or until rice is tender.
2. Beat eggs, lemon juice, and curry powder together. Add 3 tablespoons hot stock to egg mixture, stirring until well mixed. Add egg mixture to soup. Simmer, stirring constantly, for 5 minutes more.
3. Ladle soup into serving bowls, sprinkle with parsley, and serve.

Chicken Soup with Chinese Vegetables

Serves 4 to 6

6 cups chicken broth
1/2 cup bean sprouts
1/4 cup thinly sliced water
  chestnuts
1 scallion, minced
1/2 cup sliced bok choy

3 Chinese mushrooms, soaked,
  drained, and sliced
1/2 cup snow pea pods
1/2 cup diced cooked chicken
2 teaspoons soy sauce
1 tablespoon sherry
Pepper to taste

1. Place chicken broth in soup pot and bring to a boil. Add vegetables and chicken; simmer for 1 minute.
2. Add soy sauce, sherry, and pepper to soup. Simmer until heated through. Serve at once.

Chicken Velvet Soup

Serves 6

1 cooked boneless chicken
  breast, minced
1 teaspoon salt
2 egg whites, beaten until stiff
  peaks form
3 cups chicken broth
1 cup canned cream-style corn,
  drained
1 tablespoon cornstarch
2 tablespoons cold water
1 teaspoon sherry

1. Combine minced chicken and salt; fold into egg whites.
2. Place chicken broth in large saucepan and bring to a boil. Add corn, cornstarch mixed with cold water, and sherry. Cook for 2 minutes over low heat.
3. Add chicken mixture to soup. Bring to a boil, then remove from heat and serve.

Chicken and Vegetable Ball Soup

Serves 2 to 3

1½ to 2 cups chopped cooked
   chicken
2 bamboo shoots, cut into very
   thin strips
4 mushrooms, chopped
2 small carrots, finely chopped
1 egg, beaten
¼ cup plus 1 teaspoon
   soy sauce
4 teaspoons sugar
3 cups chicken stock

1. Combine chicken, bamboo shoots, mushrooms, carrots, egg,
1 teaspoon soy sauce, and 1 teaspoon sugar. Mix well and form into balls.
2. Place chicken stock, ¼ cup soy sauce, and remaining 1 tablespoon sugar in large saucepan. Bring to a boil. Drop chicken balls into boiling stock; reduce heat, simmer for 8 minutes, and serve.

Japanese Chicken Soup

Serves 4

5 cups chicken broth
1 (4-ounce) can mushroom stems
   and pieces, drain and reserve
   liquid
2 teaspoons soy sauce
1 cup cooked thin egg noodles
1 cooked boneless chicken breast,
   thinly sliced
4 thin slices lemon with rind

1. Place chicken broth in large saucepan and bring to a boil. If there is not 5 cups of broth, add enough reserved mushroom liquid to make 5 cups. Cover and simmer for 5 minutes.

2. Add mushrooms to broth and simmer until heated through. Add soy sauce and noodles. Stir well and simmer for 3 minutes more.
3. Divide sliced chicken equally into 4 bowls. Pour soup on top. Garnish with a lemon slice.

Chicken Barley Soup

Serves 4

2 quarts water
2 pounds chicken necks, skinned
1 (16-ounce) can sliced tomatoes
1 cup sliced celery
1 cup sliced onions
1 cup sliced carrots
¼ cup chopped parsley
6 tablespoons barley
1 bay leaf
¼ teaspoon marjoram

1. Place water in soup pot and bring to a boil. Add chicken necks and return to a boil. Skim as needed. Add remaining ingredients, cover, and simmer for 1 hour.
2. Remove chicken necks and refrigerate until chicken is cool enough to handle. Remove meat from bones and add to soup. Simmer until chicken is heated through and broth is hot.
3. Before serving, skim fat from surface of soup and remove bay leaf.

Turkey and Vegetable Soup

Serves 4

1¾ pounds uncooked
   turkey meat
2 tablespoons vegetable oil
2 quarts hot water
1 teaspoon salt
1 onion
1 stalk celery
2 carrots, sliced into thin
   rounds
1 kohlrabi, peeled and diced

¾ cup green beans, cut into pieces
¾ cup shelled peas
¾ cup cauliflower florets
⅛ teaspoon freshly ground
   black pepper
1 teaspoon soy sauce
Chopped chervil for garnish

1. Brown turkey meat in oil in large saucepan. Add water and salt and bring to a boil. Add onion and celery; simmer for 1 hour. Skim soup as needed during first 30 minutes of cooking time; then cover pan partially, allowing some steam to escape.
2. Remove turkey, onion, and celery from broth by pouring broth through a sieve. Dice turkey and discard vegetables.
3. Return broth to pan. Add carrots, kohlrabi, beans, peas, and cauliflower; simmer for 15 minutes.
4. Return turkey to soup and cook until heated through. Season with pepper and soy sauce. Sprinkle with chopped chervil, and serve.

Creamy Turkey-Vegetable Soup

Serves 6

1 small onion, chopped
2 tablespoons butter or
   margarine
2 cups water
2 chicken bouillon cubes
2 cups diced cooked turkey
½ cup chopped celery
1½ cups diced potatoes
1 cup diced carrots
2½ cups milk
2 tablespoons flour
1 teaspoon salt
⅛ teaspoon pepper

1. Saute onion in butter until translucent. Add water, bouillon cubes, turkey, and vegetables. Cover and boil gently until vegetables are tender.
2. Add a small amount of milk to the flour, stirring until mixture is smooth. Add remaining milk, salt, and pepper.
3. Stir flour-milk mixture into soup. Simmer, stirring occasionally, until soup thickens slightly. Remove from heat, and serve.

Indian Rice Salad

Serves 4

1 cup long-grain brown rice
2¹/₂ cups water
¹/₂ chicken bouillon cube
2 bananas
1 teaspoon lemon juice
1¹/₄ cups plain yogurt
1 tablespoon sour cream
1 tablespoon sesame oil
2 tablespoons white wine
  vinegar
¹/₂ cup chicken broth, with fat
  skimmed off
1 fresh pineapple
¹/₂ pound cooked chicken,
  cut into thin strips
1 onion, finely chopped
1 small red chili pepper, seeded
  and finely chopped
2 teaspoons grated fresh ginger or
  ¹/₂ teaspoon ginger powder
1 teaspoon curry powder
Lettuce leaves for garnish

1. Place rice, water, and bouillon cube in saucepan, cover, and cook over low heat for 35 minutes, or until rice is done.
2. Peel bananas. Slice 1 banana and sprinkle with lemon juice; set aside. Mash second banana and combine with yogurt, sour cream, oil, vinegar, and chicken broth; stir into smooth sauce.
3. Cut a few pineapple slices and reserve for garnish. Peel and core remaining pineapple, and cut enough small cubes to fill ³/₄ cup. Mix rice with chicken strips, sliced banana, onion, chili, and pineapple cubes. Fold in yogurt sauce and season with ginger and curry powder.
4. Arrange rice salad in center of serving dish. Garnish with lettuce and reserved pineapple slices.

Luncheon Salad

Serves 4 to 5

2 cups chopped cooked
  chicken
2 cups grated carrot
2 tablespoons finely chopped
  onion
2 unpeeled sweet apples, cored
  and chopped
3 stalks celery, chopped
2 teaspoons Dijon mustard
¹/₂ cup mayonnaise
Salt and pepper to taste
Lettuce leaves
1 tablespoon chopped parsley

1. Combine chicken, carrot, onion, apples, and celery in bowl.
2. Mix mustard with mayonnaise. Add to ingredients in bowl and toss lightly. Season with salt and pepper.
3. Arrange lettuce on individual dishes. Pile chicken mixture in center and sprinkle with parsley.

Waldorf Chicken Salad

Serves 4

4 sweet apples, peeled, cored,
  and diced
Juice of ¹/₂ lemon
¹/₂ cup mayonnaise
Salt and pepper to taste
1 cup diced cooked chicken
2 stalks celery, chopped
1 tablespoon chopped walnuts
Lettuce leaves

1. Mix apples with lemon juice to prevent discoloring. Season mayonnaise with salt and pepper. Combine mayonnaise with apples, chicken, celery, and walnuts. Mix lightly.
2. Arrange lettuce on serving plate. Pile salad in middle, and serve.

Chicken Salad Deluxe

Serves 5 to 6

¹/₄ pound mushrooms, sliced
1 teaspoon Dijon mustard
2 tablespoons white wine
  vinegar
Salt and pepper to taste
6 tablespoons olive oil
1¹/₂ cups diced cooked chicken
1 small red pepper, seeded and
  cut into strips
¹/₂ cup chopped cooked green
  beans
1 head iceberg lettuce
¹/₂ cup halved seedless green
  grapes
¹/₄ cup toasted flaked almonds

1. Place mushrooms in shallow bowl. Combine mustard, vinegar, salt, pepper, and olive oil; pour dressing over mushrooms and set aside for 1 hour, stirring occasionally.
2. Combine chicken, red pepper, and green beans. Add mushrooms and dressing, season to taste, and toss lightly. Refrigerate until ready to serve.
3. To serve, line deep salad bowl or large platter with lettuce leaves. Spoon chicken mixture over lettuce. Sprinkle with grapes and toasted almonds.

Fruity Chicken Salad

Serves 6 to 8

3 cups diced cooked chicken
1 cup halved seedless green grapes
1 cup diced celery
1¹/₂ cups blanched, salted almonds
1 cup diced green pepper
¹/₂ cup sour cream
1 tablespoon fresh lemon juice
¹/₄ teaspoon nutmeg
1 cup mayonnaise
Lettuce leaves
Sliced cantaloupe, peaches, or
  strawberries for garnish

1. Combine all ingredients and chill
for several hours. Serve on lettuce and
garnish with cantaloupe, peaches, or
strawberries.

Citrus Chicken Salad

Serves 4 to 6

1 (2¹/₂-pound) roasted chicken
2 medium oranges
2 slices fresh pineapple
1 cup cooked long-grain rice
2 tablespoons pineapple juice
1 tablespoon fresh orange juice
¹/₂ teaspoon salt
2 egg yolks
1 teaspoon mild mustard
Pinch of paprika
¹/₄ cup oil
5 mint leaves

1. Remove skin from chicken and take
meat off bone, cutting it into even
pieces.
2. Peel oranges carefully, removing all
white strings, then separate into
sections. Quarter sections and remove
seeds.
3. Peel pineapple and cut into wedges,
removing cores. Combine chicken with
rice, oranges, and pineapple wedges.
4. Mix pineapple juice, orange juice,
and salt together. Whisk egg yolks
with mustard and paprika, adding oil
drop by drop and whisking con-
tinuously until thick mayonnaise
forms. Stir fruit juice into this
mayonnaise, then fold into salad.
5. Shred mint leaves and sprinkle over
salad.

Molded Chicken Salad

Serves 6

1 envelope unflavored gelatin
¹/₄ cup cold water
1 cup hot chicken broth
2 tablespoons chopped green
  pepper
2 tablespoons chopped red pepper
2 cups diced cooked chicken
1 tablespoon chopped onion
1 cup chopped celery
1 cup cooked rice
¹/₂ teaspoon salt
¹/₄ cup French dressing
  (recipe below)
¹/₈ teaspoon paprika
¹/₂ cup mayonnaise
Lettuce

1. Combine gelatin and cold water.
Let stand for 10 minutes. Add chicken
broth and stir until gelatin dissolves.
2. Place green and red peppers in
bottom of 2-quart mold. Cover with 2
tablespoons gelatin mixture and chill
until firm. Combine all remaining
ingredients except lettuce and stir into
remaining gelatin. Pour into mold and
chill until firm. Unmold and serve on
bed of lettuce.
3. To make French dressing, combine
1 teaspoon salt, ¹/₂ teaspoon pepper, 1
teaspoon Dijon mustard, ²/₃ cup olive
or peanut oil, and ¹/₃ cup white wine
vinegar.

Chicken and Polenta Salad

Serves 4

1 cup coarsely ground polenta
3 cups water
¹/₂ vegetable bouillon cube
1 green pepper, quartered
  lengthwise, stem and seeds
  removed
1 red pepper, quartered
  lengthwise, stem and seeds
  removed
2 tablespoons olive oil
1 to 2 tablespoons cider vinegar
1 teaspoon chopped fresh
  rosemary or ¹/₈ teaspoon dried
  rosemary
1 teaspoon chopped fresh thyme or
  ¹/₈ teaspoon dried thyme

¹/₂ teaspoon paprika
¹/₈ teaspoon pepper
1 pound cooked boneless chicken
  breasts, skinned and shredded
2 medium tomatoes, skinned and
  quartered
2 tablespoons chopped chives

1. Place polenta, water, and bouillon
cube in large saucepan. Bring to a boil,
then cover tightly and turn heat off.
Let pan sit for 1 hour.
2. Blanch green and red peppers in
boiling, salted water for 5 minutes.
Drain and cut peppers into thin strips.
3. Combine cooked polenta with oil,
vinegar, herbs, paprika, black pepper,
green and red pepper strips, and
chicken. Mix well.
4. To serve,
arrange tomato
quarters on
top of salad
and sprinkle
with chopped
chives.

Chicken Salad with Asparagus

Serves 6

1 (3-pound) chicken
¹/₂ teaspoon salt
¹/₈ teaspoon pepper
¹/₄ teaspoon paprika
1 (16-ounce) can peas, drained
1 (14¹/₂-ounce) can asparagus
  pieces, drained
1 (8-ounce) can sliced mushrooms,
  drained
1 (8-ounce) container plain yogurt
2 tablespoons mayonnaise
1 teaspoon dill weed
¹/₂ teaspoon salt
¹/₈ teaspoon pepper

1. Preheat oven to 350 degrees.
2. Place chicken in center of large,
square piece of aluminum foil.
Sprinkle with salt, pepper, and

paprika. Wrap with foil and bake for 1 hour. Cool and remove meat from bone; cut into bite-size pieces.

3. Combine chicken pieces, peas, asparagus, and mushrooms in large bowl. Mix yogurt, mayonnaise, dill, salt, and pepper together and gently combine with other ingredients.

4. Marinate salad in refrigerator for 2 hours before serving.

Hunan-Style Chicken Salad

Serves 4

1 pound cooked chicken,
    shredded
3 cucumbers, cut into julienne
    slices
1 leek, white part only, very
    thinly sliced
1 tablespoon minced fresh ginger
    or $^1/_2$ teaspoon ginger powder
2 tablespoons soy sauce
2 tablespoons red wine vinegar
2 tablespoons sugar
1 teaspoon crushed red pepper
1 tablespoon sesame oil
1 tablespoons sesame seeds,
    toasted in hot frying pan

1. Combine chicken and cucumbers in serving dish. Sprinkle with leek pieces and ginger. Refrigerate until chilled.

2. Mix soy sauce, vinegar, sugar, red pepper, and oil together, blending thoroughly. Stir in sesame seeds.

3. Just before serving, toss chicken mixture with dressing.

Tropical Chicken Salad

Serves 6 to 8

2 cups diced cooked chicken
4 slices pineapple, diced
2 bananas, diced
1 cup chopped celery
$^1/_2$ teaspoon salt
$^1/_3$ cup mayonnaise
2 tablespoons lemon juice
Salad greens

1. Toss all ingredients together except salad greens. Refrigerate about 1 hour, until chilled.

2. Line salad bowl with crisp salad greens. Spoon chicken salad on top, and serve.

Chicken Salad California

Serves 6

3 ripe avocados
$^1/_4$ cup orange juice
2 cups diced cooked chicken
2 oranges, peeled, sectioned,
    and diced
1 cup diced celery
$^1/_2$ cup mayonnaise
3 tablespoons chili sauce
$^1/_8$ teaspoon paprika
1 teaspoon salt
2 tablespoons chopped pimento
Salad greens
Orange sections for garnish

1. Peel avocados, halve lengthwise, and brush with orange juice.

2. Combine chicken, oranges, and celery. Mix mayonnaise, chili sauce, and seasonings together. Add mayonnaise mixture to chicken, blending thoroughly.

3. Fill avocado halves with chicken mixture. Top with chopped pimento. Serve on bed of salad greens and garnish with additional orange sections.

Chicken Salad with Lychees

Serves 5 to 6

3 cups diced cooked chicken
2 to 3 stalks celery, chopped
1 green pepper, seeded and
    chopped
Salt and pepper to taste
$^3/_4$ cup French dressing
Salad greens
1 (10$^1/_2$-ounce) can mandarin
    oranges, drained

1 (8-ounce) can lychees,
    drained
$^3/_4$ cup mayonnaise
$^1/_4$ cup sour cream
2 teaspoons curry powder
2 tablespoons grated onion
2 tablespoons chopped parsley

1. Combine chicken, celery, and green pepper. Add salt, pepper, and French dressing. Toss lightly together and refrigerate for about 30 minutes.

2. Arrange salad greens around large platter. Pile chicken mixture in center.

3. Place mandarin orange segment in each lychee and arrange around edge of platter.

4. Blend mayonnaise, sour cream, curry powder, grated onion, and parsley together; chill well. Serve dressing separately.

Chicken Stuffed Apples

Serves 4

2 cups diced cooked white
    chicken meat
$^1/_2$ cup canned pineapple chunks,
    drained
1 cup seedless grapes, peeled
2 stalks celery, chopped
1$^1/_4$ cups mayonnaise
4 large apples
1 teaspoon grated lemon rind
2 tablespoons slivered almonds,
    lightly browned in butter.

1. Mix chicken with pineapple chunks, grapes, and celery. Toss with mayonnaise.

2. Polish apples and cut in half. Scoop out fruit with grapefruit knife or spoon. Remove core and dice scooped-out apple. Add diced apples to mayonnaise mixture.

3. Fill apple halves with chicken mayonnaise. Sprinkle top with grated lemon rind and almonds.

Rice and Chicken Salad

Serves 4 to 6

1 cup rice, cooked al dente
1 teaspoon Dijon mustard
¹/₂ teaspoon salt
2 teaspoons red wine vinegar
6 tablespoons olive oil
¹/₂ cup finely diced Swiss cheese
¹/₄ cup diced pitted black olives
2 tablespoons diced pitted
  green olives
¹/₄ cup diced sweet red or
  green pepper
3 tablespoons diced sour
  pickles
1 whole boneless chicken
  breast, boiled and diced

1. After rice is cooked, rinse in cold water. Drain well and set aside.
2. Mix mustard, salt, and vinegar together in large salad bowl. Use fork to stir in oil. Toss drained rice with dressing; coat well. Stir in remaining ingredients, tossing gently.
3. Serve salad cool, but not chilled.

Chicken Nectarine Salad

Serves 4

1 cup shredded cooked
  chicken
¹/₄ cup grated zucchini
¹/₄ cup grated carrot
2 tablespoons finely chopped
  scallion
2 teaspoon tarragon wine
  vinegar
1 teaspoon salad oil
¹/₄ teaspoon seasoned salt
2 fresh nectarines
3 to 4 tablespoons mayonnaise
Crisp lettuce

1. Toss chicken, vegetables, vinegar, oil, and salt together; chill.
2. When ready to serve, halve nectarines. Remove pit and cut into thin slices. Add nectarine slices and mayonnaise to chicken mixture.
3. Line salad bowls with lettuce. Spoon chicken mixture on top, and serve.

Chicken Salad with Bacon

Serves 4

1 small head iceberg lettuce
1 small red pepper, seeded and
  cut into strips
1 cucumber, thickly sliced
1 cup small whole mushrooms
2 cups coarsely chopped cooked
  chicken
2 hard-boiled eggs, quartered
4 slices crisp-fried bacon,
  halved
2 tablespoons wine vinegar
6 tablespoons salad oil
Salt to taste
¹/₄ cup mashed Roquefort
  cheese

1. Tear lettuce into large pieces; place in salad bowl. Add red pepper, cucumber, mushrooms, and chicken. Toss lightly, then top with eggs and bacon.
2. Mix vinegar, oil, salt, and cheese together well. Serve dressing with chicken salad.

Curried Chicken Salad

Serves 6

2 tablespoons butter
3 tablespoons minced onion
1¹/₄ teaspoons curry powder
¹/₃ cup mayonnaise
1 tablespoon lemon juice
¹/₂ teaspoon salt
¹/₈ teaspoon cayenne pepper
3 cups diced cooked chicken
1 (1-pound, 4-ounce) canned
  pineapple chunks, drained
¹/₂ cup coarsely chopped nuts
¹/₃ cup golden raisins
1 red apple, cored and diced
Lettuce

2 tablespoons shredded coconut

1. Melt butter in small frying pan over medium heat. Stir in onion and curry powder. Saute, stirring constantly, for 3 to 5 minutes. Remove from heat and cool.
2. Combine curry mixture with mayonnaise, lemon juice, salt, and cayenne pepper; blend thoroughly.
3. Combine chicken, pineapple, nuts, raisins, and apple in large bowl. Add curry dressing and toss gently until mixed.
4. Line salad bowl with lettuce. Add salad and sprinkle with shredded coconut.

Sorrento Salad

Serves 6

3 cups diced cooked chicken
1 cup chopped celery
¹/₄ cup chopped red pepper,
  optional
¹/₂ teaspoon salt
¹/₂ teaspoon pepper
²/₃ cup blue-cheese dressing
2 cups orange sections
2 cups grapefruit sections
¹/₂ cup diced avocado
1 avocado, cut into wedges
Orange or grapefruit juice
Salad greens

1. Combine chicken, celery, and red pepper in bowl. Sprinkle with salt and pepper. Add dressing, tossing to mix well. Chill thoroughly.
2. Dice enough orange and grapefruit sections to make ¹/₂ cup each. Add diced fruit to chicken mixture.
3. Coat diced avocado and avocado wedges with orange juice. Add diced avocado to chicken mixture.
4. Line large salad bowl with salad greens. Spoon salad into bowl. Arrange remaining orange and grapefruit sections and avocado wedges around salad. Serve with additional blue-cheese dressing.

Chicken and Fruit Salad

Serves 4

1¼ pounds boneless chicken
  breasts, skinned and cut in
  ½-inch thick strips
2 tablespoons butter
1 teaspoon salt
½ teaspoon pepper
2¼ cups strawberries,
  halved
¾ cup bean sprouts
2 teaspoons chopped crystallized
  or fresh ginger
1 teaspoon powdered ginger
1 tablespoons basil vinegar
1 tablespoon soy sauce
⅛ teaspoon salt
⅛ teaspoon cayenne pepper
2 tablespoons olive oil

1. Saute chicken strips in butter for 8
minutes, stirring frequently. Season
with salt and pepper; remove from
pan and drain on paper towels. Let
cool.
2. Combine strawberries, bean
sprouts, cooled chicken, and chopped
ginger in salad bowl.
3. In separate bowl, combine
powdered ginger, vinegar, soy sauce,
salt, and cayenne pepper. Add oil,
then toss salad gently with this
dressing.
4. Cover salad and let sit for 10
minutes at room temperature for
flavor to fully develop, then serve.

Chicken and Fresh Asparagus Salad

Serves 4 to 6

1 (2¼-pound) chicken
1½ teaspoons salt
1 clove
½ bay leaf
1 onion
⅔ cup sliced leeks, white part
  only
1 medium carrot, sliced
1 stalk celery, halved
4½ cups fresh asparagus,
  cut into 2-inch pieces
2 tablespoons cider vinegar
⅛ teaspoon pepper

⅛ teaspoon sugar
¼ cup corn oil
2 tablespoons chopped chives

1. Sprinkle chicken and giblets with 1
teaspoon salt. Cover with water and
bring to a boil. Skim as needed.
2. Use clove to spike bay leaf onto
whole onion; add to chicken.
3. Reduce heat and simmer for 1½
hours. After chicken has cooked for 30
minutes, add leeks, carrot, and celery
to pan; continue to cook, uncovered,
for remaining time.
4. At end of cooking time, remove
chicken from pan. Strain broth, then
bring it again to a boil. Add asparagus
stem pieces and simmer in broth for
15 minutes, adding asparagus tips
after 8 minutes.
5. Remove chicken meat from bone
and cut in even pieces. Remove
asparagus pieces from broth and add
to chicken; cool.
6. Mix vinegar With ½ teaspoon salt,
pepper, sugar, and oil. Toss chicken
and asparagus with dressing. Sprinkle
with chives, and serve.

Winter Turkey Salad

Serves 4

2 cups chopped cooked turkey
¼ cup sliced celery
2 tablespoons finely chopped
  pimento
2 tablespoons capers
1 tablespoon finely chopped
  scallion
1 tablespoons finely chopped
  parsley
½ cup mayonnaise
1 teaspoon Dijon mustard
Salt and pepper to taste
3 drops Tabasco sauce
Juice of ½ lemon
Lettuce leaves

1. Toss turkey, celery, pimento,
capers, scallion, and parsley together.
Combine mayonnaise, mustard, salt,
pepper, and Tabasco; stir lightly into
turkey mixture. Sprinkle with lemon
juice and toss lightly.
2. To serve, arrange lettuce leaves in
salad bowl and place turkey salad in
center.

Turkey and Barley Salad

Serves 4

1¼ cups barley
4 cups water
1 (1¾-pound) turkey drumstick
⅛ teaspoon pepper
1 carrot, chopped
1 celery stalk, chopped
1 vegetable bouillon cube,
  dissolved in 1 cup boiling
  water
½ cup pitted prunes,
  quartered
1 leek, white part only, cut
  into very thin rings
2 tablespoons sunflower oil
2 tablespoons red wine vinegar
2 tablespoons sour cream
½ teaspoon salt

1. Place barley and water in bowl;
cover and soak for 12 hours. After
soaking, transfer barley and water to
large saucepan.
2. Rub drumstick well with pepper
and place on barley in pan. Cover and
simmer gently for 50 minutes, turning
drumstick over after 30 minutes.
3. Add carrot and celery to turkey for
final 15 minutes of cooking time. Add
more water if necessary.
4. Drain barley. Remove turkey meat
from bone and cut into 1¼-inch
pieces.
5. Bring 1 cup water to a boil and
dissolve bouillon cube in it.
6. Combine barley with prunes, leek,
turkey, bouillon, oil, vinegar, sour
cream, and salt. Before serving, add a
little more red wine vinegar and salt, if
desired.

Turkey Breast and Potato Salad

Serves 4

4 large potatoes
Scant 1 cup chicken broth
$^1/_8$ teaspoon pepper
2 red onions thinly sliced
2 ripe avocados
3 to 4 tablespoons white wine
  vinegar
2 tablespoons sunflower oil
10 ounces smoked turkey
  breast, diced
$^1/_2$ to 1 teaspoon seasoning salt
2 tablespoons chopped fresh
  dill for garnish

1. Place potatoes in saucepan, cover with water, and bring to a boil. Cover and cook for 30 minutes, or until done.
2. Place chicken broth in separate saucepan and bring to a boil.
3. Drain cooked potatoes and rinse with cold water; peel and dice. Add hot broth and pepper to diced potatoes. Add sliced onions, avocados, vinegar, and oil.
4. Stir turkey breast and seasoning salt into potato salad. Sprinkle with chopped dill, and serve.

Turkey Salad with Yogurt

Serves 4

4 cups water
1 teaspoon salt
1 (2$^1/_4$-pound) turkey drumstick
2 bananas, peeled and sliced
2 red apples, peeled, cored, and
  diced
Juice of $^1/_2$ lemon
1 small pineapple, cut into small
  cubes
1$^3/_4$ cups seedless red grapes,
  halved
1$^3/_4$ cups heavy whipping cream
2$^1/_2$ cups plain full-cream yogurt
$^1/_8$ teaspoon salt
$^1/_8$ teaspoon pepper
1 tablespoon brandy
6 sprigs fresh mint for garnish

1. Bring water and salt to a boil in large saucepan. Add drumstick, cover, and simmer for 1 hour.

2. Combine banana slices and apples; sprinkle with lemon juice. Add pineapple and grapes.
3. Remove drumstick from broth and let cool. Remove meat from bone and cut into small cubes. Add to fruit.
4. Whip cream until stiff. Mix whipped cream with yogurt, salt, pepper, and brandy. Pour this sauce over fruit and turkey; mix well.
5. Garnish with mint sprigs, and serve.

Apple and Turkey Salad

Serves 4

1 cup long-grain brown rice
$^1/_2$ teaspoon salt
$^1/_2$ teaspoon curry powder
3 cups water
3 boneless turkey breasts
Juice of $^1/_2$ lemon
$^1/_8$ teaspoon pepper
1 large apple, peeled, cored,
  and sliced
2 tablespoons sour cream
2 tablespoons sesame oil
2 tablespoons lemon juice
$^1/_4$ cup chicken stock with
  all fat removed
$^1/_4$ cup sesame seeds
2 tablespoons chopped fresh dill
  for garnish
Lettuce leaves

1. Place rice in saucepan with $^1/_4$ teaspoon salt, $^1/_4$ teaspoon curry powder, and water. Cover and cook over low heat for 35 minutes.
2. Sprinkle turkey with lemon juice and pepper. Lay turkey on top of rice during last 20 minutes of cooking time, turning over after 10 minutes.
3. Drain rice. Cut turkey into strips.
4. Set a few apple slices aside and sprinkle with lemon juice. Chop remaining slices and combine with rice, turkey strips, sour cream, sesame oil, lemon juice, chicken stock, and remaining salt and curry powder.
5. Heat dry frying pan. Place sesame seeds in pan and toast, stirring well, until browned.
6. To serve, arrange rice salad on serving plate, sprinkle with sesame seeds, and garnish with dill, lettuce, and reserved fruit slices.

Turkey Stuffed Tomatoes

Serves 4

4 large red tomatoes
Salt to taste
2 stalks celery, chopped
3 tablespoons cooked corn
1 cup diced cooked turkey
$^1/_2$ cup mayonnaise
4 slices lemon

1. Cut off tops of tomatoes, remove seeds, and reserve any juice that comes from tomatoes. Turn upside down on rack to drain.
2. Lightly sprinkle diced cucumber with salt and set aside for 20 minutes. Rinse and drain. Combine cucumber, celery, corn, and turkey.
3. Mix mayonnaise and reserved tomato juice together, and add enough to turkey and vegetables to make a creamy mixture. Spoon mixture into tomatoes, and serve garnished with lemon slices.

Special Turkey Salad

Serves 4

14 ounces cooked turkey breast,
  cut into strips
1$^1/_4$ cups celery
2 yellow peppers, seeded and
  cut into strips
1 small onion, grated
$^1/_4$ cup low-fat mayonnaise
1 (6-ounce) container plain
  low-fat yogurt
2 teaspoons hot mustard
2 teaspoons maple syrup
$^1/_2$ teaspoon salt
$^1/_8$ teaspoon pepper
Green celery tops for garnish

1. Mix turkey, celery, and yellow peppers together in bowl.
2. Mix grated onion with mayonnaise, yogurt, mustard, maple syrup, salt, and pepper.

3. Toss turkey mixture in dressing, cover, and let stand at room temperature for 10 minutes before serving. Garnish with green celery tops, and serve.

Turkey Salad in Curried Mayonnaise

Serves 4 to 6

3 cups shredded cooked turkey
3 cups mixed cooked vegetables, such as peas, green beans, corn, and celery
4 tomatoes
1 bunch watercress
1 tablespoon butter
1 shallot, peeled and chopped
1/2 tablespoon curry powder
1 teaspoon flour
1/2 cup turkey stock
2 teaspoons coconut
2 teaspoons chutney
3 teaspoons lemon juice
Salt and pepper to taste
1 to 1 1/2 cups mayonnaise
1/8 teaspoon paprika
1 to 2 lemons, quartered

1. Cool turkey and cooked vegetables. Quarter tomatoes; remove seeds, strain, and reserve any juice that comes from tomatoes. Wash watercress and dry thoroughly.
2. Melt butter in frying pan. Add shallot and saute until translucent. Add curry powder and saute for 1 or 2 minutes more. Sprinkle in flour and saute for 3 to 5 minutes. Add stock, blending well. Bring to a boil, stirring constantly.
3. Stir in coconut, chutney, and 2 teaspoons lemon juice; simmer for 10 to 15 minutes. Strain and cool. Season with salt and pepper.
4. Season cooled vegetables with salt and pepper; sprinkle with remaining lemon juice. Place in salad bowl. Arrange turkey in center of bowl.
5. Thin mayonnaise with a small amount of reserved tomato juice. Spoon mayonnaise carefully over turkey and sprinkle with paprika. Arrange tomato quarters and watercress sprigs alternately around edge of bowl. Serve garnished with lemon quarters.

Smoked Turkey Salad

Serves 4 to 6

3/4 teaspoon salt
1/4 teaspoon pepper
1 teaspoon dried mustard
1 1/2 teaspoons sugar
1 egg
3/4 cup salad oil
1 teaspoon lemon juice
1 teaspoon wine vinegar
1 to 2 tablespoons boiling water
1/2 pound egg noodles
3 to 4 tablespoons light cream
1 pound smoked turkey breast, thinly sliced
1/2 cup cooked corn and pimento
2 to 3 lettuce hearts
3 to 4 tomatoes, skinned and quartered

1. Place salt, pepper, mustard, and sugar in blender or food processor. Add egg. Mix thoroughly at low speed. Add a few drops of oil and mix well. Add remaining oil in steady stream until it has been absorbed and mayonnaise is very thick. Add lemon juice, vinegar, and boiling water.
2. Boil noodles in salted water following package directions; drain and cool. Add cream to mayonnaise mixture. Toss cooled noodles with two-thirds of mayonnaise mixture and season to taste.
3. Place turkey slices on top of noodles in neat row. Mix corn and pimento with small amount of remaining mayonnaise. Garnish turkey with lettuce hearts, tomatoes, and corn and pimento.

Turkey-Nut Salad

Serves 4

1/2 cup seedless grapes
3 to 4 tablespoons almonds
Juice of 1/2 lemon
Grated rind of 1/2 orange
1 cup mayonnaise
2 cups diced cooked turkey
1/2 cup sliced celery
Lettuce or endive leaves
1/2 teaspoon paprika

1. Dip grapes first in boiling water for about 10 seconds, then in cold water; peel. Quickly dip almonds in and out of boiling water; remove skins, halve, and brown in moderate oven (350 degrees) for 2 minutes.
2. Add lemon juice and orange rind to mayonnaise. Toss turkey, peeled grapes, celery, and almonds in mayonnaise.
3. Arrange turkey mixture on lettuce or endive leaves. Sprinkle with paprika, then serve.

Turkey and Pomegranate Salad

Serves 5 to 6

2 cups diced cooked turkey
2 to 3 stalks celery, chopped
Seeds from 1 large, ripe pomegranate
1 cup chopped blanched almonds
Salt and pepper to taste
Mayonnaise
Lettuce leaves
2 slices pineapple, cut into wedges

1. Combine turkey, celery, pomegranate seeds, and almonds. Season with salt and pepper.
2. Add just enough mayonnaise to moisten. Toss salad lightly.
3. Serve on a bed of lettuce. Garnish with pineapple wedges.

Turkey and Grape Aspic

Serves 4 to 6

1½ tablespoons unflavored
  gelatin
2¾ cups clear turkey or chicken
  stock, heated
¼ cup white wine
1 pound seedless white grapes
Juice of ½ lemon
1 few tarragon leaves
1 to 1½ pounds turkey meat,
  diced
Lettuce leaves

1. To make aspic, add gelatin to ¾ cup hot stock and stir until dissolved. Add white wine and remaining stock. Cool thoroughly.
2. Dip grapes in boiling water for 10 seconds, then into cold water. Peel and remove seeds; place peeled grapes in bowl and sprinkle with lemon juice to prevent browning.
3. Pour layer of aspic into round mold. Arrange grapes with tarragon leaves in a decorative pattern. Refrigerate until set. Cover with another layer of aspic, then with a layer of turkey. Refrigerate until set again. Continue making layers of aspic, grapes, and turkey until all are used. End with layer of aspic covering the top completely.
4. Refrigerate until set. Dip mold in bowl of hot water to loosen and turn out onto lettuce-l ined plate.

Turkey Vegetable Salad

Serves 6

2 cups diced cooked turkey
1 cup cooked peas
1 cup diced celery
¾ cup chopped walnuts
1 teaspoon grated onion
½ teaspoon salt
⅛ teaspoon pepper
½ cup mayonnaise
Lettuce leaves
Walnut halves for garnish

1. Lightly mix turkey with peas, celery, chopped walnuts, onion, salt, and pepper. Toss with mayonnaise until evenly coated. Refrigerate until chilled.
2. Line salad bowl with lettuce leaves. Spoon turkey salad on top. Garnish with walnut halves, and serve.

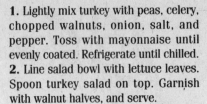

Jellied Cranberry-Turkey Salad

Serves 4 to 5

1 cup bottled cranberry juice
1 (3-ounce) package raspberry
  or cherry gelatin
½ cup port wine
1½ cups diced cooked turkey
¾ cup chopped celery
2 tablespoons chopped
  scallion
¾ teaspoon seasoned salt
⅛ teaspoon pepper
3 to 4 tablespoons mayonnaise
½ cup seedless grapes,
  halves
Romaine lettuce

1. Place cranberry juice in saucepan and bring to a boil. Add gelatin and stir until dissolved. Remove from heat. Add port wine and let cool.
2. Turn cranberry mixture into over-sized wine glasses or goblets, filling glasses until half full. Chill until firm.
3. Combine turkey, celery, scallion, salt, and pepper. Chill for several hours. Add mayonnaise and grapes, tossing gently.
4. Arrange small romaine lettuce leaves in each glass. Spoon in turkey salad, and serve.

Chicken Salad with Coconut

Serves 6

3 fresh pineapples, halved
  lengthwise
½ cup whipped cream or sour
  cream
½ cup mayonnaise
3 cups cubed cooked chicken
½ cup slivered almonds
Salt and pepper to taste
½ cup grated fresh coconut

1. Scoop fruit out of each pineapple half, leaving about ½-inch thick shell. Mince scooped-out fruit; set aside.
2. Blend whipped or sour cream and mayonnaise together in large bowl. Add chicken, almonds, salt, pepper, and minced pineapple. Toss gently.
3. Place pineapple shells on serving plate and fill them with chicken mixture. Sprinkle with coconut and serve.

Chicken Salad with Cherries

Serves 4

3 cups diced cooked chicken
¼ cup diced scallions
1 cup fresh or canned Bing
  cherries, drained if canned
1 cup mayonnaise
1 to 2 teaspoons curry powder
4 sprigs watercress
½ cup finely chopped Brazil nuts

1. Toss chicken, scallions, and cherries together gently in bowl.
2. In separate bowl, blend mayonnaise and curry powder together. Add to chicken mixture; toss gently.
3. Separate watercress leaves from stems; discard stems and arrange leaves in bottom of glass bowl. Spoon chicken salad on top.
4. Before serving, sprinkle salad with Brazil nuts.

ENTICING ENTREES: CHICKEN

Chicken and Rice Stew

Serves 4

6 cups water
1 (3-pound) chicken
1 sprig each tarragon, parsley, celery leaves, and thyme, tied together
$1/2$ cup sliced leek, white part only
2 shallots, peeled and quartered
1 teaspoon salt
1 cup long-grain rice
$2^1/4$ cups shelled peas
1 cup diced carrots
$1/8$ teaspoon cayenne pepper
2 tablespoons chopped parsley

1. Bring water to a boil in large saucepan. Add chicken and cook for 30 minutes, skimming as needed.
2. Add herbs, leek, shallots, and salt to pan. Cover and simmer for 30 minutes more.
3. Place uncooked rice in colander and wash under cold running water until water runs clear; drain.
4. Remove chicken and herbs from broth, and set aside. Add peas, carrots, and rice to broth, cover, and simmer for 20 minutes.
5. Remove chicken meat from carcass and cut into small pieces. Return chicken pieces to pot. Season with cayenne pepper, sprinkle with chopped parsley, and serve.

Chicken and Vegetable Guest Stew

Serves 4

3 tablespoons butter
1 (3-pound) chicken, cut into serving pieces
1 onion, diced

$1/2$ cup diced carrot
2 leeks, white part only, sliced
1 teaspoon salt
2 teaspoons paprika
$1/8$ teaspoon pepper
1 cup unsweetened apple juice
$1^3/4$ cups chopped, skinned tomatoes
$1/2$ cup finely sliced mushrooms
2 tablespoons chopped chives

1. Heat 2 tablespoons butter in large, heavy skillet. Add chicken pieces and brown well on all sides. Remove from pan.
2. Add onion and carrot to same pan and saute until brown. Add remaining butter and leeks; saute briefly, then lay chicken pieces on top of vegetables. Sprinkle with salt, paprika, and pepper. Pour apple juice over chicken. Cover and cook for 35 minutes over low heat.
3. Add tomatoes and mushrooms to stew the final 10 minutes of cooking time. Sprinkle with chopped chives and serve with brown or white rice.

Chicken and Pasta Stew

Serves 4

1 ($2^1/2$-pound) chicken
6 cups water
1 teaspoon salt
3 whole allspice
3 peppercorns
$1/2$ bay leaf
1 cup soup vegetables, such as chopped onion, leek, carrot, celery, or turnip
1 tablespoon vegetable oil
1 onion, diced
2 cloves garlic, peeled and diced
2 cups diced eggplant
2 cups diced zucchini

2 cups skinned and diced tomatoes
1 sprig fresh thyme or $1/4$ teaspoon dried thyme
$1/2$ cup pasta of your choice

1. Place chicken in large saucepan. Cover with water and add salt, allspice, peppercorns, and bay leaf. Bring to a boil, skimming as needed. Simmer, uncovered, for $1^1/2$ hours. Add chopped soup vegetables to chicken after first half hour of cooking.
2. Heat oil in separate saucepan. Add onion and garlic; saute until translucent. Add diced eggplant, zucchini, tomatoes, and thyme, continuing to saute for 10 minutes more.
3. Strain chicken broth. Add 1 cup strained broth to vegetables in saucepan. Bring remaining broth to a boil in another saucepan; add pasta and boil until pasta is done, following package directions.
4. Remove chicken meat from carcass and cut into bite-size pieces; add to vegetables. Pour pasta and cooking broth over chicken-vegetable mixture, stirring until well mixed. Transfer to serving dish and serve hot.

Braised Rosemary Chicken

Serves 4

1 (3-pound) chicken, cut into
   serving pieces
1 teaspoon salt
2 tablespoons butter
   cup hot chicken broth
1 sprig fresh rosemary or
   ¼ teaspoon dried rosemary
1 small cooking apple
1 small potato
½ cup dry white wine
Freshly ground black pepper

1. Rub chicken pieces well with salt. Set giblets aside. Melt butter in heavy-bottomed pot and brown chicken on all sides. Add broth, rosemary, and chicken heart and gizzard. Cover and simmer 30 minutes.
2. While chicken is cooking, chop liver. Peel apple and potato; wash potato, then grate with apple. Add grated apple and potato, liver, and white wine to chicken, adding more broth if necessary.
3. Continue to cook chicken, covered, for 10 minutes. Season to taste with salt and pepper, and serve.

Chicken à la King

Serves 4

1 red pepper, seeded and halved
2 tablespoons butter
1¾ cups finely sliced mushrooms
1¼ pounds boneless chicken
   breasts, skinned and cut into
   ½-inch-wide strips
1 cup light cream
2 tablespoons whole-wheat flour
½ cup chicken broth
1 teaspoon seasoning salt
⅛ teaspoon freshly ground black
   pepper
Juice of 1 lemon
1 tablespoon chopped parsley

1. Blanch red pepper halves in boiling salted water for 5 minutes; drain and dice. Set aside.
2. Melt butter in large frying pan. Add mushrooms and chicken strips; saute 5 minutes, stirring frequently.
3. Whisk cream with flour and broth,

then add to chicken. Add diced red pepper. Simmer for 5 minutes, adding a little more broth if necessary to form a creamy sauce.
4. Remove pan from heat; season with seasoning salt, pepper, and lemon juice. Sprinkle with parsley, and serve.

Glazed Baked Chicken

Serves 4

2 (2¼-pound) frying chickens,
   halved
2 teaspoons vegetable oil
2 tablespoons honey
1 tablespoon moderately hot
   mustard
2 teaspoons curry powder
½ teaspoon salt

1. Preheat oven to 425 degrees.
2. Cut 4 pieces of aluminum foil large enough to wrap each chicken half. Brush chicken halves with oil and lay, cut side down, on foil.
3. Combine honey with mustard, curry powder, and salt; brush chicken with this mixture. Wrap foil loosely around chicken halves, sealing edges well.
4. Place foil parcels on roasting rack and bake for 30 minutes in center of oven. Open foil and continue to cook for 20 minutes longer, until skin is crisp and brown. Place each foil parcel on individual serving plate; remove foil before serving.

Deep-Fried Chicken

Serves 4

½ cup flour
2 teaspoons salt
2 eggs
5 tablespoons water, preferably
   mineral water
4 cups safflower oil
3 pounds chicken pieces
Freshly ground black pepper to
   taste

1. Mix flour, salt, eggs, and water together to make batter. Cover and let stand for 20 minutes.
2. Heat oil to 350 degrees in skillet deep-fryer. Heat oven to 200 degrees.
3. Dip each chicken piece in batter. Fry chicken, a few pieces at a time, in

oil until crisp and brown all over. Drain on paper towels, then keep warm in oven while remaining chicken is fried. Season with salt and pepper, and serve.

Chicken with Broccoli

Serves 4

3-pounds chicken pieces
1 onion, cut into eighths
1 carrot, chopped
½ cup chopped celery
2 tablespoons safflower oil
3 tablespoons sherry vinegar
1 cup water
1 sprig fresh thyme or ¼ teaspoon
   dried thyme
1½ teaspoons salt
8 small onions
3½ cups broccoli florets
2 cups water
1 tablespoon butter
1 teaspoon sugar
5 tablespoons orange juice
½ teaspoon freshly ground white
   pepper
¼ cup corn oil

1. Brown chicken pieces and vegetables in safflower oil in large saucepan. Add vinegar, water, thyme, and 1 teaspoon salt. Cover and simmer for 30 minutes.
2. Remove chicken pieces from pan. Strain broth, then boil small onions in strained broth for 10 minutes. Remove onions from broth.
3. Boil broccoli florets for 10 minutes in 2 cups water. Drain and cool.
4. Melt butter in small saucepan. Add sugar and caramelize to a light brown. Add small onions, tossing until glazed.
5. Combine orange juice, ½ teaspoon salt, pepper, and corn oil; toss broccoli in this dressing. To serve, arrange chicken on serving platter with broccoli and glazed onions.

Chicken in a Pot

Serves 4

3 cups chicken broth
2½ pounds chicken pieces, with
   giblets
½ cup diced carrots
1 cup sliced leeks (white part only)

1 large onion, sliced into rings
2¼ cups roughly chopped
 sauerkraut, drained
1 bay leaf
4 juniper berries
1¾ cups chopped, skinned
 tomatoes
½ teaspoon salt
½ teaspoon freshly ground black
 pepper

1. Bring chicken broth to a boil in large, heavy pot. Add chicken pieces and heart, reduce heat to low, and cook uncovered for 30 minutes. Skim as needed.
2. Add carrots, leeks, onion, sauerkraut, bay leaf, juniper berries, and chicken liver to broth. Cover and simmer for 30 minutes.
3. Add tomatoes to pot 10 minutes before end of cooking time. Season well with salt and pepper, and serve.

Chicken and Ham Pie

Serves 4 to 6

1 (3-pound) chicken
4 onions, 2 whole, 2 thickly sliced
2 carrots
3 stalks celery
3 sprigs parsley
1 bay leaf
6 peppercorns
Salt to taste
4 tablespoons butter
1 cup sliced mushrooms
2 tablespoons flour
2 tablespoons mixed chopped
 parsley, thyme, and tarragon
6 slices ham, chopped
1 package frozen puff pastry
1 egg, beaten

1. Cut meat off chicken bones in large chunks and set aside. Place carcass and giblets in large saucepan with 2 whole onions, carrots, celery, herbs, and peppercorns. Cover with water, bring to a boil, and simmer for 1 hour; strain and add salt. Measure out 1½ cups strained broth and set aside.
2. Melt 2 tablespoons butter in separate saucepan. Add sliced onions and saute for 3 to 4 minutes. Add mushrooms and saute for 1 minute. Remove mushrooms and onions from pan and keep warm.

3. Melt 2 more tablespoons butter in same pan and brown chicken for 4 to 5 minutes. Sprinkle in flour, then pour on reserved broth. Bring to a boil, whisking constantly. Simmer 1 minute, then add sliced onions and mushrooms. Sprinkle in mixed chopped herbs.
4. Make a layer of ham on bottom of pie dish. Spoon in half the chicken mixture, then cover with another layer of ham. Add remaining chicken mixture and top with ham. Cool.
5. Preheat oven to 450 degrees.
6. Thaw pastry according to package directions. Roll out pastry the shape and size of dish top, cutting a thin strip to place around moistened edge of pie dish. Brush this strip with water, then place large piece of pastry on top. Crimp edges together; cut off excess pastry with sharp knife. Make 3 or 4 holes to allow steam to escape and brush pastry with beaten egg.
7. Bake for 25 minutes to cook pastry. Reduce heat to 375 degrees, cover pastry with damp waxed paper or foil and bake for 20 minutes longer. Remove from heat and cool slightly before serving.

Oven Fried Chicken with Tomato Sauce

Serves 4

3 pounds chicken pieces
2 to 3 tablespoons flour
Salt and pepper to taste
⅛ teaspoon paprika
1 to 2 eggs, beaten
6 to 8 tablespoons cornflakes
 or bread crumbs
4 tablespoons melted butter

Tomato Sauce
2 tablespoons butter
1 onion, finely chopped
1 clove garlic, peeled and crushed
1 tablespoon flour
2 tablespoons tomato paste
1 (8-ounce) can tomatoes
1 cup chicken broth
1 teaspoon fines herbes
6 peppercorns
1 strip lemon peel
⅛ teaspoon cayenne pepper
1 teaspoon sugar, optional
Salt and pepper to taste

1. Preheat oven to 400 degrees.
2. Roll chicken pieces in flour seasoned with salt, pepper, and paprika. Brush thoroughly with beaten egg and roll in cornflake or dried bread crumbs. Put chicken in well-buttered, ovenproof dish.
3. Pour melted butter over chicken. Bake for 30 to 35 minutes, or until chicken pieces are crisp and brown.
4. While chicken is baking, prepare tomato sauce. Melt butter in saucepan. Add onion and garlic, and saute until golden. Whisk in flour, tomato paste, tomatoes, and broth. Bring to a boil. Add herbs, peppercorns, lemon peel, and cayenne pepper; simmer for 20 minutes. Strain sauce and add sugar, if desired. Season with salt and pepper.
5. Serve hot chicken with sauce and rice or mashed potatoes.

Brunswick Stew

Serves 4 to 6

1 (3 to 4-pound) chicken, cut
 into serving pieces
Boiling water
1 teaspoon salt
3 potatoes, peeled and sliced
1 large onion, sliced
1 cup green lima beans
1 cup canned tomatoes
 or 5 fresh tomatoes,
 sliced
1 tablespoon sugar
1 cup frozen corn
Freshly ground black pepper
 to taste
1 tablespoon ketchup or
 Worcestershire sauce,
 optional
¼ cup butter

1. Place chicken in Dutch oven with enough boiling water to cover. Add salt and simmer for 45 minutes.
2. Add potatoes, onion, lima beans, tomatoes, and sugar to chicken. Cover and simmer for 30 minutes, or until beans and potatoes are tender.
3. Add corn, cover, and simmer for 10 minutes. Season and add ketchup or Worcestershire sauce, if desired. Add butter and stir well. Transfer to serving dish and serve hot.

Chicken Florentine

Serves 4

3 pounds chicken pieces
2 to 3 tablespoons flour,
  seasoned with salt and
  pepper
6 tablespoons butter
1 pound frozen spinach
1 tablespoon flour
3 to 4 tablespoons light
  cream
1/8 teaspoon paprika
4 to 5 tablespoons grated
  Parmesan cheese
3 tablespoons cornflake or
  bread crumbs

1. Roll chicken pieces in seasoned flour. Melt 3 tablespoons butter in large frying pan. Add chicken pieces and cook until browned, about 10 minutes.
2. Preheat oven to 400 degrees.
3. Cook frozen spinach following directions on package. Add 2 tablespoons butter and toss until melted. Sprinkle in flour. Bring spinach to a boil, then add cream and paprika. Spoon spinach mixture into buttered, ovenproof dish. Arrange chicken pieces on top.
3. Mix cheese and cornflake or bread crumbs together. Sprinkle thickly on top of chicken. Melt remaining butter and dribble on top. Bake for 25 to 30 minutes, or until topping is crisp and brown.

Chicken in White Wine Sauce

Serves 4

3 pounds chicken pieces
2 to 3 slices onion
3 to 4 sprigs parsley or
  1 teaspoon dried parsley
1/8 teaspoon nutmeg
6 peppercorns
1 bay leaf
2 cups white wine
1/2 cup chicken broth
4 tablespoons butter
3 tablespoons flour
1 teaspoon tarragon
1/4 cup whipping cream

1. Preheat oven to 350 degrees.
2. Place chicken pieces in casserole dish with onion, parsley, nutmeg, peppercorns, and bay leaf. Add wine and broth. Bake for 35 to 45 minutes, or until chicken is tender. Transfer chicken pieces to serving dish and keep warm.
3. Boil liquid left in casserole for a few minutes until slightly reduced. Strain and measure out 2 cups of liquid.
4. Melt butter in saucepan. Whisk in flour, then add the 2 cups of strained liquid. Season to taste and add tarragon and cream.
5. Spoon sauce over chicken. Serve at once, with rice or mashed potatoes.

Boiled Chicken with Mushroom Sauce

Serves 6 to 8

3 tablespoons vegetable oil
2 onions, chopped
2 to 3 stalks celery, chopped
1 (4-pound) stewing chicken, cut
  into serving pieces
1 thick slice bacon, cut into pieces
Salt to taste
4 peppercorns
1 bay leaf
2 tablespoons margarine
2 cups sliced mushrooms
1 teaspoon Worcestershire sauce
3 tablespoons flour

1. Heat oil in large saucepan. Add onions and celery; saute for 3 to 4 minutes. Add chicken pieces, giblets, and bacon. Add water to cover, salt, peppercorns, and bay leaf. Bring to a boil, cover, and simmer about 2 hours, or until chicken is tender. Transfer chicken to a serving dish and keep warm. Strain and measure out 1 1/2 cups chicken broth.
2. Melt margarine in saucepan. Add mushrooms and saute 3 minutes. Stir in Worcestershire sauce and flour. Remove from heat and gradually add reserved chicken broth. Return to heat and whisk until boiling. Boil 2 minutes. Adjust seasonings and remove bay leaf.
3. Pour sauce over chicken pieces, and serve.

Chicken Stew

Serves 6 to 8

1/2 cup pork drippings or other
  cooking fat
1 stewing chicken, cut into
  serving pieces
Flour seasoned with salt and
  pepper
2 large onions, sliced
2 to 3 tomatoes, skinned and
  quartered
6 to 8 pitted green olives, optional
2 bay leaves
1/4 teaspoon fines herbes
2 tablespoons flour
Salt and pepper to taste
Chicken broth or water
1 cup sliced mushrooms

1. Heat fat in heavy-bottomed pot. Coat chicken pieces in seasoned flour and brown on all sides. Remove chicken from pan and set aside.
2. Add onions and tomatoes to remaining fat in pan. Saute about 5 minutes. Add olives, bay leaves, and herbs. Sprinkle with 2 tablespoons flour and season with salt and pepper, mixing well.
3. Return chicken to pan. Add broth or water to cover, cover pan, and simmer for 2 to 2 1/2 hours, until chicken is tender. Add mushrooms during last 10 minutes of cooking time and remove bay leaves.
4. To serve, place chicken pieces on large serving dish. Arrange vegetables around chicken. Thicken stock with a small amount of flour, and adjust seasonings. Pour some sauce over chicken; serve remaining sauce separately.

Chicken and Vegetable Casserole

Serves 5 to 6

3 pounds chicken pieces
Flour seasoned with salt and
  pepper
1/4 pound salt pork, cut into small
  pieces
1/4 teaspoon thyme
1/8 teaspoon marjoram
1 1/2 cups sliced carrots

1 cup small white onions, peeled
1½ cups diced potatoes
1 cup sliced mushrooms
½ bay leaf
1 sprig parsley
1 clove garlic, peeled and
 crushed
1½ cups boiling water
Salt and pepper to taste

1. Preheat oven to 350 degrees.
2. Coat chicken with seasoned flour.
3. Place salt pork in frying pan and cook until crisp to make crackling. Remove pieces of crackling from pan.
4. Brown chicken on all sides in pork fat. Place in casserole dish.
5. Add remaining ingredients and crisp pieces of pork to chicken. Cover and cook in oven for 1¼ hours. Season with salt and pepper. Remove bay leaf, and serve.

Chicken Sorrento

Serves 5 to 6

3 pounds chicken pieces
Flour seasoned with salt and
 pepper
3 tablespoons vegetable oil
⅓ cup rice
1 large onion
1 orange, cut in half and seeded
 but not peeled
½ cup milk
1 cup water
3 tablespoons chopped pimento
¼ teaspoon thyme
⅛ teaspoon sugar
⅛ teaspoon cayenne pepper

1. Coat chicken pieces with seasoned flour. Heat oil in large frying pan and brown chicken on all sides. Remove chicken from pan and set aside. Add rice to pan, stirring over low heat until rice is golden brown.
2. Preheat oven to 350 degrees.
3. Put onion and unpeeled orange through a food grinder, using the coarse blade. Mix rice with onion and orange mixture, then place in casserole dish. Arrange chicken pieces on top of mixture. Add remaining ingredients.
4. Cover and bake for 1 to 1¼ hours. Adjust seasoning before serving.

Barbecued Chicken

Serves 4

4 large chicken quarters

Barbecue Sauce

6 tablespoons vegetable oil
1 onion, finely chopped
1 clove garlic, peeled and
 crushed
1 (8-ounce) can tomatoes
1 tablespoon ketchup
1 tablespoon chutney
1 tablespoon vinegar
½ cup chicken broth or water
1 tablespoon Worcestershire
 sauce
1 teaspoon Dijon mustard
1 teaspoon paprika
Juice and grated rind of
 ½ lemon
2 teaspoons brown sugar
1 tablespoon finely chopped
 parsley
1 bay leaf
Salt and pepper to taste

1. Wash chicken and pat dry.
2. Heat oil in saucepan. Add onion and garlic and saute for 5 minutes. Add remaining ingredients, except chicken. Simmer for 20 to 30 minutes. Strain and set aside to cool.
3. With a sharp knife, make small cuts in chicken pieces. Spoon cooled barbecue sauce over chicken and let stand for at least ½ hour.
4. Heat broiler or charcoal grill. Cook chicken about 30 to 45 minutes, depending on size of chicken pieces. Baste frequently with barbecue sauce. Test doneness by pricking chicken with skewer; if juice from chicken runs clear, chicken is done.
5. Heat remaining sauce and serve separately with chicken.

Chicken-Peach Casserole

Serves 6

2 tablespoons butter or margarine
1 tablespoon vegetable oil

3½ pounds chicken pieces,
 skinned
1 large onion, sliced
1 green pepper, seeded and
 cut into strips
1 tablespoon cornstarch
1 tablespoon soy sauce
3 tablespoons white wine
 vinegar
1 (30-ounce) can sliced peaches,
 drained (reserve syrup)
2 tomatoes, skinned and thickly
 sliced

1. Heat butter and oil in large frying pan. Add chicken and brown on all sides. Cover and cook over low heat for 10 minutes. Remove chicken from pan and arrange in large casserole dish.
2. Saute onion and green pepper in remaining fat until onion is transparent.
3. Preheat oven to 375 degrees.
4. Mix cornstarch with soy sauce and vinegar until smooth. Add 1 cup reserved peach syrup. Pour into saucepan, whisking until boiling. Boil until clear. Add peaches and tomatoes. Pour sauce over chicken in casserole dish.
5. Cover casserole and bake for 30 to 40 minutes, removing lid for last 5 minutes of cooking time. Adjust seasoning, and serve.

Deviled Chicken

Serves 4

6 tablespoons vegetable oil
1 teaspoon curry powder
2 teaspoons prepared mustard
1 tablespoon vinegar
½ teaspoon freshly ground black
 pepper
⅛ teaspoon cayenne pepper
1 tablespoon ketchup
8 chicken legs

1. Preheat broiler.
2. Mix oil and curry powder until smooth. Add remaining ingredients, except chicken.
3. Brush chicken legs generously with sauce. Broil about 30 minutes, or until tender and brown on both sides. Transfer to platter, and serve.

Cinnamon Orange Chicken

Serves 4

4 chicken quarters
2 tablespoons flour
Salt and pepper to taste
1 teaspoon ground cinnamon
4 tablespoons margarine
1/2 cup chicken broth
2 oranges

1. Coat chicken in flour seasoned with salt, pepper, and cinnamon.
2. Heat margarine in large frying pan. Add chicken and saute for 20 minutes, or until tender and golden all over. Remove chicken and drain on paper towels. Keep warm.
3. Pour off fat from pan. Add chicken broth and finely grated rind and juice from 1 orange. Bring to a boil, whisking constantly.
4. Arrange chicken on serving platter. Pour sauce on top. Peel remaining orange, removing skin and pith; slice thinly. Arrange orange slices on chicken and serve with rice.

Cheesy Oven-Fried Chicken

Serves 4

4 large chicken quarters
1 tablespoon flour
Salt and pepper to taste
1/2 teaspoon dry mustard
1 egg, beaten
1/4 cup soft white bread crumbs
1/4 cup grated Cheddar cheese
4 tablespoons margarine

1. Preheat oven to 400 degrees.
2. Coat chicken in flour seasoned with salt, pepper, and mustard. Brush chicken with beaten egg and roll in mixture of bread crumbs and cheese.
3. Place in casserole dish and dot with small pieces of margarine. Bake for 40 minutes, or until golden brown and tender.

Chicken with Sweet Peppers

Serves 4

2 whole boneless chicken breasts
1 clove garlic, peeled and crushed
4 tablespoons olive oil
3 tablespoons soy sauce
1/2 teaspoon salt
1/2 teaspoon freshly ground black pepper
2 teaspoons cornstarch
2 green peppers, seeded and cut into 1-inch pieces
2 red peppers, seeded and cut into 1-inch pieces.
8 scallions, cut into 1/2-inch pieces
3 stalks celery, cut into 1/2-inch pieces
1/4 teaspoon sugar
1/4 cup cold water

1. Combine chicken, garlic, 1 tablespoon oil, 2 tablespoons soy sauce, salt, pepper, and 1 teaspoon cornstarch in mixing bowl. Marinate at least 30 minutes.
2. Heat remaining 3 tablespoons oil in wok or large frying pan. Add peppers and stir-fry for 3 minutes. Add scallions and stir-fry for 2 minutes. Add celery and stir-fry for 2 minutes more. Remove peppers, scallions and celery from pan, using slotted spoon. Keep warm.
3. Place chicken in hot oil in wok or pan and stir-fry for 5 minutes. Combine 1 tablespoon soy sauce, 1 teaspoon cornstarch, sugar, and cold water; pour over chicken.
4. Add vegetables and combine carefully, cooking over low heat about 3 minutes. Serve with boiled rice.

Chicken with Lemon Sauce

Serves 6 to 8

1/2 cup butter or margarine
2 broiler chickens, halved
1 clove garlic, peeled and crushed
1 1/2 teaspoons salt
1/4 cup salad oil
1/2 cup lemon juice

2 tablespoons minced onion
1/2 teaspoon freshly ground black pepper
1/2 teaspoon thyme

1. Melt butter in heavy frying pan with lid. Add chicken and brown well on both sides.
2. Combine remaining ingredients and pour over chicken. Cover tightly. Cook over low heat about 40 minutes, or until chicken is tender. Transfer to serving dish, and serve.

Honey Chicken

Serves 4

1/2 cup flour
1 teaspoon salt
3 or 4 boneless chicken breasts
1/2 cup butter, melted
1/4 cup honey
1/4 cup lemon juice
1 tablespoon soy sauce

1. Preheat oven to 350 degrees.
2. Combine flour and salt. Dip chicken in flour-salt mixture. Arrange chicken in baking dish.
3. Pour melted butter over chicken. Bake for 30 minutes.
4. Mix remaining ingredients together, and pour over chicken. Bake 30 minutes longer, basting often. Remove from heat and serve hot.

Orange Chicken

Serves 4 to 6

4 teaspoons Dijon mustard, optional
1 (3-pound) frying chicken, quartered and skinned
1 teaspoon salt
1/4 teaspoon pepper
2 tablespoons butter, melted
1 small onion, chopped
1 cup orange juice
1/4 cup brown sugar, lightly packed

1. Preheat oven to 375 degrees.
2. Spread mustard on meaty side of chicken and sprinkle with salt and pepper. Place chicken, meaty side down, in baking pan. Add butter, onion, and orange juice. Bake for 20

minutes, basting after 10 minutes. Turn chicken over.

3. Stir sugar into pan juices. Continue baking chicken for 40 minutes, basting several times, until chicken is golden brown and tender. Remove chicken from pan and keep warm.

4. Pour pan juices into 1-quart saucepan and boil gently, stirring frequently, until sauce is reduced and thickened. Spoon sauce over chicken, and serve.

Stuffed Chicken Breasts

Serves 6

1 tablespoon butter
1¹/₂ cups shredded zucchini
1 tablespoon dill weed
Salt and pepper to taste
6 boneless chicken breast halves, skinned and pounded thin
1 egg, beaten
Bread crumbs

1 Melt butter in large frying pan. Add zucchini, dill, salt, and pepper. Cook over medium heat until zucchini becomes tender and loses moisture.

2. Divide zucchini mixture among chicken breast halves, using only enough so that chicken can be drawn up around it. Fold over sides of chicken to totally enclose zucchini. Secure with toothpicks.

3. Preheat oven to 450 degrees.

4. Dip chicken breast in egg, then coat with bread crumbs. Place in lightly greased baking dish and bake for 15 minutes, or until tender. Remove from heat and transfer to serving dish.

Chicken Marengo

Serves 4

3 pounds chicken pieces
¹/₂ teaspoon freshly ground white pepper
¹/₂ cup olive oil
1³/₄ cups sliced mushrooms
Juice of 1 lemon
6 anchovy fillets, finely chopped
2 cloves garlic, peeled and chopped

1 sprig parsley, 2 sprigs thyme, and ¹/₂ bay leaf, tied together
1 cup hot chicken broth
1³/₄ cups chopped, skinned tomatoes
12 black olives
2 hard-boiled eggs, finely chopped

1. Rub chicken pieces well with pepper and a small amount of olive oil. Sprinkle mushrooms with lemon juice.

2. Heat remaining olive oil in heavy saucepan. Add chicken pieces and cook for 10 minutes, until well browned. Add mushrooms, anchovies, garlic, herbs, and hot chicken broth. Cover and simmer over medium heat for 25 minutes.

3 Add tomatoes and olives to chicken for final 5 minutes of cooking time. Transfer to heated, deep platter. Before serving, sprinkle with chopped eggs.

Chicken with Olives

Serves 4

¹/₄ cup olive oil
1 (3-pound) chicken, cut into serving pieces
2 cloves garlic, peeled and finely chopped
1 sprig fresh rosemary or ¹/₄ teaspoon dried rosemary
1 teaspoon salt
¹/₈ teaspoon freshly ground black pepper
2 ripe tomatoes, skinned and cut into chunks
16 black pitted olives
3 tablespoons chicken broth
Basil leaves, for garnish

1. Heat oil in large, heavy frying pan with lid. Brown chicken pieces and giblets well over medium heat. Combine chopped garlic and rosemary, and sprinkle over chicken. Season with salt and pepper. Cover and cook for 15 minutes over low heat.

2. Add tomatoes, olives, and broth. Simmer for 15 minutes longer, adding more bouillon if necessary. Transfer to heated serving dish.

3. Garnish with basil leaves, and serve.

Chicken with Dried Fruit

Serves 4

³/₄ cup pitted prunes
³/₄ cup dried apricots
1 tablespoon raisins
1¹/₂ cups water
4 zwieback biscuits
3 tablespoons light cream
1 egg
2 tablespoons brandy
1 tart apple, peeled and diced
1 (3-pound) chicken
2 teaspoons paprika
Salt and pepper
3 tablespoons butter, melted
1 small onion, chopped
1 small carrot, chopped
¹/₄ cup chopped celery
1³/₄ cups sour cream

1. Place prunes, apricots, raisins, and water in saucepan and bring to a boil. Drain, reserving water. Place fruit in large wooden bowl. Chop coarsely, reserving a few whole prunes and apricots for garnish.

2. Crumble zwieback and mix with cream, egg, and brandy. Add zwieback mixture and diced apple to bowl with dried fruit.

3. Preheat oven to 400 degrees.

4. Remove giblets, chop, and set aside. Wash and dry chicken; rub inside and out with paprika and pepper, salting inside only. Fill chicken with fruit stuffing, sew up, truss, and place in roasting pan. Pour melted butter on top. Roast for 1¹/₄ hours. Remove chicken from oven and keep warm.

5. While chicken is roasting, place chopped onion, carrot, and celery in saucepan with reserved cooking water and chopped giblets. Simmer for 30 minutes. Remove from heat and strain broth.

6. Stir strained broth into roasting pan to deglaze. Stir in sour cream and boil until smooth and slightly thickened. Serve chicken with sour cream gravy separately.

Chicken in Cider

Serves 4

3 pounds chicken pieces
1 teaspoon salt
$1/2$ teaspoon freshly ground black
   pepper
$1/2$ cup butter
1 cup apple cider
3 cups carrots, cut into 2-inch
   pieces
$1/4$ cup water
1 tablespoon honey
$1/4$ cup chopped parsley
$1/2$ cup light cream
$1/2$ cup chopped fresh tarragon
   or 1 teaspoon dried tarragon

1. Rub chicken pieces well with salt and pepper. Heat $1/4$ cup butter in heavy-bottomed pan; lightly brown chicken pieces on all sides. Add cider. Cover and simmer for 45 minutes.
2. Heat remaining $1/4$ cup butter in deep pan. Add carrots, a small amount of salt, and $1/4$ cup water. Cover and steam gently for 20 minutes. Allow any remaining water to evaporate. Lightly coat carrots with honey and sprinkle with 1 tablespoon chopped parsley. Cover and keep warm.
3. Arrange chicken on warm serving dish. Reduce chicken cooking liquid by half over high heat. Stir in cream, remaining parsley, and tarragon. To serve, pour sauce over chicken.

Chicken with Cold Nut Sauce

Serves 4

1 teaspoon curry powder
1 teaspoon paprika
$1/8$ teaspoon freshly ground
   black pepper
1 teaspoon salt
1 (3-pound) chicken
3 tablespoons sunflower oil

Nut Sauce

2 slices whole-wheat bread,
   cubed
$1/2$ cup plus 2 tablespoons water
$1/2$ cup ground walnuts
3 tablespoons walnut oil

1 teaspoon red wine vinegar
1 clove garlic, peeled and finely
   chopped
$1/4$ teaspoon honey
$1/4$ teaspoon salt

1. Preheat oven to 400 degrees.
2. Combine curry, paprika, pepper, and salt; rub inside of chicken with mixture. Truss chicken, brush with sunflower oil, and lay breast side down in roasting pan.
3. Roast chicken for 1 hour, turning over after 30 minutes and basting frequently with cooking juices. Switch off oven and let chicken stand for 10 minutes.
4. To make sauce, soak bread cubes in $1/2$ cup water. Squeeze bread dry and rub through sieve. Combine bread with ground nuts. Stir walnut oil, vinegar, 2 tablespoons water, and garlic into read mixture. Season with honey and salt.
5. Serve nut sauce separately with neatly carved slices of chicken.

Chicken Croissants

Makes 10 croissants

1 package frozen puff pastry
2 tablespoons butter
2 onions, diced
1 cup finely chopped mushrooms
1 teaspoon salt
$1/4$ teaspoon freshly ground black
   pepper
1 teaspoon thyme
2 tablespoons light cream
1 egg, separated
14 ounces boneless chicken
   breasts, finely chopped
1 tablespoon condensed milk

1. Remove pastry from wrapping and thaw according to instructions.
2. Melt butter in large frying pan. Add onions and saute until transparent. Add mushrooms, salt, pepper, and thyme; continue to cook, stirring constantly, until all liquid has

evaporated. Remove from heat. Stir in cream and set aside to cool. When mixture is cool, mix in egg white and chopped chicken.
3. Preheat oven to 400 degrees.
4. Rinse baking sheet with cold water; dry. Roll out pastry and cut into 5 squares. Halve each square diagonally, then roll out resulting triangles again to make them slightly wider. Spoon $1/10$ of filling mixture along wide edge of each triangle. Roll up to form crescent, curving tips around in semicircle.
5. Beat egg yolk and condensed milk together, then brush on each croissant. Place croissants on baking sheet. Bake for 20 minutes on bottom oven shelf, or until evenly browned. Remove from heat and transfer to serving platter.

Deluxe Roast Chicken with Bread Sauce

Serves 4 to 6

$3/4$ cup butter
1 large onion, chopped
2 cups fresh bread crumbs
2 tablespoons chopped cooked
   ham
1 tablespoon chopped parsley
1 teaspoon thyme
$1/8$ teaspoon grated lemon rind
1 egg, beaten
Salt and pepper to taste
1 (5- to 6-pound) roasting chicken
4 teaspoons vegetable oil
2 cups chicken stock made from
   giblets
4 slices bacon, halved, rolled up,
   and skewered
8 Italian sausages

Bread Sauce

2 cloves
1 onion
1 cup milk
$1/2$ bay leaf
1 sprig parsley
$1/8$ teaspoon nutmeg
6 peppercorns
1 cup fresh bread crumbs
1 tablespoon butter
2 tablespoons light cream
Salt to taste

1. Preheat oven to 400 degrees.
2. Melt ¼ cup butter in saucepan. Add half the chopped onion and saute for 3 to 4 minutes, until softened. Combine sauteed onion with bread crumbs, chopped ham, herbs, and grated lemon rind. Add enough beaten egg to make fairly moist mixture. Season with salt and pepper.
3. Spoon stuffing into cavity of chicken. Put remaining onion and some salt and pepper inside neck end of bird with a small amount of butter. Fold skin flap under wings and skewer or sew to hold in place. Rub remaining butter over chicken and sprinkle with salt and pepper.
4. Heat oil in roasting pan. When hot, add chicken, baste thoroughly, then cover with foil. Roast, basting every 15 minutes and turning chicken from side to side. Allow about 20 minutes per pound. During last 15 minutes of cooking time, remove foil to allow breast to brown. Transfer chicken to hot serving dish and keep warm while making gravy.
5. Pour off fat from roasting pan. Pour in remaining chicken stock and bring to a boil. For more flavor, reduce liquid by boiling.
6. To prepare bread sauce, stick cloves into onion. Place onion, milk, herbs, and peppercorns in saucepan. Cook gently for 20 to 30 minutes, without boiling. Place bread crumbs in saucepan. Strain milk over bread crumbs; heat together stirring constantly, until creamy. Stir in butter, cream, and salt; serve hot.
7. Preheat broiler. Roll up bacon and put on skewers. Broil bacon and sausages until crisp.
8. Serve chicken surrounded by bacon rolls and sausages. Serve chicken gravy and bread sauce separately.

Chicken with Almonds

Serves 4

¼ cup vegetable oil
2 tablespoons butter or margarine
2½ pounds chicken pieces
2 onions, thinly sliced
3 tomatoes, skinned, seeded, and chopped
⅛ teaspoon cinnamon
Salt and pepper to taste
1½ cups chicken broth
5 tablespoons blanched almonds
½ cup seedless golden raisins
3 to 4 cups cooked rice

1. Preheat oven to 375 degrees.
2. Heat oil and butter in frying pan. Add chicken pieces and brown on all sides. Add onions, tomatoes, cinnamon, salt, and pepper. Cook over low heat for 3 or 4 minutes, then transfer to an ovenproof casserole dish.
3. Add chicken broth, cover, and cook for 30 minutes. Add almonds and raisins and cook for 30 minutes more.
4. Line large oval platter with hot cooked rice. Pile chicken pieces in center of platter. To serve, season sauce to taste and pour over chicken.

Chicken Cordon Bleu

Serves 4

4 boneless chicken breasts
¼ cup chopped cooked ham
¼ cup grated Swiss cheese
1 small clove garlic, peeled and crushed
2 tablespoons white wine
Salt and pepper to taste
¼ cup flour, seasoned with salt and pepper
1 large egg, beaten with 1 teaspoon oil
½ cup dried white bread crumbs
¼ cup oil
5 tablespoons butter

1. Place chicken breasts skin side down, and with a sharp knife cut a shallow slit down center of each without cutting through to skin. Then cut shallow pockets on either side of these slits.

2. Mix ham and cheese with crushed garlic and white wine. Season well. Spoon mixture into pockets in chicken breasts and seal slit with the small finger-shaped fillet that is attached to each breast. Refrigerate for 30 minutes.
3. Coat breasts well with seasoned flour, brush with egg beaten with oil, and roll in bread crumbs. Heat ¼ cup oil in frying pan. Add butter and, when butter is foaming, cook chicken until tender, golden brown, and crisp. Drain on paper towels, and serve.

Marinated Chicken with Cucumber Salad

Serves 4

1 (2½-pound) chicken, halved

Marinade

2 cups plain yogurt
1 onion, sliced
2 teaspoons curry powder
1 teaspoon ginger
2 teaspoons paprika
1 teaspoon caraway seeds
2 cloves garlic, peeled and crushed

Cucumber Salad

2 cups plain yogurt
½ cucumber, thinly sliced
¼ cup chopped chives
1 teaspoon salt
Freshly ground black pepper

1. Wash chicken and pat dry; place in deep plate. Mix all marinade ingredients together and pour over chicken halves. Refrigerate for 6 to 8 hours. Turn chicken several times while it is marinating.
2. Preheat oven to 350 degrees.
3. Transfer chicken halves to ovenproof dish. Pour marinade over chicken and brush chicken well. Bake for 45 minutes, basting occasionally.
4. To make cucumber salad, let yogurt drain through a coffee filter for 15 minutes. Mix cucumber with yogurt. Add chives, salt, and pepper. Serve salad with chicken.

Stuffed Chicken Legs

Serves 4 to 6

3/4 cup mushrooms
3 sprigs parsley
2 cloves garlic, peeled
3 tablespoons butter
1/2 teaspoon lemon juice
8 chicken legs, about
    6 ounces each
1/2 teaspoon salt
1/8 teaspoon freshly ground
    black pepper
2 tablespoons vegetable oil

1. Place mushrooms, parsley, garlic, butter, and lemon juice in blender or food processor and process to a smooth paste.
2. Preheat oven to 475 degrees.
3. Wash chicken legs and pat dry. Loosen skin from meat, working from thick end and pushing skin up toward bone. Spread mushroom filling over meat and pull skin down over it again. Rub chicken well with salt and pepper. Brush with oil and lay on rack in roasting pan. Roast for 45 minutes in center of oven. Remove from oven and transfer chicken to serving dish, spooning mushroom filling on top.

Chicken-Vegetable Stew

Serves 4

6 tablespoons butter
1 (2 1/4-pound) chicken, cut into
    serving pieces
3 small onions, chopped
1 carrot, chopped
2 leeks, white part only,
    sliced
1 teaspoon salt
2 teaspoons paprika
1/8 teaspoon pepper
1 cup unsweetened apple juice
1 pound tomatoes, skinned and
    chopped
1/2 cup finely sliced mushrooms
2 tablespoons chopped chives

1. Melt 4 tablespoons butter in large, heavy-bottomed pan. Add chicken pieces ands brown well on all sides; remove from skillet. Brown chopped onions and carrot in butter.

2. Add remaining 2 tablespoons butter and leeks. Saute briefly, then lay chicken pieces on top of vegetables in pan. Sprinkle with salt, paprika, and pepper; pour on apple juice. Cover and cook over low heat for 35 minutes.
3. Add tomatoes and mushrooms to stew for final 10 minutes of cooking time. Sprinkle with chopped chives, and serve.

Chicken and Turnip Stew

Serves 4

1 (2 1/2-pound) chicken
2 carrots
2 leeks, white part only
2 small onions
6 cups water
2 1/8 teaspoons sea salt
5 white peppercorns
2 1/4 pounds turnips, peeled and
    thinly sliced
2 shallots, peeled and halved
1 cup finely chopped parsley
1/8 teaspoon pepper

1. Place chicken in large pot with 1 carrot, 1 leek, 1 onion, water, 2 teaspoons sea salt, and peppercorns. Simmer for 1 hour, or until chicken is tender. Skim as needed during first 30 minutes of cooking time.
2. Remove chicken from broth and discard vegetables. Cook turnips, shallots, remaining carrot, leek, and onion in broth until tender.
3. Remove chicken meat from bone and cut into good-size pieces. Remove pan from heat. Stir chicken pieces and parsley into soup. Season with 1/8 teaspoon sea salt and pepper.
4. Serve with slices of hearty rye bread.

Chicken Stew with Mixed Vegetables

Serves 4

4 carrots, scraped
3 stalks celery, chopped
2 leeks, white part only, sliced
2 small onions, chopped

2 cloves garlic, peeled and
    chopped
6 cups water
1 sprig fresh thyme or
    1/4 teaspoon dried thyme
1 bay leaf
1 clove
2 teaspoons sea salt
1 teaspoon white peppercorns
1 (4-pound) stewing chicken
2 young turnips, peeled and cut
    into julienne strips
1 zucchini, cut into julienne
    strips

1. Roughly chop 2 carrots and cut remaining 2 carrots into julienne strips. Place chopped carrots, celery, 1 leek, onions, and garlic in large pot. Cover with water and bring to a boil. Add thyme, bay leaf, clove, salt, and peppercorns. Add chicken and simmer for 2 hours, skimming as need during first 30 minutes of cooking time.
2. Remove chicken from broth. Strain broth and bring to a boil again. Add remaining leek, turnips, zucchini, and carrot strips. Simmer for 10 minutes.
3. Separate chicken meat from bones and cut into small cubes. Add chicken cubes to stew. Before serving, season to taste with salt and pepper.

Creole Jambalaya

Serves 6 to 8

1/2 pound smoked pork tenderloin,
    cubed
1 (2 1/2-pound) chicken, cut into
    serving pieces
1 teaspoon salt
1/8 teaspoon white pepper
5 tablespoons oil
2 onions, diced
1 clove garlic, peeled and diced
2 green peppers, seeded and diced
1 red pepper, seeded and diced
3 cups hot chicken bouillon
1 tomato, skinned and chopped
2 cups long-grain rice
1/8 teaspoon cayenne pepper
1/8 teaspoon saffron
1/2 pound smoked garlic sausage,
    sliced
1/2 pound lean ham, cut into strips
1/2 pound cooked lobster meat, cut
    into strips

1. Combine pork cubes and chicken pieces. Mix salt, pepper, and oil together and pour over chicken and pork. Cover and marinate for 30 minutes.

2. Transfer meat and oil mixture to large, heavy-bottomed pan; saute pork and chicken until browned. Add onion, garlic, and peppers; saute until tender. Pour on 1½ cups bouillon. Cover and simmer for 30 minutes.

3. Add tomatoe, rice, remaining bouillon, cayenne pepper, and saffron to meat, mixing well. Simmer for 20 minutes.

4. Arrange sausage, ham, and lobster on top of rice combination. Simmer for 5 minutes, or until heated through, and serve.

Drumsticks with Mushrooms

Serves 4

8 chicken drumsticks
¼ cup flour
1 tablespoon butter
¼ cup olive oil
1 onion, chopped
1 clove garlic, peeled and
　chopped
1 tablespoon tomato paste
⅓ cup dry red wine
1 tablespoon salt
⅛ teaspoon white pepper
¼ teaspoon marjoram
⅛ teaspoon thyme
1½ cups sliced mushrooms
Juice of ½ lemon
3 sprigs parsley, finely chopped
1 tablespoon wine vinegar

1. Coat drumsticks with flour. Heat butter and 1 tablespoon olive oil in large skillet. Add drumsticks and cook until browned. Add onion and garlic, stirring until softened.

2. Combine tomato paste, wine, salt, pepper, marjoram, and thyme, and add to skillet with chicken. Simmer for 30 minutes.

3. Sprinkle mushrooms with lemon juice. Heat remaining olive oil in separate skillet. Add mushrooms and half the parsley; saute until all juices have evaporated.

4. Stir mushroom mixture into chicken and transfer to an attractive serving dish. Sprinkle with vinegar and remaining parsley, and serve hot.

Chicken Drumsticks with Lentils

Serves 4

2¼ cups lentils
6½ cups water
1 cup dry red wine
8 chicken drumsticks
1 chicken bouillon cube
1 bay leaf
1 dried chili pepper
⅛ teaspoon freshly ground
　black pepper
½ teaspoon thyme
1 teaspoon basil
¼ pound bacon, diced
2 onions, sliced into rings
1 clove garlic, peeled and crushed
⅛ teaspoon salt
2 tablespoons chopped parsley

1. Wash lentils several times in bowl of water. Place lentils in large saucepan, cover with water and red wine, and bring to a boil. Add drumsticks, crumbled bouillon cube, bay leaf, chili, pepper, thyme, and basil. Bring to a boil again, cover, and simmer for 45 minutes.

2. Cook bacon in skillet until crisp. Drain. Add onions to pan and saute until golden brown. Add garlic and continue sauteing until brown.

3. Spoon onion mixture over lentils and chicken. Before serving, season with salt and sprinkle with chopped parsley.

Chicken Wings in Batter

Serves 4

¾ cup flour
½ teaspoon salt
⅛ teaspoon cayenne pepper
2 eggs, separated
⅓ cup beer

4 cups plus 1 tablespoon vegetable
　oil
12 to 16 chicken wings
Lemon slices, for garnish

1. Combine flour, salt, and cayenne pepper. Beat egg yolks with beer and 1 tablespoon oil, then stir into dry ingredients. Set batter aside for 30 minutes.

2. Heat oil to 350 degrees in deep-fryer. Preheat oven to 200 degrees.

3. Beat egg whites until stiff and fold into batter. Dip chicken wings in batter. Fry wings, a few at a time, in deep fat for about 4 minutes on each side, or until crisp and golden.

4. Drain wings on paper towels, then keep warm in oven until all are done. Garnish with lemon slices.

Chicken Drumsticks in a Roasting Bag

Serves 4

8 chicken drumsticks
1 teaspoon salt
1 tablespoon paprika
2 tablespoons butter
1 onion, cut into wedges
1 cup leeks, white part only,
　cut into 1¼-inch pieces
¼ medium cauliflower, divided
　into florets
2 red peppers, seeded and
　diced
½ cup chicken broth
2 tablespoons medium-dry
　sherry
2 tablespoons chopped chives

1. Preheat oven to 425 degrees.

2. Rub drumsticks well with salt and paprika. Melt butter in frying pan. Brown drumsticks over low heat.

3. Place drumsticks in roasting bag with onion, leeks, cauliflower florets, and red peppers. Add chicken broth. Seal bag and pierce top several times.

4. Lay roasting bag in baking dish and bake for 35 minutes. Remove food carefully from bag and place drumsticks, vegetables, and cooking juices on serving dish. Before serving, sprinkle with sherry and chives.

West Indian Drumsticks

Serves 6

12 chicken drumsticks
³/₄ teaspoons salt
¹/₂ teaspoon paprika
1 tablespoon cornstarch
1 tablespoon sugar
1 cup orange juice
1¹/₂ teaspoons curry powder
1 teaspoon grated orange peel
¹/₂ teaspoon ginger
2 cloves garlic, peeled and
    crushed
¹/₂ cup chopped cashews

1. Preheat oven to 375 degrees.
2. Place chicken in large baking dish and sprinkle with ¹/₂ teaspoon of salt and paprika. Bake for 30 minutes.
3. Mix cornstarch and sugar together in large saucepan. Stir in orange juice, curry powder, orange peel, ginger, garlic, and remaining ¹/₄ teaspoon salt. Cook, stirring, over medium heat until mixture boils and thickens.
4. Pour sauce over chicken and bake about 25 minutes, or chicken is fork tender. Baste once with pan juices halfway through baking time. Before serving, sprinkle with cashews.

Marinated Chicken Legs

Serves 4

8 chicken legs, about 6 ounces
    each
1 teaspoon salt
2 cloves garlic, peeled and finely
    chopped
1 small fresh red chili, seeded
    and cut into fine rings
1 cup dry white wine
1 tablespoon Dijon mustard
¹/₈ teaspoon freshly ground black
    pepper
6 tablespoons olive oil

1. Rub chicken legs well with salt and place in flat dish. Mix garlic, chili, wine, mustard, and pepper together, and pour over chicken. Cover and refrigerate for 3 hours, turning legs occasionally.
2. Preheat oven to 400 degrees.
3. Remove chicken from dish. Pour marinade into saucepan and boil for several minutes. Brush chicken with oil and arrange in baking dish. Place on middle oven rack and roast for 45 minutes, basting with marinade several times.
4. For the last 10 minutes of cooking time, turn oven temperature up to 475 degrees and move chicken up to top shelf, so that legs become crisp and golden brown. Remove from heat, and serve.

Chicken Liver and Lentils

Serves 4

4¹/₄ cups water
1³/₄ cups red lentils
¹/₄ cup butter
1 tablespoon olive oil
¹/₄ pound uncooked ham,
    fat removed and finely
    diced
1 cup finely chopped parsley
¹/₂ cup finely chopped fresh sage
    or 1 teaspoon dried sage
3 tablespoons chicken bouillon
1 pound, 2 ounces chicken livers,
    fat and skin removed and cut
    into strips
1 teaspoon salt
¹/₈ teaspoon black pepper

1. Place water in large saucepan and bring a boil. Add lentils and cook over low heat for 8 minutes; drain lentils and set aside.
2. Heat half the butter and the oil in large saucepan. Saute ham and herbs over low heat. Add chicken bouillon; cover and cook 5 minutes longer.
3. Heat remaining butter in frying pan; cook livers for 3 to 4 minutes, stirring constantly. Season with salt and pepper, mix with lentils, and serve immediately.
4. Mashed potatoes or hot French bread go well with this dish.

Fricassee with Walnuts

Serves 4

3 tablespoons soy sauce
2 tablespoons dry sherry
¹/₂ teaspoon sugar
¹/₈ teaspoon salt
2 tablespoons cornstarch
1¹/₄ pounds chicken breast fillets,
    cubed
5 tablespoons oil
1 cup thinly sliced celery
1 medium onion, cut into julienne
    strips
1 red pepper, seeded and cut into
    julienne
¹/₂ cup chicken broth
1 cup walnut halves

1. Mix soy sauce, sherry, sugar, salt, and cornstarch together and combine with chicken cubes.
2. Heat 1 tablespoon oil in frying pan and saute celery for 1 minute. Add onion; saute for 1 minute over high heat. Add red pepper; saute for 1 minute more. Remove vegetables from pan.
3. Heat remaining oil in pan and cook chicken cubes for 3 minutes, stirring frequently. Reduce heat and stir in chicken broth.
4. Return vegetables and walnuts to pan and heat briefly. Serve with rice.

Chicken in Peanut Sauce

Serves 4

1 (2¹/₄-pound) chicken, cut
    into 4 pieces
1 teaspoon sea salt
¹/₂ teaspoons freshly ground black
    pepper
1 tablespoon butter
1 cup shelled peanuts, coarsely
    ground
2 tablespoons whole-wheat flour
1 cup diced carrots
¹/₂ teaspoon ground turmeric
³/₄ cup hot water
2 tablespoons chopped parsley

1. Rub chicken pieces with salt and pepper. Melt butter in frying pan. Brown chicken well, then cover pan and cook gently for 40 minutes, turning once.

2. Sprinkle peanuts with flour, then add to chicken. Turn chicken pieces in peanut mixture. Add diced carrots, turmeric, and hot water. Simmer for 10 minutes more, or until sauce thickens.
3. Before serving, adjust seasoning and sprinkle with parsley.

Poached Chicken

Serves 4

2 (1³/₄-pound) chickens
2 teaspoons salt
1 stalk celery
1 bay leaf
4 small onions
1 clove
4 medium carrots, quartered
 lengthwise
4 leeks, white part only,
 quartered lengthwise
4 small potatoes, peeled and
 halved
1 sprig parsley
1 sprig fresh thyme or ¹/₄ teaspoon
 dried thyme

1. Place chickens and giblets in large stock pot. Add salt and celery. Spike bay leaf onto 1 onion with clove; add to soup pot. Pour on boiling water to cover chickens. Return to boil, then simmer for 1 hour, skimming as needed during first 30 minutes of cooking time.
2. Add carrots, leeks, potatoes, parsley, and thyme to pot. Cover and poach for 30 minutes.
3. Remove chickens from stock, cut into serving pieces, and arrange on warmed dish with vegetables. Strain bouillon and serve as clear soup beforehand.

Chicken with Eggplants

Serves 4

3 medium unpeeled eggplants,
 diced
1 teaspoon salt
6 tablespoons olive oil
1 (2³/₄-pound) frying chicken,
 cut into serving pieces

2 slices bacon, diced
1 clove garlic, peeled and chopped
¹/₃ cup dry white wine
1¹/₄ cup ripe tomatoes, skinned
 and chopped
¹/₂ teaspoon oregano
¹/₄ teaspoon salt
¹/₈ teaspoon pepper
1 cup finely chopped parsley

1. Sprinkle eggplants with salt and set aside for 30 minutes to drain.
2. Heat 3 tablespoons oil in large, heavy skillet with lid. Place chicken pieces, bacon, and chopped garlic in pan; brown well. Add wine and allow it to boil away.
3. Add tomatoes, oregano, salt, and pepper. Cover and cook on low heat for 25 minutes.
4. Rinse diced eggplants and drain well. Fry in remaining oil over high heat for 7 minutes, stirring constantly. Add to chicken mixture.
5. Sprinkle parsley over dish just before serving.

Braised Herbed Chicken

Serves 4

1 (2³/₄-pound) chicken, cut into
 serving pieces
3 tablespoons butter
¹/₂ teaspoon salt
¹/₈ teaspoon freshly ground
 black pepper
Juice of ¹/₂ lemon
¹/₃ cup dry white wine
3 tablespoons chicken
 bouillon
5 shallots, peeled and finely
 chopped
1 cup finely chopped parsley
5 sprigs fresh basil, finely
 chopped
1 lemon, sliced

1. Brown chicken on all sides in butter over low heat. Season with salt and pepper; sprinkle with lemon juice and half the wine. Cover and simmer for 30 minutes, turning several times and adding bouillon as necessary. Remove chicken from pan and keep warm.
2. Cook shallots in braising juices until tender but not brown. Add remaining

wine and cook until sauce is reduced and thickened.
3. Return chicken to pan and reheat in sauce. Sprinkle with chopped herbs and serve garnished with lemon slices.

Chicken Livers in Yogurt Sauce

Serves 4

1¹/₄ cups plain yogurt
¹/₄ cup cream
1 teaspoon lemon juice
1 sprig each fresh parsley, basil,
 and chives, finely chopped
1 clove garlic, peeled and
 chopped
Salt and pepper to taste
¹/₈ teaspoon sugar, optional
1¹/₄ pounds chicken livers
3 tablespoons cooking oil
2 medium onions, cut into thin
 rings
1 tablespoon flour
¹/₂ teaspoon fines herbes
¹/₈ teaspoon salt
¹/₄ teaspoon freshly ground
 black pepper

1. Combine yogurt with cream, lemon juice, and fresh herbs. Sprinkle chopped garlic with salt and crush before adding to yogurt mixture. Season to taste, adding sugar if desired. Set aside.
2. Remove any fat or skin from chicken livers, wash, and pat dry. Heat 1 tablespoon oil in skillet. Add onion rings and saute until brown, about 5 minutes. Remove from pan.
3. Heat remaining oil in skillet. Roll livers in flour and saute, a few at a time, about 2 minutes, until brown. Sprinkle with dried herbs.
4. Add fried onions to livers and continue to saute for 1 minute. Season with salt and pepper, and serve with yogurt sauce.

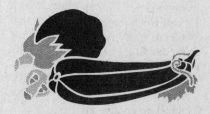

Roast Capon with Orange Pecan Stuffing

Serves 6 to 8

1 (5- to 6-pound) capon

Stuffing

1/4 cup butter or margarine
1 cup thinly sliced celery
1/4 cup chopped onion
3/4 cup water
5 cups toasted, crustless bread cubes
3/4 cup peeled and diced oranges
1/3 cup coarsely chopped pecans
1 teaspoon grated orange rind
1 teaspoon salt
1/2 teaspoon curry powder, optional

1. Wash capon and pat dry.
2. To prepare stuffing, melt butter in frying pan. Add celery, onion, and water. Cook over moderate heat until vegetables are tender. Combine bread cubes, orange pieces, pecans, orange rind, 1/2 teaspoon salt, and curry powder, mixing well. Add vegetables and mix carefully.
3. Preheat oven to 325 degrees.
4. Sprinkle remaining salt over neck and body cavities of capon. Stuff neck and body cavities loosely with bread mixture. Skewer neck skin to back. Return legs and tail to tucked position.
5. Place capon, breast side up, in open roasting pan. Do not add water to pan. Brush with melted butter or margarine. Cover capon loosely with foil, crimping it to edges of pan (foil should not touch capon). Roast about 3 hours. Remove foil 45 minutes before end of roasting time to allow bird to brown. Brush again with melted butter and continue roasting until done.

Chicken and Fennel Risotto

Serves 4

2 1/4 pounds chicken breasts, halved
1 teaspoon salt
1/8 teaspoon pepper
1/2 teaspoon tarragon
2 stalks fresh fennel
6 tablespoons olive oil
2 onions, peeled and diced
1 large clove garlic, peeled and diced
1 1/4 cups rice
1 1/2 cups chicken bouillon
3 3/4 cup dry white wine
1/2 teaspoon salt
1 cup freshly grated Parmesan cheese

1. Rub chicken well with salt, pepper, and tarragon.
2. Cut off some green leaves from fennel; wash and put aside. Trim fennel stalks; quarter heads and wash.
3. Heat oil in large frying pan with lid. Brown chicken breasts well. Add fennel, onions, and garlic; saute briefly.
4. Add rice to frying pan and saute, stirring constantly, for 3 or 4 minutes. Pour chicken bouillon and white wine over mixture. Season with salt, cover, and simmer for 20 minutes.
5. Finely chop reserved fennel leaves. Before serving, sprinkle Parmesan cheese and chopped fennel leaves over chicken.

Chicken Soufflé

Serves 4

1 1/4 pounds whole chicken breasts
Boiling water
1 small bay leaf
1/2 teaspoon peppercorns
1 teaspoon salt
2 sprigs parsley
1/2 teaspoon tarragon
2 tablespoons butter
4 shallots, peeled and diced
2 tablespoons flour
1 cup strained chicken broth
6 tablespoons light cream
1/4 cup dry white wine
1/8 teaspoon pepper
4 eggs, separated
1 tablespoon grated Parmesan cheese

1. Place chicken breasts in boiling water to cover. Add bay leaf, peppercorns, salt, parsley, and tarragon. Cover and simmer gently for 30 minutes.
2. Remove chicken meat from bone and cut into thin slivers. Strain broth.
3. Melt butter in saucepan. Saute shallots for 3 minutes. Sprinkle in flour and continue to saute, stirring constantly, until light brown. Gradually add broth, then cream and white wine. Bring to a boil, stirring constantly. Season with salt and pepper.
4. Preheat oven to 400 degrees. Butter souffle dish well.
5. Stir egg yolks, cheese, and chicken slivers into sauce. Beat egg whites until very stiff and fold carefully into mixture.
6. Spoon chicken mixture quickly into prepared souffle dish and bake in center of oven for 30 minutes. Serve immediately.

Chicken with Wine and Herbs

Serves 4

8 chicken pieces
1/4 cup flour
1 tablespoon butter
1/4 cup olive oil
1 onion, chopped
1 clove garlic, peeled and chopped
1 tablespoon tomato paste
3/4 cup dry red wine
1 teaspoon salt
1/4 teaspoon pepper
1/8 teaspoon marjoram
1/8 teaspoon thyme
1 cup finely chopped parsley
1/2 cup sliced mushrooms, sprinkled with lemon juice
1 tablespoon wine vinegar

1. Coat the chicken with flour. Heat butter with 1 tablespoon oil in large frying pan. Brown drumsticks on all sides. Add onion and garlic; saute until soft.

2. Combine tomato paste, red wine, salt, pepper, marjoram, and thyme. Add mixture to chicken and cook gently for 30 minutes.

3. Heat remaining oil in separate frying pan. Add $1/2$ cup chopped parsley and sliced mushrooms to pan; cook over high heat, stirring constantly, until all juices have evaporated.

4. Add mushroom mixture to chicken. Sprinkle with vinegar and remaining parsley before serving.

Chicken Breast with Cheese Sauce

Serves 4

1$1/4$ pounds boneless chicken breasts
$1/4$ teaspoon salt
$1/4$ teaspoon pepper
1 tablespoon flour
1 egg, lightly beaten
$1/2$ cup chopped, blanched almonds
3 tablespoons butter
3 tablespoons dry white wine
1$1/4$ cups light cream
$1/2$ cup Gorgonzola cheese
$1/8$ teaspoon grated nutmeg
Pinch of sugar

1. Rub chicken breasts on both sides with salt and pepper. Coat breasts first in flour, then in egg, and finally in chopped almonds. Press coating firmly onto chicken.

2. Melt butter in frying pan. Cook chicken over medium heat for 4 minutes on each side. Remove from pan and keep warm.

3. Add wine and cream to same frying pan; bring to a boil, stirring constantly. Cut rind off Gorgonzola, mash with fork, and add to sauce; stir until cheese melts. Season with nutmeg, sugar, and additional salt and pepper, if desired.

4. Arrange chicken on dish with cheese sauce and serve hot.

Champagne Fricassee

Serves 4

1$1/4$ pounds boneless chicken breasts
$1/8$ teaspoon pepper
1 teaspoon finely chopped fresh tarragon leaves or $1/8$ teaspoon dried tarragon
Juice of $1/2$ lemon
$1/4$ cup butter
2 shallots, peeled and chopped
$1/2$ pound shrimp, shelled and deveined
1 cup light cream
1 egg yolk
$1/4$ cup dry champagne
1 teaspoon salt
Pinch of cayenne pepper

1. Rub chicken breasts with pepper. Sprinkle with tarragon and lemon juice. Cover and marinate for 10 minutes. Remove chicken from marinade and dry thoroughly. Cut chicken into $1/2$-inch wide strips.

2. Heat butter in large, heavy skillet until foamy. Add chicken strips and cook for 4 minutes, turning frequently until evenly browned. Add shallots and saute for 1 minute.

3. Add shrimp to skillet and saute, stirring constantly, for 1 minute.

4. Beat cream with egg yolk; stir into chicken mixture and heat gently. Do not let sauce boil. Pour in champagne and continue to reheat gently, still not allowing sauce to boil. Season with salt and cayenne pepper. Transfer to serving dish and serve hot.

Viennese Fried Chicken

Serves 4

3 pounds chicken pieces
1 teaspoon salt
2 eggs
3 tablespoons milk
$1/4$ cup flour
$2/3$ cup fresh bread crumbs
$3/4$ cup lard or butter
1 cup parsley leaves
1 lemon, cut into wedges

1. Rub chicken pieces well with salt.

2. Beat eggs with milk in flat dish. Coat chicken pieces first in flour, then in egg mixture. Finally, coat chicken with bread crumbs, pressing crumbs on well.

3. Heat lard and fry crumbed chicken pieces a few at a time for about 7 minutes, turning to brown evenly. Drain on paper towels.

4. Fry parsley leaves in small bunches until crisp.

5. Arrange chicken on warm serving dish. Garnish with fried parsley and lemon wedges.

Stuffed Chicken with Brussels Sprouts

Serves 4

2 tablespoons butter
1 large onion, finely diced
2 ounces bacon, diced
$1/2$ pound chicken livers
1 tart apple, peeled, cored, and grated
1 teaspoon chopped mint
2 tablespoons fresh bread crumbs
1 teaspoon salt
$1/2$ teaspoon pepper
1 (3$1/4$-pound) frying chicken
$1/3$ cup dry white wine
$3/4$ cup cream
4$1/2$ cups Brussels sprouts
$1/8$ teaspoon grated nutmeg

1. Heat 1 tablespoon butter in frying pan. Add onion and bacon and cook until browned. Add livers and cook for 1 minute longer; cool slightly.

2. Combine apple with mint, bread crumbs, and liver mixture. Season with salt and pepper.

3. Preheat oven to 400 degrees.

4. Season chicken with salt and pepper both inside and out. Fill with stuffing and sew up opening. Melt remaining butter and sprinkle over chicken. Place in roasting pan or heavy casserole with lid, and roast for 20 minutes.

5. Pour wine and cream over chicken. Add Brussels sprouts; season with salt and nutmeg. Cook for 30 minutes longer. Remove lid and cook for 25 minutes more, or until chicken is brown.

Broiled Chicken with Mango Butter

Serves 4

1/2 cup softened butter
1 tablespoon mango chutney
Juice of 1/2 lime
1/8 teaspoon cayenne pepper
8 chicken pieces
2 tablespoons oil
1/2 teaspoon salt
1/8 teaspoon pepper

1. Combine butter with mango chutney, lime juice, and cayenne pepper, blending well. Shape into a roll, wrap in foil or wax paper, and chill for about 2 hours in freezer.
2. Preheat broiler.
3. Brush chicken pieces lightly with oil; season with salt and pepper. Broil chicken for 30 minutes, turning at least twice and brushing again with oil.
4. Divide chilled mango butter into 8 equal rounds and lay one on each portion of hot broiled chicken.

Sesame Chicken

Serves 4

1/4 cup sesame seeds
2 tablespoons sesame oil
2 tablespoons butter
1 small onion, finely chopped
1 heaping tablespoon cracked or bulgur wheat
Salt and freshly ground pepper
1 egg
1 tablespoon chopped parsley
1 (2 1/4-pound) chicken

1. Brown 1/8 cup sesame seeds in frying pan without any fat, then add 1 tablespoon each of oil and butter. Add onion and cracked wheat or bulgur; saute for 5 minutes, stirring frequently. Remove pan from heat and stir in pinch of salt and pepper. Cool slightly, then mix in egg and parsley.
2. Preheat oven to 425 degrees.
3. Stuff chicken with wheat mixture and sew up opening. Mix remaining sesame seeds with salt and pepper; coat chicken with this mixture, rubbing in well.

4. Heat remaining oil with remaining butter. Brush chicken with half of oil-butter mixture. Place, breast side down, in roasting pan. Roast for 25 minutes, then turn over and roast for 25 minutes longer. Brush with remaining oil-butter mixture and roast for 10 or 15 minutes. Baste several times with cooking juices.
5. Turn oven off and leave chicken to rest in oven for 10 minutes before serving.

Chicken with Thyme

Serves 4

3 tablespoons boiling milk
1 heaping tablespoon cracked or bulgur wheat
1 leek, white part only, finely chopped
2 tablespoons butter
1 tablespoon chopped parsley
2 teaspoons thyme
1 1/2 teaspoons sea salt
1/2 teaspoon pepper
1 egg
1 (2 1/4-pound) chicken

1. Pour hot milk over cracked wheat, cover, and let soak for 15 minutes.
2. Brown leek in 1 tablespoon butter. Add parsley and saute briefly. Stir in soaked wheat and milk; bring to a boil. Remove stuffing from heat and cool slightly. Mix in 1 teaspoon thyme, 1/2 teaspoon salt, 1/8 teaspoon pepper, and egg.
3. Preheat oven to 425 degrees.
4. Stuff chicken with wheat stuffing and sew up opening. Combine remaining thyme with rest of salt and pepper; rub well into chicken.
5. Place chicken, breast side down, in roasting pan; roast for 25 minutes. Turn chicken over and continue to roast for 25 minutes. Roast for 10 minutes more, basting frequently with cooking juices.
6. Turn off oven and let chicken sit in oven for 10 minutes before serving.

Chicken Tetrazzini

Serves 4 to 6

1 (3- to 4-pound) stewing chicken
2 onions
2 carrots
2 sprigs parsley
1/2 teaspoon thyme
1 bay leaf
8 ounces spaghetti
6 tablespoons butter
Pinch of garlic powder
1/4 cup flour
1/2 cup dry white wine
Salt and pepper to taste
1/4 pound mushrooms, sliced
3 to 4 tablespoons heavy whipping cream
1/4 cup grated Parmesan cheese
2 tablespoons bread crumbs
2 tablespoons toasted sliced almonds

1. Place chicken in large pot with water to cover. Add onions, carrots, and herbs. Bring water to a boil, then simmer for about 45 minutes, or until chicken is tender; skim froth that rises to the surface. Let chicken cool in stock, overnight if possible.
2. Skim fat from stock. Remove skin and bones from chicken, then cut chicken meat into long strips; set aside. Strain and reserve chicken stock.
3. Cook spaghetti according to package directions; drain. Toss with 1 tablespoon butter flavored with a little garlic powder. Place in ovenproof dish and keep warm.
4. To make sauce, melt 4 tablespoons butter in saucepan. Add flour, stirring until well blended. Add 1 1/2 cups of the reserved chicken stock. Bring to a boil, stirring constantly. Simmer for 2 minutes. Add wine and simmer for 3 minutes more.
5. Preheat oven to 400 degrees.
6. Place chicken in mound on top of spaghetti. Sprinkle with salt and pepper. Saute mushrooms in 1 tablespoon butter until tender, then spoon on top of chicken.
7. Stir cream into sauce; spoon sauce over chicken. Sprinkle with grated

Parmesan and bread crumbs. Bake for 10 to 15 minutes, until top is crisp and browned. Sprinkle with almonds; serve at once.

Chicken with Sweet Corn Stuffing

Serves 4

2 cobs sweet corn
1¹/₂ teaspoons salt
1 (3-pound) chicken
1 green pepper, seeded and diced
2 tablespoons butter
¹/₄ pound sausage meat
Salt to taste
¹/₂ teaspoon pepper
2 tablespoons oil
1 carrot, grated
1 onion, cut into eighths
1 clove garlic, peeled and chopped
5 tablespoons white wine
5 tablespoons chicken broth
1 cup sour cream

1. Cover corn with water in large saucepan; add ¹/₂ teaspoon salt and boil for 45 minutes. Remove corn cobs, cool slightly, and scrape kernels off cob.
2. Chop chicken heart and liver. Saute green pepper and chopped giblets in 1 tablespoon butter. Add sausage and corn, seasoning well.
3. Preheat oven to 400 degrees. Stuff chicken with corn stuffing and sew up. Brush with oil and roast for 1¹/₄ hours on bottom oven rack.
4. Saute carrot, onion, and garlic in remaining butter until nicely browned. Pour in wine and broth; simmer for 10 minutes, then strain. Stir sour cream into strained gravy and serve separately with chicken and corn stuffing.

Breast of Chicken with Kiwi Fruit

Serves 4

4 cups chicken broth
1³/₄ pounds whole chicken breasts
1 stalk celery, chopped
1 leek, white part only, chopped
4 kiwi fruits, peeled and cut into ¹/₄-inch thick slices
1 orange
1 lemon
1 tablespoon butter
1 tablespoon sugar
¹/₈ teaspoon salt
¹/₈ teaspoon cayenne pepper

1. Bring chicken broth to boil in large saucepan. Add chicken and simmer for 10 minutes, skimming as needed. Add celery and leek. Simmer for 10 minutes longer.
2. Arrange kiwi slices in fan-shaped pattern on serving dish.
Wash orange in hot water, then dry and peel one half very thinly. Finely shred peel and sprinkle over kiwi fruit. Squeeze juice from orange and lemon.
3. Melt butter in saucepan and add sugar, stirring until caramelized. Gradually add orange and lemon juices, stirring well. Boil sauce until reduced to 2 tablespoons. Season with salt and cayenne pepper.
4. Take chicken off bone, remove skin, and slice. To serve, arrange chicken on top of kiwi slices on serving dish; pour citrus sauce on top.

Chicken in Tarragon Sauce

Serves 4

¹/₄ cup olive oil
1 (2³/₄-pound) chicken, cut into serving pieces
2 cloves garlic, peeled and finely chopped
2 bay leaves
Juice of 1 lemon
Scant 1 cup dry white wine
¹/₄ cup tarragon vinegar
1 teaspoon salt
Pinch of pepper
1 tablespoon chopped fresh tarragon
¹/₂ lemon, cut into 8 wedges
12 pitted black olives

1. Heat oil in large skillet with lid. Add chicken pieces, garlic, and bay leaves; brown chicken on all sides. Sprinkle with lemon juice. Add wine, vinegar, salt, and pepper. Cover and simmer for 40 minutes, turning chicken pieces several times.
2. Remove chicken from cooking liquid and set aside. Boil cooking liquid over high heat until reduced by half.
3. Arrange chicken pieces on serving platter. Spoon reduced cooking liquid on top and sprinkle with tarragon. Garnish with lemon wedges and olives.

Chicken with Sherry Mushroom Sauce

Serves 6 to 8

3 tablespoons vegetable oil
2 onions, chopped
2 stalks celery, chopped
1 (4-pound) stewing chicken, cut into serving pieces
2 slices bacon
Water
Salt to taste
4 peppercorns
1 clove garlic, peeled and minced
2 tablespoons butter
1¹/₂ cups sliced mushrooms
¹/₂ cup heavy whipping cream
1 tablespoon sherry

1. Heat oil in large skillet with lid. Add onions and celery; saute for 3 to 4 minutes. Add chicken pieces, giblets, and bacon to pan. Cover with water; add salt, peppercorns, and garlic. Simmer, covered, for 2 hours, or until chicken is tender.
2. Remove chicken from pan. Strain chicken broth.
3. Melt butter in small frying pan. Add mushrooms and saute for 3 minutes. Stir in cream and sherry. Remove from heat and gradually add 1¹/₂ cups of strained chicken broth. Return to heat, stir until almost boiling, and simmer for 2 minutes. Adjust seasonings to taste.
4. Arrange chicken pieces on serving dish. Pour sauce over chicken, and serve. Freeze any remaining broth for future use.

Hawaiian Chicken Kebabs

Serves 4

1 (3-pound) chicken
1 red pepper, seeded and cut
   into squares
1 green pepper, seeded and cut
   into squares
1 clove garlic, peeled and
   crushed
1 small onion, grated
2 teaspoons brown sugar
1 teaspoon curry powder
1 cup tomato juice
1/2 teaspoon ground ginger
1/2 teaspoon cayenne pepper
1/2 teaspoon salt
1 tablespoon lemon juice

1. Remove chicken meat from bones and cut into bite-size pieces. Alternate chicken and peppers on skewers. Place kebabs in shallow bowl.
2. Mix all remaining ingredients in bowl, blending together well. Pour over kebabs and refrigerate for 2 hours, turning occasionally.
3. Preheat broiler or heat coals in outdoor grill. Broil kebabs for 10 to 20 minutes, or until chicken is thoroughly cooked. Baste occasionally with marinade. Remove from heat and serve.

Chicken Casserole with Vegetables

Serves 4

2 tablespoons vegetable oil
1 (3-pound) chicken, cut into
   serving pieces
3 to 4 scallions, chopped
1 (16-ounce) can tomatoes
1 (10-ounce) package frozen
   corn
1 pound fresh green beans
1 1/2 cups chicken stock
1 bay leaf
1/2 teaspoon powdered thyme
1 (8-ounce) can new potatoes

1. Preheat oven to 350 degrees.
2. Heat oil in large frying pan. Brown chicken pieces and scallions, then

transfer to casserole dish. Add all remaining ingredients except potatoes to casserole.
3. Drain potatoes, then brown in oil left in frying pan. Add potatoes to casserole. Cover and cook for 1 to 1-1/4 hours. Serve with tossed salad.

Creole Chicken

Serves 4

6 slices bacon
1 (2 1/2-pound) chicken, cut into
   serving pieces
5 tablespoons flour
1 tablespoon olive oil
3/4 cup sliced onion
1 clove garlic, peeled and
   chopped
2 stalks celery, chopped
1 green pepper, seeded and cut
   into very thin strips
2 (16-ounce) cans crushed
   tomatoes
2 teaspoons thyme
1 teaspoon pepper
1/4 teaspoon cayenne pepper
1 bay leaf
Juice of 1/2 lemon

1. Cook bacon slices in stew pot until brown and crisp. Remove from pan and drain on paper towels.
2. Dredge chicken pieces in flour, then cook in bacon fat until golden brown all over. Remove from pan. Pour olive oil into pan and add onion and garlic. Saute for 5 minutes, then add celery and green pepper. Saute for 3 minutes longer.
3. Add canned tomatoes, thyme, pepper, cayenne pepper, and bay leaf. Bring to a boil. Place chicken pieces on vegetable mixture and simmer for 30 minutes. Add water if mixture becomes too dry.
4. To serve, stir in lemon juice and sprinkle with crumbled bacon slices. Serve with rice.

Chicken Maryland with Tomato Sauce

Serves 4 to 6

1 (3-pound) chicken, cut into
   serving pieces
1/4 cup flour seasoned with salt,
   pepper, and cayenne pepper
1 egg
2 tablespoons plus 1 teaspoon oil
1 1/2 cups fresh white bread crumbs
6 tablespoons butter
3 bananas, halved
6 slices bacon, halved, rolled
   up, and skewered

Corn Fritters

1 cup cooked corn
1 egg, separated
Salt and pepper to taste
2/3 cup flour
1/2 teaspoon baking powder
1/2 teaspoon curry powder
Oil for deep frying

Tomato Sauce

3 tablespoons butter
1 onion, sliced
1 clove garlic, peeled and crushed
1 (8-ounce) can tomatoes
2 tablespoons fines herbes
Salt and pepper to taste
1 teaspoon sugar
1 teaspoon paprika
1/2 cup chicken broth

1. Roll chicken pieces in seasoned flour. Beat egg with 1 teaspoon oil, then brush over chicken. Coat chicken well with bread crumbs.
2. Heat 2 tablespoons oil and 4 tablespoons butter in large, heavy skillet. Add chicken pieces and fry over medium heat for 20 to 25 minutes, turning frequently until brown and crisp all over.
3. Fry halved bananas in 2 tablespoons butter until golden brown. Remove from pan and keep warm. Broil bacon skewers until crisp. Remove from heat and keep warm.
4. To prepare corn fritters, drain canned corn and mix with 1 egg yolk and seasoning. Sift flour, baking powder, and curry powder together; stir into corn mixture. Just before

frying, beat egg white until stiff and fold into corn mixture.

5. Heat oil until very hot but not smoking. Drop fritter mixture into oil by tablespoonfuls and fry until light brown. Drain on paper towels and keep warm.

6. To prepare tomato sauce, melt butter in saucepan. Add onion and garlic; saute for 5 to 6 minutes. Add tomatoes, herbs, seasoning, sugar, paprika, and broth. Bring to a boil, then strain or blend in blender or food processor.

7. Arrange chicken with bananas and bacon on serving platter. Serve hot tomato sauce separately.

Lemon and Garlic-Filled Chicken Breasts

Serves 4

8 boneless chicken breasts, pounded until thin
Salt and pepper to taste
1/4 pound butter, at room temperature
3 cloves garlic, peeled and crushed
Juice of 1 lemon
2 tablespoons finely chopped parsley
1 cup flour
1 egg, beaten
Bread crumbs
Oil for deep frying

1. Season chicken breasts with salt and pepper. Mix butter with garlic, lemon juice, and parsley. Spread butter mixture on chicken breasts, fold in edges, and roll up chicken; fasten with wooden toothpicks.

2. First roll breasts in flour, then dip in egg. Finally, roll in bread crumbs.

3. Heat enough oil in deep frying pan to cover chicken breasts. When oil is hot, fry chicken slowly until golden brown and thoroughly cooked. Drain on paper towels, and serve.

Marsala Chicken

Serves 4

1 (3-pound) chicken, cut into serving pieces
2/3 cup Marsala (port wine or Madeira can be substituted)
1 1/2 tablespoons butter
1 shallot, peeled and chopped
1 teaspoon salt
1/4 teaspoon pepper
5 tablespoons water
2 teaspoons flour
5 tablespoons creme fraiche or heavy whipping cream
Chopped walnuts for garnish

1. Place chicken pieces and wine in plastic bag. Fold up bag and refrigerate for 2 to 3 hours, turning bag occasionally. Remove chicken but reserve wine. Dry off chicken with paper towels.

2. Melt butter in deep frying pan. Brown chicken pieces, then add shallot and saute 1 minute. Season with salt and pepper. Add reserved wine and water. Cover and cook chicken for 15 to 20 minutes, or until chicken is tender. Transfer chicken to warm, deep dish.

3. To prepare gravy, stir flour into cooking juices in frying pan. Boil for 3 minutes, then add cream. Reduce heat to low and stir until sauce is smooth and hot.

4. Season to taste, then pour sauce over chicken. Sprinkle with chopped nuts.

Paprika Chicken

Serves 4

1 (3-pound) chicken, cut into serving pieces
2 tablespoons flour, seasoned with salt and pepper
2 tablespoons oil
1/4 cup butter
4 onions, sliced
1 clove garlic, peeled and crushed
2 teaspoons paprika
2 tablespoons tomato sauce
1 cup white wine
1 cup chicken stock
1 tablespoon chopped parsley
1 teaspoon thyme
Salt and pepper to taste
1 cup sour cream

1. Roll chicken in seasoned flour. Heat oil and 2 tablespoons butter in frying pan. Add chicken and cook until golden brown. Transfer chicken pieces to Dutch oven.

2. Add remaining butter and onions to frying pan. Cook over low heat until onions are tender but not brown, about 5 minutes. Add garlic and cook for 1 minute more. Add paprika and remaining seasoned flour, then tomato sauce. Stir until smooth. Add wine and stock; bring to a boil, stirring constantly.

3. Pour sauce over chicken pieces. Add parsley, thyme, salt, and pepper. Cook over low heat about 1 hour, or until chicken is tender. Spoon sour cream on top, and serve with buttered noodles or rice.

Chicken with Peanut Butter Sauce

Serves 4

1 (3-pound) chicken, cut into serving pieces
Salt and pepper to taste
3 tablespoons oil
2 onions, sliced
1 teaspoon curry powder
2 tablespoons tomato sauce
3 cups chicken broth
1/2 tablespoon chopped parsley
1/2 tablespoon thyme
1 bay leaf
1 cup peanut butter

1. Season chicken with salt and pepper. Heat oil in frying pan and brown chicken pieces on all sides. Transfer chicken to large pot and keep warm.

2. Add onions to frying pan and saute until translucent. Add curry powder and tomato sauce. Stir until smooth, then add 1 cup broth. Bring to a boil. Add parsley, thyme, and bay leaf. Pour mixture over chicken pieces. Simmer for 1 hour, or until chicken is tender.

3. Combine peanut butter with 2 cups broth over low heat. Season with salt and pepper. When sauce is smooth, pour over chicken. Simmer for 10 to 15 minutes more. Serve with boiled rice.

Chicken Pie

Serves 4 to 5

1 (2½-pound) chicken,
  quartered
1 teaspoon salt
1 teaspoon pepper
2 bay leaves
3 carrots
2 onions, quartered
2 stalks celery
3 sprigs parsley
2 slices cooked ham
2 hard-boiled eggs, sliced
2 tablespoons butter
2 tablespoons flour
2 tablespoons sherry
1 tablespoon lemon juice
1 teaspoon sugar
Pinch of ground mace
1 egg yolk
1 uncooked, 8-inch pastry
  crust
Egg or milk to glaze

1. Preheat oven to 425 degrees.
2. Place chicken in large frying pan
with lid. Add salt, pepper, bay leaves,
carrots, onions, celery, and parsley.
Add just enough water to cover.
Simmer, covered, for 30 minutes.
Remove chicken and vegetables from
pan and strain broth.
3. Cut meat from chicken in fairly
large chunks; chop cooked vegetables.
Alternate layers of chicken,
vegetables, ham, and eggs in
ovenproof baking dish.
4. Melt butter in saucepan. Stir in
flour, then 1 cup of strained chicken
broth. Add sherry, lemon juice, sugar,
and mace. Cook, stirring constantly,
until sauce thickens. Stir in egg yolk
and reheat without boiling.
5. Pour sauce over chicken and
vegetables. Cover with pastry. Cut a
line from center of pie toward each
corner; fold each pastry triangle back,
leaving an open square. Glaze pastry
with beaten egg or milk. Bake 30
minutes, or until pastry is golden
brown.

Chicken in Light Pastry Crust

Serves 4 to 6

1 (3-pound) chicken
4 onions, 2 whole, 2 thickly
  sliced
2 carrots
3 stalks celery
2 sprigs parsley
1 bay leaf
6 peppercorns
Salt to taste
¼ cup butter
1 cup sliced mushrooms
2 tablespoons flour
1½ cups chicken broth
¼ teaspoon thyme
¼ teaspoon tarragon
Pinch of mace
6 slices cooked ham, chopped
1 (8-ounce) package frozen puff
  pastry
1 egg, beaten

1. Preheat oven to 450 degrees.
2. Cut meat off chicken bones in large
chunks. Put carcass and giblets in pan
with 2 whole onions, carrots, celery,
parsley sprigs, bay leaf, and
peppercorns. Cover with water and
simmer for 1 hour. Strain and season
with salt.
3. Melt 2 tablespoons butter in large,
deep skillet. Saute sliced onions for 3
to 4 minutes. Add mushrooms and
saute for 1 minute; remove onions and
mushrooms from pan and keep warm.
4. Heat remaining butter in skillet and
cook chicken meat for 4 to 5 minutes.
Sprinkle in flour; add broth. Bring to a
boil, stirring constantly. Reduce heat
and simmer for 1 minute, then add
sliced onions and mushrooms. Stir in
thyme, tarragon, and mace.
5. Layer bottom of pie plate with
chopped ham. Spoon in half of chicken
mixture, then cover with another layer
of ham. Repeat chicken and ham
layers. Let cool.
6. Preheat oven to 450 degrees.
7. Roll out pastry to slightly larger
than pie plate. Cut thin strip from
outside edge of pastry. Moisten edge
of pie plate and cover with thin pastry
strip. Brush pastry strip with water,
then place large piece of pastry on
top. Crimp edges together; cut off
excess with sharp knife. Make 4 holes
to allow steam to escape. Brush
pastry with egg.
8. Bake for 25 minutes, then cover
pastry with damp wax paper or foil.
Reduce heat to 375 degrees and cook
for 20 minutes more. Remove from
oven and cool slightly before serving.

Chicken Pilau

Serves 4

2 tablespoons oil
½ cup butter
4 to 6 chicken pieces
1 large onion, sliced
1 cup chopped dried
  apricots
½ teaspoon cinnamon
Grated rind of 1 orange
Salt and pepper to taste
1 cup plain yogurt
1½ cups long-grain rice
2 tablespoons slivered
  almonds

1. Heat oil and 2 tablespoons butter in
large, deep skillet. When butter is
foaming, cook chicken pieces until
golden brown. Remove from pan and
let cool. Add onion to pan and saute
until golden. Add apricots; sprinkle
with cinnamon, orange rind, salt, and
pepper.
2. Remove bones from chicken pieces
and shred meat. Mix yogurt with onion
mixture. Cover shredded chicken with
yogurt mixture and set aside for 20
minutes.
3. Cook rice in boiling, salted water
for 10 to 12 minutes. Drain and rinse
with boiling water. Let dry for 3 to 4
minutes. Heat 3 tablespoons butter in
heavy pan or casserole dish. Stir half
the rice into pan. Pour chicken
mixture over rice, then cover with
remaining rice. Season with salt and
pepper.
4. Preheat oven to 350 degrees.
5. Melt 2 tablespoons butter and
spoon over rice. Cover pan and bake
for 15 to 20 minutes.
6. Brown almond slivers in remaining
tablespoon of butter. Sprinkle
almonds on top of rice, and serve
immediately.

Chicken Supreme

Serves 4

¹/₂ cup butter
4 whole chicken breasts
1 cup sliced mushrooms
2 teaspoons lemon juice
1 tablespoon chopped parsley
Salt and pepper to taste
3 tablespoons flour
1¹/₄ cups chicken broth
¹/₄ teaspoon mace
¹/₂ cup light cream
2 egg yolks
2 tablespoons white wine or
   lemon juice

1. Preheat oven to 375 degrees.
2. Melt 5 tablespoons butter in large frying pan. Add chicken breasts and cook over low heat for 4 to 5 minutes on each side. Remove from pan and transfer to buttered, ovenproof dish. Cover with foil and bake for 10 to 15 minutes, or until chicken is tender.
3. Meanwhile, add mushrooms and 1 teaspoon lemon juice to butter left in frying pan. Saute for 5 to 6 minutes. Add parsley, salt, and pepper. Place mushrooms in bottom of serving dish.
4. Place cooked chicken on top of mushrooms and keep warm in 250 degree oven.
5. Melt 3 tablespoons butter in saucepan. Stir in flour and, when smooth, add broth. Bring slowly to a boil, stirring constantly. Boil, continuing to stir, for 2 minutes. Add salt, pepper, and mace.
6. Mix cream with egg yolks. Stir 3 tablespoons hot sauce into cream and egg mixture, then pour into saucepan with remaining sauce. Stirring constantly, reheat slowly over pan of hot water. Do not allow sauce to boil. Add white wine or lemon juice. Spoon sauce over chicken and serve with boiled rice.

Chicken Stewed with Apples

Serves 6

1 (3¹/₂-pound) chicken, cut into
   serving pieces
Salt and pepper to taste
¹/₄ cup oil
1 onion, sliced
2 stalks celery, sliced
2 large apples, peeled, cored, and
   sliced
2 tablespoons flour
1¹/₂ cups chicken broth or water
Pinch of thyme
Pinch of marjoram
Boiled rice

1. Season chicken with salt and pepper. Heat 3 tablespoons oil in deep frying pan. Add chicken, a few pieces at a time, and brown well. Remove from pan. Saute onion, celery, and apples in same frying pan for 5 minutes; remove from pan.
2. Add remaining tablespoon oil to pan. Stir in flour, mixing well. Gradually add broth or water, stirring until boiling. Return chicken, vegetables, and apples to sauce. Add thyme, marjoram, salt, and pepper. Cover and simmer for 1 hour, or until chicken is tender.
3. To serve, put some boiled rice on large serving platter. Arrange chicken pieces on top and pour on sauce.

Chicken Contadine

Serves 4

6 chicken pieces
Flour seasoned with salt and
   pepper
2 tablespoons butter
1 onion, finely chopped
¹/₂ cup dry vermouth
2 teaspoons tomato sauce
¹/₂ teaspoon cinnamon
¹/₂ cup heavy whipping cream
¹/₂ cup chopped parsley

1. Preheat oven to 375 degrees.
2. Skin chicken pieces and coat with seasoned flour. Melt butter in large frying pan and saute onion until translucent. Add chicken pieces and brown on all sides. Transfer chicken and onions to casserole dish.
3. Pour vermouth into same frying pan and ignite. When flames die down, stir in tomato sauce and cinnamon. Mix well, then pour over chicken. Bake for 1 hour, or until chicken is tender.
4. To serve, stir in cream and sprinkle with parsley.

Skillet Apricot Chicken

Serves 4

2 tablespoons flour
¹/₂ teaspoon salt
³/₄ teaspoon garlic powder
¹/₄ teaspoon ginger
1 (3-pound) chicken, cut into
   serving pieces
1 tablespoon vegetable óil
³/₄ cup orange juice
¹/₄ cup honey
2 chicken bouillon cubes,
   crumbled
¹/₂ teaspoon rosemary
1 (3-inch) stick cinnamon
¹/₂ cup dried apricots
¹/₂ cup sliced scallions

1. Mix flour, salt, garlic powder, and ginger together. Roll chicken pieces in flour mixture. Heat oil in large frying pan and brown chicken on all sides.
2. Combine orange juice, honey, bouillon, and rosemary. Pour orange juice mixture over chicken. Add cinnamon stick, apricots, and scallions; bring to a boil. Reduce heat, cover, and simmer for 25 minutes. Uncover and cook over medium heat for 3 to 5 minutes, spooning sauce over chicken frequently until chicken is glazed. Transfer to serving dish and serve hot.

Barbecued Chicken with Herb Butter

Serves 4

¹/₂ cup dry white wine
2 tablespoons oil
Juice of ¹/₂ lemon
1 small onion, chopped
¹/₂ teaspoon tarragon
1 (3-pound) chicken, cut into
  serving pieces

Herb Butter

¹/₂ cup butter or margarine
¹/₄ cup chopped parsley
2 teaspoons rosemary

1. Combine wine, oil, lemon, onion, and tarragon. Pour over chicken and marinate for 3 to 4 hours, turning chicken frequently. Drain.
2. Place butter, parsley, and rosemary in small saucepan. Heat until butter is melted. Use half of herb butter to baste chicken; refrigerate remaining herb butter until firm.
3. Cook chicken in broiler or over coals in outdoor grill until crisp and golden, basting several times with herb butter. Cut chilled herb butter into pats and serve on chicken.

Lemon Chicken

Serves 6 to 8

¹/₂ cup butter
2 (2¹/₂-pound) chicken,
  split in half
1 clove garlic, peeled and
  mashed
1¹/₂ teaspoons salt
¹/₄ cup salad oil
¹/₂ cup lemon juice
2 tablespoons minced onion
¹/₂ teaspoon pepper
¹/₂ teaspoon thyme

1. Melt butter in heavy skillet with lid. Add chicken and brown on all sides.
2. Combine garlic, salt, oil, lemon juice, onion, pepper, and thyme; pour over chicken. Cover pan tightly and cook over low heat for 40 minutes, or until chicken is tender.

Beer Batter Chicken

Serves 3 to 4

2 eggs, beaten
²/₃ cup beer
1 cup flour
¹/₂ teaspoon salt
2 tablespoons oil or melted
  shortening
1 (3-pound) chicken, cut into
  serving pieces
Oil for deep frying

1. Combine eggs and beer. Gradually stir in flour, salt, and 2 tablespoons oil until batter is smooth. Dip chicken into batter.
2. Heat oil in deep, heavy frying pan to 375 degrees. Add chicken and fry for 15 to 20 minutes, until chicken is golden and crisp. Drain on paper towels, and serve.

Chicken-Stuffed Bread

Serves 6

1 round loaf country-style bread
2 tablespoons butter, melted
1 egg, beaten

Filling

1 tablespoon butter
1 onion, thinly sliced
1 to 2 tablespoons flour
³/₄ cup vegetable broth
¹/₂ teaspoon thyme
¹/₂ teaspoon salt
¹/₈ teaspoon pepper
1 pound cooked chicken,
  sliced
1 (8-ounce) can mushrooms,
  chopped, liquid reserved
¹/₄ pound fresh mushrooms,
  chopped

1. Preheat oven to 350 degrees. Cut lid off bread and scoop out. Brush bread, inside and out, with melted butter and then with egg. Heat in oven for 5 minutes.
2. To make filling, melt butter in saucepan. Saute onion until lightly browned. Stir in flour, then broth. Add seasonings and simmer for 3 to 4 minutes. Add chicken slices, mixing well.

3. Pour liquid from canned mushrooms into saucepan. Add canned and fresh mushrooms and simmer for 15 minutes. Season with salt and pepper.
4. Cover bottom of bread with half the mushrooms. Place chicken mixture over mushrooms, then cover chicken with remaining mushrooms. Replace bread lid and warm bread in oven for 7 to 10 minutes.
5. Serve bread warm with a green salad.

Brandied Cherry Chicken

Serves 4

1 (8-ounce) can pitted Bing
  cherries
¹/₄ cup port wine
1 (3-pound) chicken, quartered
1 tablespoon vegetable oil
¹/₄ cup brandy
³/₄ cup hot water
1 large onion, thinly sliced
¹/₂ teaspoon salt
¹/₈ teaspoon pepper
1¹/₂ tablespoons cornstarch

1. Drain cherries, reserving ¹/₄ cup syrup. Place cherries in bowl and pour reserved syrup and wine on top. Cover and refrigerate for 2 hours.
2. Remove excess fat from chicken. Heat oil in large frying pan over medium-high heat. Add chicken and lightly brown on all sides. Remove from heat. Pour brandy over chicken and ignite. When flame goes out, add water, onion, salt, and pepper. Cover and cook over low heat for 40 to 45 minutes, or until chicken is tender. Transfer chicken to serving platter.
3. Pour cooking juices into measuring cup; remove as much fat as possible. Drain cherries, reserving marinating liquid. Blend cherry liquid into cornstarch, then spoon into saucepan. Add chicken juices and cook over moderate heat, stirring constantly, until sauce thickens. Add cherries and simmer for 2 to 3 minutes, until cherries are hot.
4. Pour cherry sauce over chicken, and serve.

Chicken in Cider and Mustard

Serves 4

1 tablespoon butter
1 (3-pound) chicken, cut into
    serving pieces
1 large onion, thinly sliced
$\frac{1}{2}$ teaspoon salt
$\frac{1}{2}$ teaspoon pepper
$\frac{2}{3}$ cup apple cider
1 tablespoon Dijon mustard
2 sprigs fresh thyme or $\frac{1}{2}$
    teaspoon dried thyme
$\frac{2}{3}$ cup light cream

1. Melt butter in deep skillet. Add chicken and brown on all sides. Add onion, salt, pepper, and cider. Mix mustard, thyme, and cream together; stir mixture into chicken.
2. Simmer chicken for 30 to 35 minutes. Serve with boiled potatoes and carrots.

Cranberry Sauce Chicken

Serves 4

$\frac{1}{2}$ cup flour
1 teaspoon salt
$\frac{1}{8}$ teaspoon pepper
6 chicken pieces
Oil
2 tablespoons brown sugar
1 tablespoon cornstarch
$\frac{3}{4}$ cup cranberry juice cocktail
1 (16-ounce) can cranberry sauce
1 teaspoon ground nutmeg
1 teaspoon ground marjoram
1 tablespoon minced onion

1. Mix flour, salt, and pepper together in paper bag. Place chicken in bag and shake until well coated with flour mixture.
2. Pour oil to depth of $\frac{1}{4}$ inch in bottom of heavy skillet. Heat oil and brown chicken on all sides. Cover tightly. Reduce heat and simmer for 20 to 30 minutes, turning occasionally, until chicken is tender. Drain on paper towels.
3. Mix brown sugar and cornstarch together in saucepan. Gradually stir in cranberry juice until smooth. Add cranberry sauce, spices, and onion. Cook over medium heat, stirring constantly, until mixture comes to a boil.
4. To serve, place chicken on serving platter and spoon cranberry sauce on top.

Batter-Fried Chicken Breasts

Serves 4 to 6

6 to 8 boneless chicken breasts,
    halved
2 teaspoons salt
$\frac{1}{8}$ teaspoon pepper
1 egg, lightly beaten
$\frac{1}{2}$ cup milk
$1\frac{1}{2}$ cups plus 2 tablespoons
    flour
Oil for deep frying

1. Season chicken breasts with salt and pepper. Mix egg and milk together in shallow bowl. Add 2 tablespoons flour and mix until very smooth. Dip each chicken piece in batter. Dredge chicken in remaining flour until well coated.
2. Heat oil in heavy frying pan to 375 degrees. Fry 4 or 5 chicken pieces at a time for 12 to 15 minutes, or until chicken is golden brown on all sides. Drain on paper towels. Keep warm in 250 degree oven until all chicken is fried.

Fruit-Stuffed Chicken Breasts

Serves 6

$\frac{3}{4}$ cup butter
1 cup diced apple
$\frac{1}{2}$ cup coarsely chopped nuts
1 (20-ounce) can crushed
    pineapple, drained and syrup
    reserved
$\frac{1}{2}$ cup golden raisins
1 cup bread crumbs
1 teaspoon salt
1 teaspoon cinnamon
$\frac{1}{2}$ teaspoon nutmeg
$\frac{1}{4}$ teaspoon ginger
$\frac{1}{4}$ teaspoon ground cloves
6 whole boneless chicken breasts

Fruit Sauce

1 tablespoon sugar
1 tablespoon cornstarch
$\frac{1}{8}$ teaspoon salt
$\frac{1}{2}$ teaspoon cinnamon
$\frac{1}{4}$ teaspoon nutmeg
$\frac{1}{8}$ teaspoon ginger
1 cup orange juice
Reserved pineapple syrup and
    pineapple
$\frac{1}{4}$ cup golden raisins
1 tablespoon butter
1 orange

1. Melt $\frac{1}{2}$ cup butter in frying pan. Add apple and nuts and saute for 10 minutes. Remove from heat. Drain pineapple, reserving syrup. Add $\frac{1}{2}$ cup pineapple, raisins, bread crumbs, $\frac{1}{2}$ teaspoon salt, cinnamon, nutmeg, ginger, and cloves.
2. Lay chicken breasts flat. Sprinkle with $\frac{1}{2}$ teaspoon salt. Place $\frac{1}{3}$ cup fruit stuffing on top, then fold sides over and fasten with skewers or string.
3. Preheat oven to 375 degrees. Place remaining $\frac{1}{4}$ cup butter in 9 x 13-inch baking pan lined with foil. Place pan in oven until butter melts, about 5 minutes. Put breasts, top side down, in melted butter. Return pan to oven and bake for 25 minutes. Turn chicken over and bake for 20 minutes more.
4. In saucepan, combine sugar, cornstarch, salt, cinnamon, nutmeg, and ginger. Stir in orange juice. Add reserved pineapple syrup and remaining crushed pineapple, raisins, and butter.
5. Peel orange and cut peel into slivers. Divide orange into sections and set aside. Stir orange peel into fruit sauce mixture. Cook, stirring constantly, over medium heat until sauce boils and thickens. Add orange sections and simmer until thoroughly heated.
6. Place chicken breasts on serving platter and serve with fruit sauce.

Glazed
Apricot Chicken

Serves 4

6 chicken breasts
1 (10-ounce) jar apricot
  preserves
1 envelope dried onion soup
  mix
2 cups red Russian salad
  dressing

1. Preheat oven to 350 degrees.
2. Place chicken in casserole dish or Dutch oven. Cover chicken with apricot preserves, then sprinkle with onion soup mix. Pour on Russian dressing. Fill empty salad dressing bottle with water; pour water over chicken.
3. Bake chicken for 30 minutes, basting often. Serve over boiled rice.

Chicken Hot Pot

Serves 4

1 (2¹/₂- to 3-pound) chicken, cut
  into serving pieces
1 tablespoon flour, seasoned with
  salt and pepper
¹/₄ cup butter
1 large onion, sliced
2 cups canned tomatoes
2 teaspoons brown sugar
2 teaspoons prepared mustard
4 medium-size potatoes, peeled
  and sliced
2 apples, peeled, cored,
  and sliced

Cream Slaw

1 small head white cabbage,
  shredded
1 small green pepper, seeded and
  shredded

2 teaspoons prepared mustard
¹/₂ teaspoon paprika
2 teaspoons lemon juice
¹/₂ cup sour cream

1. Dredge chicken with seasoned flour. Melt butter in frying pan and brown chicken on all sides. Remove from pan.
2. Lightly brown onion in same frying pan. Add tomatoes, brown sugar, and mustard; cook over low heat until hot.
3. Preheat oven to 350 degrees. Arrange potatoes in bottom of buttered casserole dish. Season lightly with salt and pepper, then add apples. Add tomato mixture, then place chicken pieces on top. Cover and cook for 1¹/₂ hours.
4. Mix cabbage and green pepper together. Blend mustard, paprika, lemon juice, and sour cream together well. Toss cabbage and green pepper lightly in sour-cream dressing. Serve with chicken.

Jambalaya

Serves 4 to 6

3 tablespoons vegetable oil or
  bacon drippings
1 (3-pound) chicken, cut into
  serving pieces
2 cups sliced celery
2 cups sliced scallions
1 cup chopped green peppers
1 cup uncooked rice
2 cups boiling chicken broth
1 teaspoon salt
¹/₂ teaspoon garlic salt
¹/₄ teaspoon black pepper
¹/₄ teaspoon red pepper.

1. Heat oil or bacon drippings in large skillet or Dutch oven. Add chicken and brown on all sides. Remove chicken from pan and pour off all but 2 tablespoons of drippings.
2. Preheat oven to 375 degrees.
3. Add celery, scallions, and green peppers to drippings left in pan; saute for 5 minutes. Stir in rice, broth, and seasonings.
4. Return chicken to pan, cover, and bake for 30 minutes, or until chicken is tender. Fluff with fork before serving.

Chicken in
Lemon-Dill Butter

Serves 4

¹/₂ cup butter
2 tablespoons lemon juice
1 teaspoon salt
1 clove garlic, peeled and minced
¹/₂ teaspoon paprika
1 cup sliced mushrooms
1 tablespoon dill weed
1 (3-pound) chicken, cut into
  serving pieces

1. Melt butter in large skillet with lid. Add all ingredients except chicken and bring to a boil. Add chicken and bring to boiling point, but do not actually boil. Cover skillet and simmer for 30 minutes, or until chicken is tender.
2. Transfer chicken to serving platter. Serve with noodles or rice, covered with remaining cooking liquid.

Chicken and Oyster
Casserole

Serves 4

1 (2¹/₂-pound) chicken, cut into
  serving pieces
1 cup water
¹/₂ cup vinegar
1 clove garlic, peeled
Pinch of thyme
1 bay leaf
1 teaspoon salt
1 pint oysters
2 tablespoons butter
1 tablespoon flour
2 tablespoons sherry
1 tablespoon minced parsley
3 tablespoons bread or cracker
  crumbs

1. Place chicken in large pot. Add water, vinegar, garlic, thyme, bay leaf, and salt. Simmer for 30 minutes, or until chicken is tender. Remove chicken from pot and let cool; reserve cooking liquid. Cut chicken meat from bones and remove skin; cut chicken into bite-size pieces.
2. Drain oysters, adding oyster liquor to reserved chicken cooking liquid. Melt 1 tablespoon butter in frying pan. Stir in flour, then add chicken-and-

oyster liquid. Simmer, stirring constantly, until sauce thickens slightly. Add sherry and parsley.

3. Preheat oven to 350 degrees. Place chicken and oysters in 2-quart baking dish and pour sauce on top. Sprinkle with bread or cracker crumbs and dot with remaining butter. Bake for 15 minutes. Serve on hot biscuits.

Pot-Roasted Chicken

Serves 4

1 (3-pound) chicken
2 tablespoons vegetable oil
2 tablespoons butter
1 clove garlic, peeled and minced
4 medium-size onions, quartered
4 medium-size potatoes, quartered
6 carrots, cut into 2-inch pieces
1 (10¹/₂-ounce) can condensed chicken broth
1 soup can water
1 teaspoon rosemary
¹/₃ teaspoon pepper
1 teaspoon salt

1. Using kitchen string, tie legs to tail of chicken. Hook wing tips under back. Heat oil, butter, and garlic in Dutch oven. Brown chicken, then remove from pot. Add onions, potatoes, and carrots to pan drippings; saute for 5 minutes. Remove vegetables and set aside. Stir broth, water, rosemary, and pepper into pan drippings.

2. Preheat oven to 350 degrees. Return chicken to pot; surround with vegetables. Sprinkle with salt and bake for 1 hour, basting several times with cooking liquid. Serve chicken and vegetables with cooking liquid.

Chicken in Red Wine

Serves 4

3 tablespoons oil
1 clove garlic, peeled and minced
1 (3-pound) chicken, cut into serving pieces
¹/₄ teaspoon thyme
Salt and pepper to taste
1 cup dry red wine
2 sprigs parsley
12 small white onions, peeled
6 carrots, cut into 1-inch pieces

1. Heat oil in Dutch oven. Add garlic and saute briefly. Brown chicken on all sides. Add thyme, salt, pepper, and red wine. Simmer for 25 minutes.

2. Add parsley, onions, and carrots. Simmer for 10 minutes, or until vegetables are tender.

Summer Chicken

Serves 4

1 (3-pound) chicken
1 lemon
1 teaspoon salt
¹/₄ to ¹/₂ teaspoon freshly ground pepper
4 sprigs fresh tarragon
2 tablespoons butter
¹/₂ cup water

1. Preheat oven to 350 degrees.
2. Rub chicken inside and out with lemon, salt, and pepper. Fill chicken

with 3 tarragon sprigs and butter. Sew up chicken. Finely chop remaining tarragon sprig and sprinkle over chicken.

3. Place chicken on rack in roasting pan. Roast for 1 to 1¹/₄ hours, or until chicken is tender. Baste chicken with water several times during baking.

4. Transfer chicken to serving platter. Stir water into pan juices and bring to a boil. Serve gravy with chicken.

Poached Chicken with Vegetables

Serves 4

1 small onion
2 cloves garlic, peeled
3 sprigs parsley
1 teaspoon tarragon
1 (3-pound) chicken
1¹/₂ cups dry white wine
1 cup chicken broth
1 teaspoon salt
4 carrots, scraped
4 small turnips, peeled and quartered
4 small leeks, cleaned and blanched 5 minutes in boiling water
2 tablespoons flour
¹/₂ cup heavy whipping cream
2 egg yolks
2 to 3 teaspoons prepared white horseradish

1. Preheat oven to 325 degrees.
2. Place onion, garlic, parsley, and tarragon in cavity of chicken; truss. Place chicken in large Dutch oven. Add wine, broth, and salt. Bring to a boil. Cover and bake in oven for 45 minutes. Add vegetables. Bake, covered, for 30 minutes longer. Transfer chicken and vegetables to serving platter and keep warm.

3. Whisk flour into cream. Skim any fat from pan juices. Stir cream into pan juices and heat until thickened. Add a few tablespoons gravy to egg yolks, then add egg yolks to pan. Heat, stirring constantly, until hot but not boiling. Add horseradish. Serve sauce separately with chicken.

Chicken Breasts with Sherry

Serves 4

2 boneless chicken breasts, skinned and halved
¼ cup butter, softened
1 tablespoon chopped chives
1 tablespoon parsley
½ clove garlic, peeled and minced
½ teaspoon salt
⅛ teaspoon pepper
4 slices Swiss cheese
2 tablespoons vegetable oil
2 tablespoons flour
1 cup water
¼ cup dry sherry
2 teaspoons chicken stock

1. Pound each chicken breast half with flat side of meat mallet to ¼ inch thick. Form butter into 4 balls. Roll butter balls in mixture of chives, parsley, garlic, salt, and pepper. Place 1 butter ball on each slice of Swiss cheese. Place cheese on chicken breasts; roll so butter is completely enclosed. Secure with wooden toothpicks.
2. Heat oil in frying pan; brown chicken rolls for about 4 minutes on each side. Transfer to shallow baking dish with lid.
3. Preheat oven to 350 degrees.
4. Stir flour into drippings left in frying pan. Heat, stirring constantly, until smooth. Combine water, sherry, and stock; add to pan drippings and heat to boiling, stirring constantly. Spoon sauce over chicken.
5. Cover baking dish and bake for 30 minutes. Take chicken from oven, remove toothpicks, and serve.

Chicken with Hunter Sauce

Serves 4

1 (3-pound) chicken, cut into serving pieces
½ cup flour, seasoned with salt and pepper
2 tablespoons vegetable oil
2 tablespoons butter
2 shallots, peeled and chopped
½ pound sliced mushrooms
½ cup white wine
¼ cup brandy
1 cup beef broth
1 tablespoon tomato paste
¼ teaspoon thyme
½ teaspoon tarragon
1 tablespoon flour

1. Dredge chicken in seasoned flour. Heat oil and 1 tablespoon butter in Dutch oven or large frying pan. Add chicken pieces; cook until lightly browned. Remove chicken from pan.
2. Add shallots and mushrooms to pan; saute until liquid from mushrooms has evaporated. Add chicken, wine, brandy, broth, and tomato paste. Sprinkle with thyme and tarragon. Cover and simmer for 30 minutes, until chicken is tender. Transfer chicken to serving dish.
3. Mix 1 tablespoon flour and 1 tablespoon butter together. Add to sauce in pan, stirring until thickened. Serve sauce separately.

Chicken with Artichokes

Serves 4

2 tablespoons butter
2 whole chicken breasts, halved
1 clove garlic, peeled and minced
½ teaspoon salt
¼ teaspoon pepper
½ cup chicken broth
¼ cup white wine
1 (10-ounce) package frozen artichoke hearts, thawed
1 tablespoon cornstarch mixed with 1 tablespoon cold water
2 tablespoons lemon juice
3 eggs, beaten
2 tablespoons chopped parsley

1. Melt butter in heavy skillet. Brown chicken breasts, then add garlic; saute for 3 minutes. Add salt, pepper, chicken broth, and wine. Cover and simmer for 30 minutes. Add artichoke hearts and simmer, covered, for 10 minutes more.
2. Remove chicken from pan and keep warm. Measure out 1 cup of cooking liquid, adding more broth if needed, and place in saucepan. Heat, then stir in cornstarch mixture. Stir, until sauce thickens.
3. Gradually beat lemon juice into eggs. Slowly beat in hot sauce, then return mixture to saucepan. Cook over very low heat, stirring constantly, until thickened.
4. To serve, arrange chicken and artichokes on serving platter. Pour sauce over chicken and garnish with chopped parsley.

Oregano Chicken

Serves 4

1 (3-pound) chicken, cut into serving pieces
½ cup olive oil
¼ cup lemon juice
2 cloves garlic, peeled and minced
½ teaspoon salt
1 teaspoon oregano
½ teaspoon pepper
2 tablespoons butter, melted

1. The day before cooking, place chicken in large freezer bag. Combine oil, lemon juice, garlic, salt, oregano, and pepper; pour over chicken. Tie bag shut and turn bag several times to coat chicken with marinade. Refrigerate for 24 hours, turning bag occasionally.
2. Preheat broiler or heat coals in outdoor grill. Remove chicken from bag, and discard marinade. Broil or grill for 30 minutes, turning once and brushing with melted butter. Place on platter, and serve.

Roast Chicken and Potatoes

Serves 6 to 8

2 (3-pound) frying chickens
1 teaspoon salt
1 teaspoon pepper
2 cloves garlic, peeled and
    crushed
5 tablespoons butter, melted
6 to 8 medium potatoes,
    peeled and cut into lengthwise
    wedges
2 medium onions, peeled and
    cut into wedges
⅓ cup lemon juice
½ cup water

1. Preheat oven to 425 degrees.
2. Rub chickens with salt, pepper, and garlic. Place in large roasting pan, breast side up, and brush all over with 3 tablespoons melted butter.
3. Roll potatoes in remaining 2 tablespoons melted butter. Place potatoes and onions in roasting pan with chicken. Roast for 25 minutes. Reduce heat to 325 degrees and continue roasting for 45 to 50 minutes longer, until leg joints move easily.
4. Pour lemon juice over chicken, then transfer chicken, potatoes, and onions to platter and keep warm. Skim fat from pan juices. Add water and bring to a boil, stirring constantly. Pour into sauceboat. Slice chicken, and serve gravy separately.

Broiled Chicken with Cucumber Sauce

Serves 4

¼ cup olive oil
¼ cup lemon juice
1 cup dry white wine
1 teaspoon oregano
1 (2½-pound) chicken,
    quartered

Cucumber Sauce

1 cup plain yogurt
⅓ cup olive oil
1 clove garlic, peeled and
    crushed
1 teaspoon salt
1 cucumber, peeled, seeded,
    and finely chopped

1. Combine oil, lemon juice, wine, and oregano. Place chicken in baking dish and cover with marinade. Marinate for 3 hours.
2. Preheat broiler.
3. Broil chicken 4 inches from heat source, turning once, for about 30 minutes, or until chicken is tender. Baste occasionally with marinade.
4. To make cucumber sauce, combine yogurt, oil, garlic, salt, and cucumber. Place chicken on platter; discard any leftover marinade. Spoon cucumber sauce on top of chicken, or serve separately.

Chicken with Yogurt

Serves 4

1 (3-pound) chicken, cut into
    serving pieces
Juice of 1 lemon
Salt and pepper to taste
6 tablespoons butter
2 cloves garlic, peeled and minced
2 medium onions, sliced
½ cup white wine
1 cup chicken broth
1 teaspoon rosemary
1 cup plain yogurt
2 tablespoons flour

1. Rub chicken with lemon juice, salt, and pepper. Melt butter in large, heavy skillet. Brown chicken on all sides. Add garlic and onions; saute until lightly browned. Add wine, chicken broth, and rosemary. Reduce heat to low, cover, and simmer for 30 minutes, or until chicken is tender.
2. Combine yogurt and flour, blending well. Remove skillet from heat and let cool for 10 to 15 minutes. Gradually add yogurt and flour mixture. Cook, stirring constantly, over very low heat until slightly thickened. Pour sauce over chicken, and serve.

Roast Stuffed Chicken

Serves 4 to 5

1 (4-pound) roasting chicken
½ cup butter
1 cup chopped onion
1 cup sliced mushrooms
7 thin slices white bread, crusts
    removed and cubed
¼ cup minced parsley
1 egg, lightly beaten
Salt and pepper to taste
½ teaspoon paprika
1 tablespoon dry sherry

1. Remove liver from giblet pack and set aside. Discard remaining giblets.
2. Preheat oven to 350 degrees.
3. Melt 6 tablespoons butter in heavy skillet. Add onion and liver; saute for 3 minutes. Add mushrooms and saute, stirring, until liver is well browned and onion translucent. Remove pan from heat.
4. Finely chop chicken liver. Combine bread cubes, onion, mushrooms, butter, liver, parsley, egg, salt, and pepper in mixing bowl; mix well. Stuff chicken with mixture; truss. Secure neck opening with skewer.
5. Melt remaining butter and combine with paprika, sherry, salt, and pepper; mix well. Place chicken in roasting pan. Brush well with butter mixture. Roast for 1¼ to 1½ hours, or until juices run clear when breast is pierced with sharp knife. Baste several times with butter mixture while cooking.
6. Remove stuffing and place in serving dish. Carve chicken, and serve.

Chicken with Brandy Cream

Serves 4

3 tablespoons butter
1 tablespoon oil
1 cup slivered onion
1/2 pound mushrooms, sliced
1/4 cup flour
Salt and pepper to taste
4 boneless chicken breasts, skinned and halved
2 tablespoons brandy
1 cup heavy whipping cream
1/2 teaspoon tarragon
1 egg yolk

1. Heat 2 tablespoons butter and oil in heavy skillet over moderate heat. Add onion and saute until translucent. Add mushrooms and saute for 3 minutes, stirring occasionally. Remove from pan with slotted spoon and set aside.
2. Combine flour, salt, and pepper; dredge chicken breasts in mixture. Melt remaining tablespoon butter in skillet. Add chicken and brown well on both sides over moderate heat. Warm brandy in separate saucepan, then pour over chicken and ignite. Add cream and tarragon. Cook over low heat until thoroughly heated. Do not boil.
3. Beat egg yolk well. Add 2 tablespoons sauce in skillet to egg yolk, then stir egg yolk into chicken. Add mushrooms and onions. Cook, stirring constantly, until thickened and hot; do not let sauce boil. Remove from heat and serve immediately.

Chicken with Garlic and Oil

Serves 4

1/2 cup olive oil
1 (2 1/2- to 3-pound) chicken, cut into serving pieces
4 medium potatoes, peeled and cut into 1/2-inch-thick wedges
6 medium carrots, cut into julienne strips
1 medium onion, very thinly sliced
2 cloves garlic, peeled and chopped
Juice of 1 lemon
Salt and pepper to taste

1. Preheat oven to 350 degrees.
2. Pour olive oil into bottom of 14 x 10 x 2 1/2-inch pan or other large roasting pan. Dip chicken pieces into oil and turn until well coated. Turn chicken skin side up and distribute evenly in pan.
3. Arrange potatoes, carrots, and onions around chicken. Sprinkle garlic and lemon juice on top. Season with salt and pepper. Bake for 1 hour, basting every 15 minutes. Remove from oven, and serve.

Chicken with Sausage

Serves 4

3 tablespoons olive oil
2 pounds chicken pieces
4 sweet Italian sausage links
1 medium onion, sliced
1 large green pepper, seeded and sliced
1 cup sliced mushrooms
1 (16-ounce) can Italian-style plum tomatoes, broken up with fork
3 tablespoons tomato paste
1/2 cup red wine
1 teaspoon basil
Pinch of sugar
Salt and pepper to taste

1. Heat oil in heavy skillet. Fry chicken, a few pieces at a time, until golden brown, turning frequently. Remove from skillet and drain on paper towels.
2. Add sausages to skillet; prick with fork. Fry until well browned and thoroughly cooked, about 10 minutes. Remove from pan. Discard all but 3 tablespoons drippings.
3. Add onion, green pepper, and mushrooms to skillet; saute for 5 minutes. Add tomatoes, tomato paste, wine, and seasonings; stir well. Bring to a boil, then add chicken and sausage. Cover and simmer for 35 to 40 minutes. Transfer to serving dish, and serve with plain pasta.

Chicken Shoemaker's Style

Serves 4

1 (2 1/2- to 3-pound) chicken, quartered
2 tablespoons olive oil
3 tablespoons butter
Salt and pepper to taste
1 clove garlic, peeled and minced
2 tablespoons chopped scallion
1 cup sliced mushrooms
1/2 teaspoon tarragon
1/2 cup chicken broth
1/2 cup white wine
1/4 pound chicken livers
1 tablespoon chopped parsley

1. Cut each chicken quarter into 3 or 4 parts. Cut each wing or thigh in half. Heat oil and 2 tablespoons butter in large skillet over moderate heat. Add chicken and saute until browned. Season with salt and pepper. Remove from pan.
2. Add garlic, scallions, and mushrooms to skillet and saute for 5 minutes. Add tarragon, broth, wine, and chicken. Bring to a boil, then cover and simmer for 30 minutes.
3. Melt remaining butter in small frying pan. Add livers and saute for 5 minutes. Add livers to chicken and simmer for 5 minutes longer. Garnish with parsley, and serve.

Chicken in Dill Sauce

Serves 6

2 (2 1/2-pound) chickens, cut into serving pieces
1 1/2 quarts boiling water
1 onion, quartered
2 celery stalks with leaves, chopped
3 peppercorns
5 tablespoons flour
1/3 cup cold water
1 teaspoon salt
2 tablespoons finely chopped fresh dill
1/2 cup sour cream

1. Cover chicken with boiling water in large pot. Add onion, celery, and peppercorns. Cover and simmer for 2-1/2 hours, or until chicken is fork-tender. Remove chicken from stock and keep warm.

2. Strain stock; measure out 2 1/4 cups. Reheat 2 1/4 cups stock. Form paste with flour and water. Slowly stir flour paste into heated stock; stir until stock thickens. Add salt, dill, and sour cream, stirring until well blended.

3. Place chicken in serving dish. Pour sauce over chicken, and serve.

Rice with Chicken

Serves 4

1/2 cup olive oil
2 chicken breasts
3 chicken legs and thighs
2 tablespoons sherry
1/2 cup chopped onions
1 green pepper, chopped
1 cup long-grain rice
1 1/2 cups boiling chicken broth
1 teaspoon garlic powder
1 bay leaf
1/2 teaspoon salt
1/4 teaspoon pepper
Pinch of saffron
2 medium tomatoes, skinned and quartered
1/4 cup freshly grated Parmesan cheese

1. Heat oil in large frying pan until haze forms above pan. Reduce heat and brown chicken well on all sides. Remove chicken from pan; drizzle with sherry.

2. Add vegetables to frying pan; cook until limp. Add rice and saute until opaque and well coated with oil. Add boiling chicken broth and seasonings; return to boil.

3. Preheat oven to 350 degrees.

4. Pour rice mixture into greased, 2 1/2-quart casserole dish. Top with browned chicken. Cover and bake for 45 minutes. Place tomato quarters on top of chicken. Sprinkle with Parmesan cheese. Remove from oven, and serve.

Chicken Cutlets

Serves 6

2 tablespoons flour
2 cups hot chicken stock
3 egg yolks, beaten
3 cups finely diced cooked chicken
12 mushrooms, finely diced
Salt and pepper to taste
1 egg, beaten
Bread or cracker crumbs
Oil for deep-frying

1. Mix flour with 1/4 cup chicken stock. Add to remaining stock. Stir until thickened. Add egg yolks to sauce, stirring vigorously. Add chicken, mushrooms, and seasonings. Cook, stirring constantly, for 5 minutes. Cool and then chill mixture for several hours until stiff.

2. Shape mixture into cutlets. Dip each cutlet into egg, then into bread crumbs. Chill again.

3. Heat oil in deep frying pan. Fry cutlets until well browned. Drain on paper towels, and serve.

Cinnamon Stick Chicken

Serves 4

1 (3-pound) chicken
Salt and pepper to taste
1/4 cup butter
1 1/2 cups finely chopped onions
1 tablespoon chopped garlic
6 plum tomatoes, skinned, chopped, and drained
2 tablespoons tomato paste
1/2 cup chicken stock
2 cinnamon sticks

1. Season chicken with salt and pepper. Melt butter in large, heavy skillet. Add chicken, a few pieces at a time, and brown on all sides. Remove from pan and set aside.

2. Pour off most of fat in skillet. Add onions and garlic; saute until onions are lightly browned. Add remaining ingredients and bring to a boil. Return chicken to pan and baste each piece with sauce. Cover and simmer for 30 minutes.

3. Remove chicken to platter and spoon sauce over it. Serve at once.

Chicken with Rice and Cherries

Serves 4

1 (3-pound) chicken, cut into serving pieces
Salt and pepper to taste
1/4 cup olive oil
2 medium onions, finely sliced
1/2 cup chicken stock
1 (2-pound) can pitted black cherries, drained
1/4 cup sugar
2 tablespoons water
1/4 pound butter, melted
2 cups cooked long-grain rice

1. Sprinkle chicken with salt and pepper. Heat oil in large skillet and brown chicken pieces, a few at a time. Transfer browned chicken to heated plate. Add onions to pan and saute for 5 minutes, until lightly browned. Return chicken to skillet, add chicken stock, and bring to a boil. Reduce heat, cover, and simmer for 30 minutes. Transfer chicken to platter, reserving cooking liquid.

2. Combine cherries, sugar, and water in saucepan. Simmer for 5 minutes, stirring frequently. Remove from heat and set aside.

3. Preheat oven to 350 degrees.

4. Mix half the melted butter with reserved cooking liquid. Add 1 cup cooked rice and cook over low heat for 5 minutes. Transfer rice mixture to casserole dish. Cover with chicken pieces and half the cherries. Mix remaining rice with remaining melted butter, add to casserole. Top with remaining cherries and their cooking liquid.

5. Bake, covered, for 20 minutes, or until piping hot. Remove from oven, and serve at once.

Chicken with Sesame Seeds

Serves 6 to 8

$^1\!/_2$ cup flour
Salt and pepper to taste
1 teaspoon paprika
2 (3-pound) chickens, cut into serving pieces
3 tablespoons oil
2 tablespoons light brown sugar
$^1\!/_2$ teaspoon powdered ginger
1 cup dry red wine
2 tablespoons soy sauce
$^1\!/_3$ cup sesame seeds

1. Combine flour, salt, pepper, and paprika in paper bag. Add chicken and shake bag until chicken is well coated with flour mixture. Heat oil in large frying pan and brown chicken pieces. Remove from pan and place in casserole dish.
2. Preheat oven to 350 degrees.
3. Add brown sugar, ginger, wine, and soy sauce to fat remaining in frying pan. Stir until well blended. Pour over chicken.
4. Place sesame seeds in dry frying pan and cook over moderate heat until lightly toasted. Sprinkle sesame seeds over chicken. Bake chicken for 1 hour. Remove from oven, and serve.

Baked Rice with Chicken

Serves 6 to 8

6 tablespoons butter
3 cups uncooked white rice
4 boneless chicken breasts, halved
Salt and pepper to taste
1$^1\!/_2$ cups milk
1 cup heavy whipping cream
4 cups chicken stock

1. Heavily grease bottom and sides of 3-quart casserole dish, using 4 tablespoons butter. Spread 1$^1\!/_2$ cups rice on bottom of dish. Place chicken, skin side up, on top of rice. Season with salt and pepper.
2. Preheat oven to 400 degrees.
3. Combine milk, cream, and 2 cups stock in saucepan. Bring to a boil, then pour over chicken. Cover with remaining rice and dot with 2 tablespoons butter. Bake, uncovered, for 15 minutes.
4. Place remaining stock in saucepan and simmer until hot. Pour half of hot stock over chicken after initial 15 minutes of cooking. Bake for 15 minutes more. Pour on remaining stock and bake for 30 minutes.
5. Remove casserole from oven ad cover tightly, allowing to stand at room temperature for 20 minutes. Loosen edges of casserole with sharp knife and let stand for 10 minutes more. Place heated serving platter on top of casserole dish and invert so molded rice slides out onto platter. Serve at once.

Savory Baked Stuffed Chicken Breasts

Serves 4

4 boneless chicken breasts
1$^1\!/_2$ cups cooked rice
1 medium onion, chopped
2 tablespoons chopped parsley
2$^1\!/_2$ teaspoons salt
Pepper to taste
$^3\!/_4$ cup corn oil
$^1\!/_4$ cup flour
$^1\!/_2$ teaspoon paprika
$^3\!/_4$ cup lemon juice
$^1\!/_4$ cup water
3 tablespoons sugar
1$^1\!/_2$ teaspoons Tabasco sauce

1. Preheat oven to 450 degrees.
2. Place chicken breasts, skin side down, on plate. Combine rice, onion, parsley, $^1\!/_2$ teaspoon salt, pepper, and $^1\!/_4$ cup of corn oil, blending together well. Spoon onto chicken breasts. Roll up breasts and fasten with wooden toothpicks. Mix flour and paprika together. Dust each breast lightly with flour mixture.
3. Place chicken pieces, skin side up, in shallow baking pan lined with aluminum foil. Bake for 25 minutes. Reduce heat to 325 degrees.
4. Combine remaining corn oil, lemon juice, water, remaining salt, sugar, and Tabasco sauce in saucepan. Heat to boiling. Baste chicken with sauce and bake for 25 minutes more, until chicken is tender. Baste chicken frequently with sauce during baking. Remove chicken from oven, and serve.

Chicken Fricarole

Serves 8

1 (5- to 6-pound) stewing chicken, cut into serving pieces
1 stalk celery, cut into pieces
2 tablespoons chopped parsley
1 small onion, sliced
1 bay leaf
6 peppercorns
2 teaspoons salt
$^1\!/_2$ cup chopped onions
2 tablespoons butter
1 pound medium-wide egg noodles
2 cups chopped cooked asparagus pieces
1 cup diced cooked ham
$^1\!/_2$ cup sliced stuffed olives
1 (10$^1\!/_2$-ounce) can condensed cream of chicken soup
1 cup grated American cheese

1. Preheat oven to 350 degrees.
2. Place chicken in large casserole dish with celery, parsley, sliced onion, bay leaf, peppercorns, and salt. Add water to barely cover. Cover and bake for 2 hours. Pour off and reserve broth, removing peppercorns and bay leaf.
3. Saute chopped onions in butter until translucent. Cook noodles according to package directions. Add onions, noodles, asparagus pieces, ham, and olives to chicken. Combine soup with chicken broth and $^1\!/_2$ cup cheese. Pour over casserole. Sprinkle with remaining cheese.
4. Return casserole to oven and continue to cook, uncovered, for 45 minutes, or until bubbling hot and lightly browned; stir several times during cooking. Remove from oven, and serve hot.

Cream Chicken Casserole

Serves 10

3/4 cup flour
1 1/2 tablespoons paprika
2 teaspoons salt
1/4 teaspoon pepper
1/4 teaspoon thyme
1 teaspoon dill seed
2 (3- to 3 1/2-pound) chickens, cut into serving pieces
3/4 cup butter
1 cup chopped onion
1 tablespoon chopped pimento
1 cup light cream or evaporated milk
1 cup chicken bouillon
1/4 cup fresh lemon juice

1. Preheat oven to 325 degrees.
2. Combine flour, paprika, salt, pepper, thyme, and dill in paper bag. Add chicken, a few pieces at a time, and shake until chicken is well coated with flour mixture. Heat butter in large frying pan. Add chicken and brown on all sides. Remove from pan.
3. Add onions to pan and saute until lightly browned. Add pimento. Stir in remainder of seasoned flour until well blended. Add cream or evaporated milk, stirring well. Stir in bouillon and lemon juice.
4. Place chicken in casserole dish and pour sauce on top. Cover and bake for 50 to 60 minutes. Remove from oven, and serve hot.

Tangy Chicken

Serves 8

2 (2 1/2- to 3-pound) chickens, cut into serving pieces
2 1/2 cups water
2 bay leaves
1 onion, stuck with 2 cloves
2 stalks celery
2 teaspoons salt
1/4 teaspoon pepper
1/4 teaspoon thyme
3 tablespoons flour
1 lemon, sliced
Parsley sprigs for garnish

1. Place chicken in deep kettle with tight-fitting lid. Add water, bay leaves, onion, celery, salt, pepper, and thyme. Cover and bring to a boil. Reduce heat and simmer for 40 to 50 minutes. Remove chicken from pot; set aside and keep warm.
2. Strain broth and measure out 2 1/2 cups; let cool. Combine flour with 1/2 cup cooled stock, stirring until smooth. Add lemon slices to remaining stock. Gradually add flour mixture to remaining stock. Cook, stirring constantly, until sauce thickens. Add chicken and simmer until chicken is thoroughly heated. Garnish with parsley, and serve.

Capon Casserole with Savory Dressing

Serves 8 to 10

1/2 cup flour
Salt and pepper to taste
1 (5- to 6-pound) capon, cut into serving pieces
1/2 cup shortening
1/4 cup chopped onion
1/2 cup chopped celery and leaves
5 cups dry bread cubes
1/8 teaspoon garlic salt
1/4 teaspoon sage
1/4 teaspoon thyme
1/2 cup sliced stuffed olives
1/2 cup butter, melted
2 cups chicken broth.

1. Preheat oven to 350 degrees.
2. Combine flour, salt, and pepper in paper bag. Add capon pieces and shake until capon is well coated with flour mixture. Fry capon in hot shortening until evenly browned. Drain, then arrange around sides of large casserole dish.
3. Saute onion and celery in remaining shortening for 5 minutes. Combine onion and celery with bread cubes, seasonings, olives, butter, and 1/2 cup chicken broth. Place stuffing in center of casserole. Pour remaining broth over capon. Cover and bake for 1 1/2 hours, or until capon is tender. Remove cover and continue to bake for 15 minutes more. Remove from oven, and serve.

Chicken Baked with Fresh Tomatoes

Serves 6 to 8

1/3 cup flour
1/2 teaspoon paprika
3 teaspoons salt
2 (2 1/2-pound) chickens, cut into serving pieces
1/3 cup bacon drippings or butter
1 clove garlic, peeled and chopped
3/4 cup chopped onion
3/4 cup chopped green pepper
4 medium tomatoes, skinned and quartered
2 cups beer
1/4 cup tomato paste
1/2 teaspoon thyme

1. Preheat oven to 350 degrees.
2. Season flour with paprika and salt. Coat chickens with flour mixture. Heat bacon drippings or butter in large frying pan. Add garlic and chicken, a few pieces at a time, and cook until browned. Transfer chickens to large, greased casserole dish. Discard garlic.
3. Add onions and green peppers to frying pan and saute until tender; add to casserole with chickens. Arrange tomatoes over chickens.
4. Blend beer, tomato paste, 2 teaspoons salt, and thyme together. Pour over chickens and bake for 1 1/4 hours. Remove from oven, and serve.

Baked Chicken

Serves 6

2 (2¹/₂-pound) chickens, cut
 into serving pieces
¹/₂ cup melted butter
¹/₄ cup lemon juice
1 tablespoon tarragon
Pinch of pepper

1. Preheat oven to 350 degrees.
2. Arrange chickens in shallow baking
dish. Combine remaining ingredients,
mixing well. Brush chickens thoroughly
with butter mixture. Bake for 1 hour,
basting chickens occasionally. Remove
from oven, and serve.

Baked Chicken
with Prune Dressing

Serves 4

2 large onions, sliced
¹/₂ cup butter
2 teaspoons poultry seasoning
1 teaspoon salt
Pepper to taste
8 cups dry bread cubes
2 cups chopped pitted prunes
¹/₂ cup boiling water
1 (3-pound) chicken, cut into
 serving pieces
Whole plumped prunes for
 garnish

1. Preheat oven to 350 degrees.
2. Saute onions in butter until golden
brown. Add poultry seasoning, salt,
and pepper. Combine bread cubes and
prunes. Add onion mixture and water,
mixing well. Place stuffing on bottom
of casserole dish.
3. Place chicken pieces on top of
stuffing. Brush with melted butter,
cover, and bake for 1¹/₂ hours, or until
chicken is tender. Uncover dish during
last ¹/₂ hour of cooking time to brown
chicken. Garnish with whole prunes,
and serve.

Chicken Fricassee

Serves 4

3 tablespoons butter
1 tablespoon flour
1 cup skim milk
¹/₄ cup egg substitute or
 1 egg yolk, beaten
¹/₄ teaspoon marjoram
¹/₄ teaspoon thyme
¹/₂ teaspoon salt
2 cups cubed cooked chicken
 breasts
1 cup long-grain rice
1 onion, finely chopped
3 stalks celery, finely chopped

1. Preheat oven to 325 degrees.
2. Melt 1 tablespoon butter in saucepan. Stir in flour, blending well.
Gradually add milk. Cook, stirring
constantly, until sauce thickens. Whisk
in egg substitute or egg yolk and
spices.
3. Place chicken in shallow, greased
baking dish. Cover with white sauce.
Bake for 20 minutes, or until hot.
4. While chicken is cooking, cook rice
according to package directions. Melt
remaining butter in frying pan. Add
onion and celery; saute for 5 minutes.
Toss with hot rice.
5. Remove chicken from oven, and
serve with hot rice.

Chicken
in Fruit Sauce

Serves 4

1 (2¹/₂-pound) chicken, cut into
 serving pieces
¹/₂ cup flour, seasoned with salt
 and pepper
¹/₄ cup corn oil
¹/₄ cup sherry
¹/₂ cup crushed pineapple in
 natural juice
³/₄ cup orange juice
¹/₄ cup pitted dates
¹/₄ teaspoon ground cinnamon
¹/₈ teaspoon ground cloves
2 tablespoons cold water
1 tablespoon cornstarch
¹/₄ cup sliced almonds

1. Dredge chicken in seasoned flour
until well coated. Heat oil in heavy
skillet; brown chicken well on all
sides. Combine sherry, pineapple,
orange juice, dates, cinnamon, and
cloves. Pour sauce over chicken.
Cover and cook over low heat for 1¹/₂
hour to 2 hours, until chicken is
tender.
2. Combine water and cornstarch; stir
well. Increase skillet heat to high and
stir in cornstarch mixture. Cook for 15
minutes, stirring constantly, until
sauce thickens.
3. Sprinkle chicken with almonds, and
serve with boiled rice and oranges.

Chicken Lentil
Casserole

Serves 4 to 5

1 cup lentils
2¹/₂ cups water
3 tablespoons butter
¹/₂ pound mushrooms, sliced
1 medium onion, chopped
1 large carrot, chopped
1 medium potato, chopped
1 tablespoon flour
1¹/₂ cups chicken broth
³/₄ teaspoon salt
¹/₈ teaspoon pepper
³/₄ teaspoon dill weed
1 cup chopped cooked chicken
1 cup buttered whole-wheat bread
 crumbs

1. Wash lentils. Place in saucepan and
cover with water. Bring to a boil.
Cover and simmer for 20 minutes.
2. Preheat oven to 350 degrees.
3. Melt 2 tablespoons butter in frying
pan. Add mushrooms and saute for 3
minutes. Remove mushrooms from
pan and set aside. Add remaining
butter to pan. Saute onion, carrot, and
potato for 3 minutes. Stir in flour,
blending well. Add broth, salt, pepper,
and dill. Bring to a boil, stirring

constantly. Boil for 1 minute, then remove from heat. Add mushrooms and chicken.

4. Drain lentils. Stir lentils into chicken mixture. Pour into 1½-quart casserole dish. Top with buttered bread crumbs and bake for 30 minutes, or until lightly browned and bubbling. Remove from oven, and serve hot.

Bird of Paradise

Serves 4

½ cup butter, melted
½ cup honey
¼ teaspoon ginger
2 cloves garlic, peeled and minced
¼ cup lemon juice
2 (2-pound) chickens, halved
Salt and pepper to taste
2 pineapple slices, quartered
8 kumquats
8 maraschino cherries

Polynesian Sauce

Reserved basting sauce
½ cup kumquat syrup
⅓ cup lightly toasted chopped nuts
½ cup pineapple juice

1. Preheat oven to broil.
2. Combine melted butter, honey, ginger, garlic, and lemon juice. Sprinkle chicken with salt and pepper. Place chicken on broiler pan, skin side down, and brush with butter sauce. Broil chicken, 7 to 8 inches from heat source, for 30 minutes, brushing occasionally with seasoned butter. Turn, brush with butter, and broil for 15 minutes longer. Reserve remaining sauce.
3. Thread a pineapple piece, kumquat, and cherry on each of 4 skewers. Thread chicken half lengthwise on each skewer. Repeat with remaining fruit. Broil for 2 minutes, turning once.
4. Combine all Polynesian sauce ingredients in saucepan, and heat. Serve chicken with Polynesian sauce and boiled rice.

Twin Roast Chickens

Serves 8

2 (2½- to 3-pound) chickens
Salt and pepper to taste
1 (8-ounce) package prepared stuffing mix
2 tablespoons butter, melted
8 canned peach halves, drained
Pickle relish

1. Preheat oven to 375 degrees.
2. Season chickens inside and out with salt and pepper. Prepare stuffing according to package directions. Stuff and truss chickens. Place chickens on rack in shallow roasting pan. Brush with melted butter and roast for 30 minutes per pound.
3. During last 20 minutes of roasting, place peaches, cut side down, around chicken. To serve, place chickens on heated serving platter; garnish with peach halves. Fill center of peaches with pickle relish.

Golden-Crisped Chicken

Serves 12

2½ cups cornflake crumbs
1 tablespoon salt
½ teaspoon pepper
3 (2½-pound) chickens, cut into serving pieces
1 cup evaporated milk

1. Preheat oven to 350 degrees.
2. Mix cornflake crumbs with salt and pepper in pie plate or shallow baking dish. Line 2 shallow baking pans with aluminum foil. Dip chicken pieces in evaporated milk, then roll immediately in seasoned cornflake crumbs.
3. Place chicken, skin side up, in foil-lined pans; do not crowd. Bake for 1½ hours, or until tender. At end of 1 hour, exchange place of pans on racks; continue to bake. Remove from oven, and serve.

Spiced Cranberry Chicken

Serves 3

½ cup flour
1 teaspoon salt
⅛ teaspoon pepper
6 chicken fryer legs and thighs
Oil

Cranberry Spice Sauce

2 tablespoons brown sugar
1 tablespoon cornstarch
¾ cup cranberry juice cocktail
1 (16-ounce) can whole cranberry sauce
1 teaspoon nutmeg
1 teaspoon marjoram
1 tablespoon minced onion

1. Mix flour, salt, and pepper together. Dredge chicken pieces in seasoned flour until well coated. Heat ¼ inch of oil in large frying pan. Add chicken and brown on all sides. Cover tightly, reduce heat, and cook gently for 20 to 30 minutes, until chicken is tender, turning occasionally. Drain on paper towels.
2. Mix brown sugar and cornstarch together in saucepan. Gradually stir in cranberry juice cocktail until smooth. Add whole cranberry sauce, spices, and minced onion. Cook over medium heat, stirring constantly, until mixture comes to a boil.
3. To serve, place chicken on platter and spoon cranberry spice sauce on top.

Patio Chicken

Serves 4

1 (2½-pound) chicken, cut into
  serving pieces
¼ cup butter, melted
1 cup bread crumbs
1 teaspoon onion salt
1 teaspoon garlic salt
½ teaspoon pepper
1 tablespoon chopped parsley
½ teaspoon curry powder
1 cup mayonnaise

1. Preheat oven to 400 degrees.
2. Brush chicken with melted butter.
Roll in mixture of bread crumbs, onion
salt, garlic salt, pepper, parsley, and
curry powder. Arrange crumb-coated
chicken, skin side up, on foil-lined
cookie sheet. Do not overlap any
pieces. Cook for 15 minutes. Remove
from oven.
3. Brush chicken generously with
mayonnaise. Reduce heat to 300
degrees; bake for 1 hour, or until
chicken is tender. Remove from oven,
and serve.

Skillet Herb-Fried Chicken

Serves 6 to 8

⅔ cup evaporated milk
1¼ cups flour
1½ teaspoons salt
½ teaspoon paprika
⅛ teaspoon pepper
¼ teaspoon rosemary
¼ teaspoon thyme
2 (2½-pound) chickens, cut
  into serving pieces
Corn oil for frying

1. Pour evaporated milk into bowl.
Combine flour, salt, paprika, pepper,
rosemary, and thyme in shallow dish.
Dip chicken in evaporated milk, then
dredge in flour mixture.

2. Pour corn oil in heavy skillet to
depth of ½ inch; heat. Add chicken,
skin side down, to skillet and cook,
uncovered, for 15 to 25 minutes on
each side, turning once, until chicken
is crisp and brown. Drain on paper
towels, then serve.

Easy Chicken Cacciatore

Serves 4

1 (2½-pound) chicken, cut into
  serving pieces
¼ cup flour seasoned with salt
  and pepper
¼ cup olive or salad oil
1 cup canned pearl onions,
  drained
1 green pepper, seeded and cut
  into strips
1 (4-ounce) can mushrooms,
  drained
1 small clove garlic, peeled and
  minced
1 (10½-ounce) can condensed
  tomato soup
½ cup water
2 tablespoons vinegar or lemon
  juice
1 tablespoon Worcestershire sauce
½ teaspoon oregano

1. Dredge chicken pieces in seasoned
flour. Heat olive oil in large skillet.
Add chicken and brown on all sides.
Remove from pan. Add onions, green
pepper, mushrooms, and garlic to
same skillet. Blend in tomato soup,
water, vinegar or lemon juice,
Worcestershire sauce, and oregano.
2. Return chicken to skillet. Cover and
simmer, stirring occasionally for 30
minutes, or until chicken is tender.
Remove from heat, and serve over
cooked spaghetti.

Baltimore Dinner Belle

Serves 4

1 egg
⅓ cup milk
¾ cup fine cracker crumbs
¼ cup flour
1 tablespoon cornmeal
½ teaspoon salt

½ teaspoon paprika
1 (3-pound) frying chicken,
  cut into serving pieces
¼ cup butter
¼ cup olive or salad oil

1. Beat egg and milk together in bowl.
Combine cracker crumbs, flour,
cornmeal, salt, and paprika. Dip
chicken pieces in egg mixture, then
coat with cracker crumb mixture.
2. Heat butter and salad oil in heavy
skillet. Add chicken and brown on all
sides. Turn heat very low. Flick a small
amount of water over chicken with
your fingers, then cover and cook for
30 minutes, or until tender. Remove
from pan, and serve.

Savory Chicken

Serves 4

1 (3½-pound) chicken, cut into
  serving pieces
½ teaspoon thyme
½ teaspoon marjoram
1 egg, slightly beaten
2 tablespoons milk
¼ cup flour
½ cup fine cracker crumbs
1 teaspoon salt
¼ teaspoon pepper
¼ cup wine vinegar
¼ cup butter, melted

1. Sprinkle chicken with thyme and
marjoram; let stand for 1 hour.
2. Preheat oven to 350 degrees.
3. Beat egg with milk. Combine flour
with cracker crumbs, salt, and pepper.
Dip chicken in egg mixture, then
dredge in flour mixture. Place in
greased baking pan; do not crowd.
Bake, uncovered, for 1½ hours, or
until chicken is tender. Turn
occasionally during cooking; sprinkle
twice with wine vinegar and once with
melted butter. Remove from oven, and
serve hot.

Crusty Baked Delmarva Chicken

Serves 6

2 eggs
2 teaspoons Worcestershire
  sauce
1 teaspoon onion juice
2 (3-pound) chickens,
  cut into serving pieces
2 cups bread crumbs
1 teaspoon sage
$1/2$ teaspoon paprika
Pinch of garlic salt
$1/2$ teaspoon salt
$1/8$ teaspoon pepper
$1/4$ cup vegetable oil
4 slices bacon
$1/3$ cup milk

1. Preheat oven to 350 degrees.
2. Beat eggs, Worcestershire sauce, and onion juice together until thoroughly mixed. Dip chicken pieces in this mixture. Combine bread crumbs, sage, paprika, garlic salt, salt, and pepper. Roll chicken in bread crumb mixture.
3. Pour oil in flat baking dish. Arrange chicken in dish; spread bacon slices over chicken. Bake for 1 hour, then add milk. Cover with lid or foil, and continue to bake for 15 to 20 minutes. Remove from oven, and serve hot.

Chicken Dillicassee

Serves 6 to 8

1 ($4^1/2$-pound) stewing chicken, cut
  into serving pieces
6 cups boiling water
1 onion, quartered
2 celery tops
3 peppercorns
5 tablespoons flour
$1/3$ cup water

Salt to taste
Pinch of cayenne pepper
2 tablespoons minced fresh dill
  or $1/2$ teaspoon dried dill
1 egg yolk
$1/3$ cup light cream
6 to 8 biscuits, split in half

1. Place chicken in kettle and cover with boiling water; add onion, celery tops, and peppercorns. Cover and simmer for $2^1/2$ hours, or until tender. Remove to warm platter.
2. Strain broth; pour $2^1/2$ cups strained broth into saucepan. Mix flour with water until smooth. Add to broth and cook, stirring constantly, until sauce is thick and smooth. Season with salt, cayenne pepper, and dill. Beat egg yolk with cream, and stir into sauce. Pour sauce over chicken pieces. Serve chicken surrounded with split biscuits.

Chicken Barbecued in a Skillet

Serves 4

$1/4$ cup shortening
1 (3-pound) chicken, cut into
  serving pieces
$1/3$ cup thinly sliced onion
$1/3$ cup chopped green pepper
1 small clove garlic, peeled and
  minced
1 ($10^1/2$-ounce) can condensed
  tomato soup
2 tablespoons brown sugar
2 tablespoons Worcestershire
  sauce
2 tablespoons lemon juice or
  vinegar
2 teaspoons prepared mustard
Dash of Tabasco sauce

1. Heat shortening in heavy skillet; add chicken and brown on all sides. Remove chicken from pan. Add onion, green pepper, and garlic to skillet; saute for 5 minutes. Mix in remaining ingredients and simmer until thoroughly blended.
2. Return chicken to skillet. Spoon sauce over chicken, cover, and simmer for 30 minutes, turning occasionally. Remove from heat, and serve

Hens en Croute

Serves 4

3 cups flour
$1^1/2$ cups shortening
1 teaspoon salt
Pinch of ginger
About $1/4$ cup cold water
$1/2$ cup prepared stuffing
4 boneless chicken breasts,
  skinned and halved
1 egg yolk, mixed with 3
  tablespoons water

Sauce Supreme

6 tablespoons butter
1 onion, finely chopped
$1/4$ cup flour
1 cup heavy whipping cream
Salt and pepper to taste
$1/2$ cup dry white wine

1. Mix flour, shortening, salt, ginger, and cold water together to form dough. Roll out on floured surface, and cut into 8 circles.
2. Preheat oven to 425 degrees.
3. Place about 1 tablespoon stuffing on each piece of chicken. Roll up chicken and place each on a circle of dough. Wrap dough up to completely encase chicken breast. Place on buttered baking sheet; brush with egg yolk. Bake for 20 to 30 minutes, until browned.
4. To make sauce, melt butter in saucepan. Add onion and saute until translucent. Add flour and cream. Heat, stirring constantly, until sauce thickens. Season with salt and pepper. Stir in wine, and heat thoroughly. Serve sauce separately with chicken breasts.

Baked Filled Chicken Breasts

Serves 8

8 (1-ounce) slices boiled ham
4 boneless chicken breasts,
   skinned and halved
   lengthwise
8 slices bacon
1 (10½-ounce) can cream of
   mushroom soup
1 cup sour cream

1. Preheat oven to 300 degrees.
2. Place ham slice on each chicken breast. Roll up and wrap with slice of bacon; secure with wooden toothpicks.
3. Place chicken rolls in deep, buttered baking pan. Mix soup with sour cream; pour over chicken. Cover pan with foil and bake for 1 hour. Uncover and bake for 15 minutes longer, or until chicken is cooked thoroughly. Remove from oven, and serve.

Peach-Stuffed Chicken Breasts

Serves 6

6 boneless chicken breasts,
   skinned and halved
   lengthwise
1 teaspoon salt
3 fresh peaches, peeled and cut
   into small pieces
½ cup finely chopped onion
½ cup chopped cashews
½ teaspoon powdered ginger
¼ cup butter

Fresh Peach Sauce

2 fresh peaches, peeled and
   sliced
½ cup brown sugar
2 teaspoons mustard
¼ teaspoon salt
1 cup sour cream
1 tablespoon brandy

1. Preheat oven to 350 degrees.
2. Pound chicken breasts to flatten; sprinkle with salt. Combine peaches, onion, cashews, and ginger. Place mixture on each piece of chicken, roll up, and secure with wooden toothpicks.
3. Melt butter in foil-lined baking pan. Place stuffed chicken breasts in pan and bake for 25 minutes. Turn chicken over and bake for 20 minutes longer.
4. To make sauce, combine peaches, brown sugar, mustard, salt, sour cream, and brandy in saucepan. Simmer for 5 minutes, until thoroughly heated. Serve sauce separately with chicken breasts.

Curry-Glazed Chicken

Serves 8

2 (3-pound) chickens, cut into
   serving pieces
6 tablespoons flour
1½ teaspoons salt
1 teaspoon powdered ginger
¾ cup butter

Curry Glaze

6 slices bacon, diced
1 medium apple, peeled, cored,
   and diced
2 tablespoons flour
1 tablespoon curry powder
1 tablespoon sugar
1 cup condensed beef broth
2 tablespoons ketchup
2 tablespoons lemon juice

1. Preheat oven to 400 degrees.
2. Shake chicken pieces in bag with flour, salt, and ginger. Melt butter in baking pan; roll chicken in butter, coating well. Arrange chicken, skin side up, in single layer. Bake, uncovered, for 20 minutes. Turn chicken over, brush with more butter, and bake for 20 minutes more, until browned.
3. To prepare curry glaze, fry bacon gently until browned. Add apple, flour, curry powder, sugar, beef broth, ketchup, and lemon juice. Heat together, stirring constantly, until boiling and thickened. Brush chicken with glaze and bake for 20 minutes longer. Remove from oven, and serve with boiled rice.

Chicken Hawaiian

Serves 12

6 coconuts
1¼ cups butter
5 cups flour
4 cups milk
1½ teaspoons salt
1 pound mushrooms, sliced
2 cups diced celery
½ cup pimentos
4 to 5 cups cooked diced
   chicken
1 cup shortening
2 to 3 tablespoons cold water
2 egg yolks, beaten with
   2 tablespoons water

1. Saw coconuts in half. Scrape about 2 tablespoons coconut meat from each half; grate and set aside. Keep coconut milk in refrigerator and reserve for use in another recipe.
2. To make cream sauce, melt 1 cup butter in saucepan. Stir in 3 cups flour, blending well. Add milk and 1 teaspoon salt; cook, stirring constantly, until sauce thickens.
3. Melt remaining butter in frying pan. Add mushrooms and saute for 5 minutes. Combine grated coconut, cream sauce, mushrooms, celery, pimento, and chicken. Divide mixture among 12 coconut shell halves.
4. Preheat oven to 350 degrees.
5. Make pastry by mixing 2 cups flour, shortening, ½ teaspoon salt, and cold water together. Roll out dough on floured board until quite thin; cut into 12 circles to fit top of filled coconut shells. Crimp edges and make several slits in top for steam to escape. Brush with egg yolks.
6. Cover baking sheet with crumpled foil. Place shells on foil (the crumpled foil should prevent shells from tipping) and bake for 1 hour. Remove from oven, and serve.

Arroz con Pollo

Serves 6

2¹/₂ pounds chicken pieces
2¹/₂ tablespoons butter
2 small cloves garlic, crushed
2 teaspoons salt
¹/₈ teaspoon pepper
¹/₈ teaspoon paprika
3 slices bacon finely diced
¹/₄ cup chopped onion
¹/₄ cup chopped green pepper
1 cup long-grain rice
2 cups boiling chicken broth
¹/₂ cup canned tomatoes, crushed
Pinch of saffron
¹/₂ cup cooked peas

1. Preheat oven to 350 degrees.
2. Place chicken, skin side up, in baking dish. Combine butter, 1 clove garlic, 1 teaspoon salt, pepper, and paprika; brush on chicken. Bake for 45 to 55 minutes, or until chicken is golden brown.
3. In ovenproof skillet, saute bacon until lightly browned. Add onion, green pepper, and remaining garlic. Saute for 5 minutes. Add rice and saute for 2 minutes. Stir in chicken broth, tomatoes, saffron, and remaining salt. Cover tightly and bake at 350 degrees for 45 minutes, or until rice is tender and liquid is absorbed.
4. Add peas and fluff lightly with fork. To serve, arrange cooked chicken over rice.

Chicken Ole

Serves 8

¹/₄ cup butter
¹/₄ cup oil
2 (2¹/₂-pound) chickens, cut into serving pieces
Water
1 small carrot
6 peppercorns
2 celery stalks with leaves

2 cloves garlic, peeled and minced
Salt to taste
2 large onions, chopped
4 green peppers, seeded and chopped
¹/₄ cup unbleached flour
4 cups canned tomatoes, with juice
2 cups ripe, pitted black olives
2 cups canned corn
8 slices bacon

1. Heat butter and oil in frying pan. Add chicken and brown on all sides. Transfer chicken to large kettle. Cover with water. Add carrot, peppercorns, celery, garlic, and salt. Bring to a boil, then reduce to simmer. Cook for 1 hour, or until chicken is tender. Remove chicken from broth and let cool slightly. Take meat from bones. Reserve 2 cups of chicken broth.
2. Saute onions and green peppers for 5 minutes in same frying pan in which chicken was browned. Add reserved broth and flour; stir constantly until sauce thickens. Add tomatoes and olives.
3. Preheat oven to 375 degrees.
4. Layer corn, chicken, and tomato mixture in casserole dish. Top with bacon and bake for 25 to 30 minutes. Remove from oven, and serve hot.

Chicken with Mushrooms

Serves 4 to 5

¹/₂ cup butter
1 (3- to 4-pound) chicken, cut into serving pieces
1 large onion, chopped
1 cup sliced mushrooms
Salt to taste
1¹/₂ cups water
1 cup sour cream
1 tablespoon flour

1. Melt butter in large frying pan. Add chicken and brown on all sides. Add onion and saute until translucent. Add mushrooms, salt, and water. Cover and simmer for 45 minutes, until chicken is tender. Remove chicken from pan.
2. Mix sour cream and flour together; blend into pan juices. Bring gravy to a boil, stirring until smooth and thickened. Serve gravy separately with chicken.

Chicken Breasts with Fontina

Serves 6 to 8

4 eggs
¹/₃ cup flour
Salt and pepper to taste
Vegetable oil for frying
8 boneless chicken breast halves, skinned and flattened to about ¹/₄-inch thick
¹/₄ cup butter
¹/₂ pound mushrooms, sliced
1 tablespoon lemon juice
8 slices fontina cheese
1 cup tomato sauce
¹/₄ cup chopped parsley or chives

1. Place eggs, flour, salt, and pepper in food processor or blender container; process until smooth. Transfer to bowl and refrigerate for 30 minutes.
2. Preheat oven to 375 degrees.
3. Heat ¹/₂ inch oil to 350 degrees in large skillet. Dip chicken breasts in chilled batter. Fry, a few at a time, until golden brown on both sides. Drain on paper towels.
4. Pour oil from skillet; wipe pan clean. Melt butter in skillet; add mushrooms and lemon juice. Cook over high heat for 3 to 4 minutes. Remove from heat.
5. Arrange chicken on bottom of baking pan. Place a slice of cheese over each breast. Combine mushrooms with tomato sauce; spoon over chicken.
6. Bake chicken for 10 minutes. Sprinkle with parsley or chives; serve immediately.

Chicken and Herbs

Serves 4

3 pounds chicken pieces
Salt and pepper to taste
1 (10-ounce) can condensed
  cream of chicken soup
$^1/_4$ cup water
$^1/_2$ cup sherry
1 cup button mushrooms
$^1/_2$ teaspoon allspice
$^1/_2$ teaspoon oregano
$^1/_2$ teaspoon parsley flakes
$^1/_2$ teaspoon minced onion
$^1/_2$ teaspoon garlic salt
$^1/_2$ teaspoon Worcestershire
  sauce
$^1/_2$ teaspoon poultry seasoning
Paprika to taste

1. Preheat oven to 350 degrees.
2. Season chicken with salt and pepper; place in large baking dish.
3. Combine soup, water, sherry, and mushrooms in bowl; blend well. Pour soup mixture over chicken.
4. Mix allspice, oregano, parsley flakes, minced onion, garlic salt, Worcestershire sauce, and poultry seasoning together in separate bowl; sprinkle over chicken.
5. Sprinkle chicken with paprika and bake for 1 hour, or until chicken is tender. Do not turn chicken; baste several times with pan liquid. Serve hot, with wild rice.

Chicken à la Queen

Serves 6

2 sprigs minced parsley
1$^1/_2$ tablespoons minced onion
$^1/_2$ clove garlic, peeled and finely
  minced
2 tablespoons butter
6 tablespoons flour
1$^1/_2$ cups chicken broth
1$^1/_2$ cups light cream

$^3/_4$ teaspoon salt
$^1/_2$ teaspoon pepper
2 pimentos, chopped
$^1/_2$ cup chopped green pepper
$^3/_4$ cup button mushrooms
1 (5-pound) cooked chicken,
  skinned, boned, and cut into
  large cubes
3 egg yolks, beaten
3 tablespoons dry sherry

1. Place parsley, onion, garlic, and butter in top of double boiler. Cook for 4 minutes; do not brown. Stir in flour. Gradually add broth and cream. Cook, stirring frequently, for 20 minutes.
2. Add salt, pepper, pimentos, green pepper, mushrooms, and chicken; mix well.
3. Just before serving, stir in egg yolks and sherry. Cook over low heat, stirring constantly, until heated thoroughly. Serve on bed of rice or in patty shells.

Chicken Bundles

Serves 4

1 cup bran cereal
$^1/_4$ cup finely chopped almonds
$^3/_8$ teaspoon pepper
$^1/_8$ teaspoon sage
$^1/_8$ teaspoon thyme
5 tablespoons butter, melted
$^1/_2$ teaspoon lemon juice
2 tablespoons finely chopped
  onion
1 tablespoon chopped pimentos
1 cup cubed cooked chicken
1 (8-ounce) can refrigerated
  crescent dinner rolls
2 tablespoons margarine
1 tablespoon flour
$^1/_4$ teaspoon salt
$^1/_2$ cup sour cream
$^2/_3$ cup milk
1 (2$^1/_2$-ounce) jar sliced
  mushrooms, drained
$^1/_2$ teaspoon chopped parsley

1. Preheat oven to 350 degrees.
2. In small mixing bowl, combine $^1/_4$ cup cereal, 2 tablespoons almonds, $^1/_8$ teaspoon pepper, sage, thyme, 3 tablespoons melted butter, lemon juice, onion, pimentos, and chicken. Mix well; set aside.

3. Crush remaining cereal to coarse crumbs; mix with remaining almonds. Set aside.
4. Separate crescent roll dough into 4 squares (2 triangles each). Firmly press perforations to seal. Place about $^1/_3$ cup chicken filling in center of each square. Gather corners together, pinching to seal.
5. Brush bundles with remaining melted butter. Roll in cereal crumb mixture. Place on ungreased baking sheet. Bake for 25 minutes, or until lightly browned.
6. While bundles are baking, melt margarine in small saucepan. Stir in flour, salt, remaining pepper, and parsley. Gradually add milk, stirring until smooth. Add mushrooms and cook over medium heat, stirring constantly, until bubbly and thickened.
7. Add sour cream. Cook, stirring constantly, until heated thoroughly; do not boil. Serve sour cream sauce over chicken bundles.

Sautéed Chicken in Rosemary Sauce

Serves 4 or 5

5 tablespoons extra virgin
  olive oil
1 (2$^1/_2$-pound) chicken, skinned
  and cut into 10 pieces
Salt and pepper to taste
1 cup water
3 tablespoons red wine vinegar
2 cloves garlic, peeled and
  finely chopped
3 tablespoons chopped fresh
  rosemary or 1$^1/_2$ teaspoons
  dried rosemary

1. Heat oil in large skillet. Add chicken pieces, salt, and pepper. Cook over low heat, turning occasionally, until browned.
2. Add water and cook over high heat until liquid is almost evaporated. Add vinegar, garlic, and rosemary. Cover and simmer for 20 minutes, or until chicken is tender.
3. Transfer chicken and sauce to serving dish; serve at once.

ENTICING ENTREES: TURKEY

Thanksgiving Turkey

Serves 12

1 (9-pound) turkey
2½ teaspoons salt
1½ teaspoons freshly ground
   black pepper
1 lemon, halved
2 onions
½ cup butter
3 sprigs parsley, chopped
6 slices bread, cubed
½ cup milk
2 eggs
2 teaspoons dried sage
½ bouillon cube
1 teaspoon curry powder
3 cups chicken bouillon
2 tablespoons cornstarch
2 tablespoons water

1. Rub turkey inside with 2 teaspoons salt and ½ teaspoon pepper. Squeeze lemon and rub outside of turkey with juice.
2. Chop onions with liver. Melt ¼ cup butter in saucepan. Add onions, liver, and parsley; saute for 3 minutes. Combine onion and liver mixture with bread cubes, milk, eggs, sage, remaining salt and pepper, and bouillon cube.
3. Preheat oven to 325 degrees.
4. Stuff turkey and sew up openings, then truss. Put turkey into roasting pan. Melt remaining ¼ cup butter in small saucepan. Stir in curry powder and brush turkey all over with this mixture. Use some melted butter to grease piece of aluminum foil. Place foil over turkey. Roast on bottom oven rack for 3 to 3½ hours.
5. At end of 1½ hours, add gizzard, heart, and neck. Pour on just enough hot bouillon to keep turkey moist, and baste frequently with cooking juices. Test to see if done after 3 hours by piercing thickest part of leg with skewer. The juices will run clear when turkey is cooked. Remove turkey from oven and let stand, covered with foil.
6. Carve turkey and arrange on warm serving platter. Keep warm in switched-off oven.
7. Pour off fat from roasting pan. Discard gizzard; finely chop heart and meat from neck. Stir remaining bouillon into roasting pan to deglaze; transfer liquid to small saucepan and bring to a boil. Add finely chopped giblets.
8. Mix cornstarch with water to form paste. Add to gravy, stirring until thickened. Adjust seasonings and serve gravy separately with turkey.

Roast Turkey with Chestnut Dressing

Serves 6 to 8

1 (10- to 12-pound) turkey
Salt to taste
¼ cup butter
1 large onion, chopped
2 stalks celery, chopped
¼ pound ground veal
¼ pound ground pork
1 turkey liver, chopped
Pepper to taste
½ teaspoon paprika
6 cups soft bread cubes
¼ cup chopped parsley
1 pound chestnuts, roasted,
   peeled, and chopped
1 egg, well beaten
5 slices bacon

1. Lightly salt turkey cavity; set aside while preparing dressing.
2. Melt butter in large frying pan. Add onion and celery; saute for 5 minutes. Using slotted spoon, transfer to large mixing bowl.
3. Add veal, pork, and liver to frying pan; saute until lightly browned. Season with salt, pepper, and paprika; add to onion mixture. Add bread cubes, parsley, chestnuts, and egg, mixing well.
4. Preheat oven to 325 degrees. Stuff turkey with dressing and truss. Place in roasting pan, breast side up. Lay bacon strips in single layer over turkey. Roast about 4 hours, to internal temperature of 185 degrees. Remove from oven and cover with tent of aluminum foil. Let stand 20 minutes before carving.

Turkey Cutlets with Savory Tomato Sauce

Serves 4

1 tablespoon butter or
   margarine
2 pounds turkey cutlets
2 cups tomato juice
2 tablespoons onion, minced
½ teaspoon savory
Salt or garlic salt and pepper
   to taste
Parsley sprigs for garnish

1. Melt butter in nonstick frying pan. Add turkey cutlets in single layer. Cook over moderate heat for 1 to 2 minutes on each side, until turkey is thoroughly cooked. Remove to serving platter and keep warm. Drain frying pan.
2. Add tomato juice, onion, savory, salt, and pepper to frying pan. Cook, uncovered, over high heat until juice is reduced by half. To serve, pour sauce over cutlets and garnish with fresh parsley.

Italian Style Roast Turkey

Serves 8 to 10

1 (8- to 9-pound) turkey
Salt and pepper to taste

Stuffing

1 cup pitted prunes
Boiling water
2 cups peeled chestnuts
Bouillon
2 cups sausage meat
3 tablespoons butter
1 turkey liver
1 large onion, sliced
2 pears, peeled and roughly chopped
Salt and pepper to taste
¼ cup white wine

For Braising

3 tablespoons butter
2 onions, sliced
2 carrots, sliced
4 stalks celery, chopped
3 slices bacon
2 cloves garlic, peeled
1 sprig fresh rosemary or ¼ teaspoon dried rosemary
8 peppercorns
1 sprig parsley
1 sprig thyme or ¼ teaspoon dried thym
2 bay leaves
2 cups red wine
1 to 2 cups turkey stock

For Roasting

3 tablespoons vegetable oil
1 tablespoon butter

1. Preheat oven to 325 degrees. Season turkey inside with salt and pepper.
2. To prepare stuffing, place prunes in saucepan with just enough boiling water to cover; reduce heat and simmer for 20 minutes. Drain and chop roughly. If using fresh chestnuts, cook in boiling water 5 minutes, then remove outer and inner skins. Place chestnuts in saucepan with bouillon to cover and simmer for 30 minutes; drain and chop roughly.
3. Mix chestnuts and prunes with sausage. Melt butter in frying pan; saute turkey liver and onion 3 to 4 minutes. Remove from pan, cool, and chop. Add chopped liver, onion, and pears to other ingredients. Add salt, pepper, and wine. Cook, stirring constantly, until thoroughly blended and hot. Cool before stuffing turkey.
4. Stuff turkey and sew up. Melt 3 tablespoons butter in large ovenproof casserole. Add sliced onion, carrot, celery, and bacon; saute for 3 to 4 minutes. Add garlic, rosemary, peppercorns, parsley, thyme, and bay leaves. Place turkey on top of this mixture, pour on red wine, and cover with enough stock to come halfway up the turkey. Cover casserole and braise turkey for 3½ hours, turning from side to side every half hour to allow all sides to cook evenly.
5. Remove turkey from casserole, reserving pan liquids and vegetables. Heat 3 tablespoons oil and 1 tablespoon butter in roasting pan. Add turkey and baste. Roast 30 minutes, basting every 10 minutes, until turkey is brown and tender.
6. Remove garlic cloves from pan liquids. Boil pan drippings and vegetables until slightly reduced. Strain and serve separately as sauce.

Roast Turkey with Fruit Stuffing

Serves 18 to 20

1 (14-pound) turkey
Salt and pepper to taste
½ cup butter
3 pounds tart apples, peeled, cored, and sliced
⅔ cup chopped, pitted prunes
Sugar to taste
6 slices bacon, halved, rolled, and skewered
1 pound link sausages
Watercress for garnish

1. Season turkey inside with salt and pepper.
2. Melt ¼ cup butter in saucepan. Add apples, cover, and cook over low heat until apples are tender. Occasionally shake pan gently to prevent apples from sticking. Stir in prunes and sugar; simmer for 10 minutes more. Cool, then spoon stuffing into turkey.
3. Preheat oven to 375 degrees. Truss turkey, then rub outside with remaining butter. Roast for 15 minutes per pound, plus 15 minutes over. If turkey becomes too brown, place pieces of foil over breast.
4. Add bacon rolls and sausages to roasting pan for last 30 minutes of cooking time. Serve turkey on large platter surrounded by bacon and sausages. Garnish with watercress.

Turkey Ragout

Serves 4

2 tablespoons olive oil
1 large onion, finely chopped
2 cloves garlic, peeled and finely chopped
3 slices bacon, finely chopped
1 large carrot, finely diced
½ cup diced celery
1½ pounds turkey breast, cubed
1 heaping teaspoon flour
⅓ cup chicken bouillon
¾ cup dry red wine
½ teaspoon salt
½ teaspoon freshly ground black pepper
⅛ teaspoon thyme
⅛ teaspoon marjoram
½ bay leaf

1. Heat oil in large frying pan with lid. Add onion, garlic, and bacon; saute until brown. Add carrot and celery, and continue to saute briefly, stirring well. Add cubed meat and brown thoroughly.
2. Sprinkle flour over turkey mixture and stir well. Gradually add bouillon and bring to a boil. Add wine and continue to boil, uncovered, until sauce is reduced by half; stir frequently.
3. Season with salt, pepper, thyme, marjoram, and bay leaf. Cover and simmer for 15 minutes. Transfer to serving dish, and serve.

Turkey Breast Cutlets with Lemon and Wine Sauce

Serves 4

2 tablespoons flour
3 tablespoons freshly grated
  Parmesan cheese
1/2 teaspoon salt
1/4 teaspoon pepper
1/4 teaspoon nutmeg
1 egg, well beaten
1/2 cup milk
1 pound boneless turkey breast,
  skin removed
Flour
1/4 cup sweet butter
5 tablespoons dry white wine
Juice of 1/2 lemon
Chopped fresh parsley
Lemon wedges for garnish

1. Combine flour, cheese, salt, pepper, and nutmeg in shallow bowl. Add egg and milk; beat until well blended.
2. Cut turkey breast crosswise into 6 slices. Pound each slice with meat mallet until thin. Dredge lightly in flour; shake off excess.
3. Heat butter in large, heavy skillet over moderate heat until foam subsides. Dip turkey in batter and fry until golden. Remove from pan and keep warm.
4. Add wine to pan and cook over low heat for 2 minutes, stirring to loosen browned bits from pan. Add lemon juice, mixing well. To serve, pour sauce over turkey cutlets. Sprinkle with chopped parsley and garnish with lemon wedges.

Country Stew

Serves 4

2 cloves
1 bay leaf
1 onion
3 cups water
1/2 teaspoon salt
1 3/4 pounds boned turkey thighs
2 carrots, sliced
2 leeks, white part only, chopped
1 cup heavy whipping cream
2 tablespoons freshly grated
  horseradish

1. Use cloves to spike bay leaf onto onion. Bring water to a boil in large pot. Add salt, spiked onion, and turkey; boil for 45 minutes, skimming as needed during first 20 minutes.
2. When turkey has been cooking for 20 minutes, add carrots and leeks. Cover and cook for remaining 25 minutes.
3. Whip cream until just stiff and stir in horseradish. To serve, arrange turkey and vegetables in serving bowl, discarding onion. Serve horseradish cream separately.

Turkey and Cheese Roulades

Serves 4

3 tablespoons butter
1 small onion, diced
2 carrots, cut into julienne
  strips
2 tablespoons chopped mixed
  fresh herbs, such as dill,
  thyme, parsley, and chervil
  or 1/2 teaspoon fines herbes
1/2 cup cream cheese
1 egg yolk
1 tablespoon mustard
Salt and pepper to taste
4 turkey cutlets, sliced thin
1 cup hot chicken bouillon
1/4 cup dry vermouth
2 tablespoons sour cream

1. Heat 1 tablespoon butter in frying pan. Saute onion and carrots for 5 minutes. Remove from pan and cool slightly.
2. Mix herbs with cream cheese, egg yolk, mustard, salt, and pepper. Spread herb and cheese mixture over turkey cutlets. Divide cooled vegetables evenly among cutlets and spread on top of herb-cheese mixture. Roll turkey up and fasten with wooden toothpicks.
3. Melt remaining butter in frying pan and brown roulades well over medium heat. Add chicken bouillon and vermouth. Cover and simmer for 20 minutes.
4. Stir sour cream into cooking juices and serve with roulades.

Turkey and Vegetable Roll-Ups

Serves 4

1/2 cup raisins
1/4 pound uncooked ham, cubed
1 cup chopped parsley
1 tablespoon capers
4 turkey cutlets, sliced thin
1/4 teaspoon salt
1/4 teaspoon pepper
1/4 cup olive oil
1 onion, chopped
1 (3-ounce) can tomato paste
1/2 cup water
1 cup light cream
1 small bay leaf
1/4 teaspoon rosemary
Pinch of thyme
1 red pepper, seeded and cut
  into strips
Pinch of sugar, optional

1. Combine raisins, ham cubes, parsley, and capers.
2. Sprinkle turkey with salt and pepper. Spread raisin mixture over cutlets. Roll up and fasten with wooden toothpicks.
3. Heat oil in frying pan. Brown turkey rolls well, then add onion and cook for 1 minute. Add tomato paste, water, cream, and herbs. Simmer for 20 minutes. Add red pepper strips during last 10 minutes of cooking time. Before serving, season sauce with sugar, if desired.

Turkey Wings with Peaches

Serves 4

1½ pounds turkey wings
1 small bay leaf
1 carrot
1 small onion
3 peppercorns
¼ teaspoon salt
Water
1 cup egg noodles
1 teaspoon salt
¼ cup butter
3 cups fresh peach slices
½ teaspoon freshly ground
   pepper
1 tablespoon chopped fresh dill
1 tablespoon chopped chives

1. Place turkey wings in saucepan with bay leaf, carrot, onion, peppercorns, and ⅛ teaspoon salt. Cover with water, then cover pan and simmer for 1 hour. Remove wings from cooking liquid and let cool. Remove meat from bones and cut into pieces.
2. Cook noodles in boiling salted water following package directions; drain.
3. Melt butter in frying pan and saute peach slices for 5 minutes, turning frequently.
4. Combine noodles, peach slices, and turkey. Cook over low heat until heated through. Serve sprinkled with freshly ground pepper, chopped dill, and chives.

Turkey Drumsticks with Tomatoes

Serves 4

2 turkey drumsticks, weighing 1¼
   pounds each
Salt and pepper to taste
2 cloves garlic, peeled and finely
   chopped
¼ teaspoon rosemary
3 tablespoons wine vinegar
3 tablespoons olive oil
5 anchovy fillets, finely chopped,
   optional
1 (16-ounce) can tomatoes,
   roughly chopped

1 tablespoon capers
2 egg yolks
Juice of ½ lemon
1 tablespoon butter

1. Rub drumsticks with salt, pepper, garlic, and rosemary. Pour vinegar over drumsticks, cover, and marinate for 2 hours. Turn drumsticks several times while marinating.
2. Heat oil in Dutch oven. Brown turkey on all sides. Add anchovies, if desired. Stir in tomatoes and capers. Simmer for 1¼ hours, adding more tomato juice if needed.
3. Remove turkey meat from bone and cut into 1½-inch pieces. Reheat turkey in sauce.
4. Before serving, beat egg yolks with lemon juice. Stir egg mixture and butter into sauce and cook, stirring, over low heat until sauce is hot. Transfer to serving dish, and serve hot.

Turkey with Coriander

Serves 4

¼ cup oil
½ tablespoon crushed coriander
4 (6-ounce) turkey cutlets,
   thickly cut
Salt and pepper to taste
4 shallots, peeled and chopped
1 clove garlic, peeled and crushed
1 (16-ounce) can tomatoes,
   drained (reserve juice) and
   chopped
½ chicken bouillon cube,
   crumbled
½ teaspoon sugar
¼ teaspoon cayenne pepper
½ cup chopped parsley

1. Heat oil in heavy skillet and toss coriander in it quickly. Season turkey with salt and pepper, then add to skillet. Brown over high heat for 1 minute on each side. Remove turkey from skillet.
2. Add shallots and garlic to skillet and saute for 3 to 5 minutes. Add

tomatoes, reserved tomato juice, bouillon cube, sugar, and cayenne pepper. Boil, stirring constantly, until liquid is slightly reduced.
3. Add turkey to sauce, together with any juice that has collected. Cover pan and cook over low heat for 5 minutes. Sprinkle with chopped parsley and serve with noodles.

Stuffed Turkey with Chestnut Sauce

Serves 8

Oil
1 (7-pound) turkey
1 teaspoon salt
1 teaspoon pepper
1 teaspoon paprika
3 tart apples, peeled, cored,
   and diced
1¾ cups chopped hazelnuts
½ cup finely chopped marzipan
¼ teaspoon cinnamon
Juice of ½ lemon
1 cup hot chicken broth
⅓ cup butter
½ cup white wine
¾ cup canned chestnut puree
1¾ cups light cream
2 tablespoons brandy

1. Preheat oven to 400 degrees. Brush roasting pan with oil.
2. Rub turkey inside with salt, pepper, and paprika. Combine two-thirds of diced apples with nuts, marzipan, cinnamon, and 1 tablespoon lemon juice. Stuff turkey with this mixture. Sew up openings and truss turkey. Sprinkle remaining lemon juice on remaining apples.
3. Roast turkey, breast side down, for 1 hour, basting occasionally with broth. Turn turkey over and continue to roast for 1½ hours longer. Transfer turkey to platter and let stand in switched-off oven for 15 minutes.
4. Melt butter in saucepan. Add remaining apples. Strain turkey cooking juices and add to apples. Stir in wine, chestnut puree, cream, and brandy. Season with salt and pepper, and, if desired, add a pinch of cinnamon. Serve chestnut sauce separately with turkey.

Breast of Turkey with Yogurt Sauce

Serves 4

2 cloves garlic, peeled and
    chopped
¹/₂ teaspoon salt
¹/₄ teaspoon pepper
6 tablespoons sunflower oil
2¹/₄ pounds turkey breast
    on bone
1 yellow pepper, seeded and
    chopped
1 red pepper, seeded and
    chopped
1 cup leeks, white part only,
    cut into ¹/₂-inch pieces
¹/₂ cup hot chicken broth
2¹/₄ cups peeled and diced
    cucumbers
1¹/₄ cups plain full-cream yogurt
¹/₂ cup chopped fresh chervil

1. Mix chopped garlic with salt and pepper, then crush garlic and combine with 1 tablespoon oil. Coat turkey with this mixture, cover, and refrigerate for 30 minutes.
2. Preheat oven to 400 degrees.
3. Heat remaining oil in small saucepan. Place turkey breast in roasting pan and pour hot oil on top. Roast in center of oven for 30 minutes. Arrange chopped peppers and leeks around turkey. Pour on hot broth and roast for 10 minutes longer. Add cucumbers and cook for 5 more minutes.
4. Transfer turkey and vegetables to warm serving dish. Keep warm in switched-off oven.
5. Stir yogurt into roasting pan to deglaze. Heat gently over low heat. Pour yogurt into sauceboat and sprinkle with chervil. Serve with turkey and vegetables.

Turkey Breasts with Zucchini

Serves 4

¹/₄ cup sunflower oil
4 shallots, peeled and sliced
4¹/₂ cups thinly sliced zucchini
1 cup hot chicken broth
1 teaspoon paprika
Salt and pepper to taste

4 boneless turkey breasts
Juice of ¹/₂ lemon
2 tablespoons chopped parsley
2 teaspoons soy sauce

1. Heat 2 tablespoons oil in large frying pan. Saute shallots until transparent, then add zucchini. Cover and cook over low heat for 5 minutes. Add chicken broth, paprika, salt, and pepper. Cover again, leaving small crack for steam to escape, and simmer for 10 minutes. Remove lid and cook until almost all liquid has evaporated.
2. Flatten turkey slightly and rub well with pepper. Heat remaining oil in large frying pan and saute turkey for 2 to 3 minutes on each side, or until well browned.
3. Season vegetables to taste with salt and lemon juice. Stir in parsley and arrange on serving dish with turkey. Before serving, sprinkle soy sauce over turkey.

Turkey Breasts with Sage

Serves 4

1 large clove garlic, peeled and
    crushed
1 turkey liver, cubed
1 slice lemon peel, chopped
2 ounces uncooked ham, without
    fat, chopped
3 anchovies, finely chopped,
    optional
1 tablespoon capers
¹/₄ cup olive oil
4 boneless turkey breasts
1 teaspoon salt
¹/₂ teaspoon pepper
4 leaves fresh sage, cut into
    fine strips, or ¹/₄ teaspoon
    dried sage
Juice of ¹/₂ lemon

1. Combine garlic, turkey liver, lemon peel, ham, anchovies if desired, and capers. Heat oil in 2 large frying pans. Add half of turkey liver mixture to each pan. Saute for 1 minute, then lay 4 turkey breasts on top of each pan. Season with salt, pepper, and sage. Sprinkle with lemon juice.

2. Cook turkey breasts for 2 to 3 minutes on each side. Transfer to warm serving dish. Arrange turkey liver mixture around breasts. Serve with boiled rice.

Boiled Turkey

Serves 6 to 8

¹/₄ cup butter
¹/₂ cup sliced mushrooms
1¹/₂ cups lean ground veal
³/₄ cup lean ground ham
³/₄ cup white bread crumbs
¹/₄ cup milk
Salt and pepper to taste
¹/₂ teaspoon thyme
1 teaspoon onion powder
1 (6-pound) turkey
4 onions
3 carrots, sliced
3 stalks celery, sliced
8 peppercorns
2 chicken bouillon cubes
3 tablespoons flour
¹/₂ cup white wine

1. Melt 1 tablespoon butter in frying pan and saute mushrooms for 5 to 6 minutes; let cool. Add mushrooms to ground veal and ham.
2. Soak bread crumbs in milk for 15 minutes, then squeeze out as much milk as possible. Add to meat and mushroom mixture. Season with salt, pepper, thyme, and onion powder. Stuff turkey with this mixture. Sew up opening carefully to prevent stuffing from escaping during boiling. If cheesecloth is available, wrap turkey in large piece of cheesecloth and tie securely.
3. Place turkey in pan of cold water that just covers bird. Add onions, carrots, celery, peppercorns, and bouillon cubes. Bring water slowly to a boil, then reduce heat to simmer. Cook for 30 minutes per pound.
4. Remove turkey from cooking liquid. Strain stock and boil until stock is reduced by half. Melt remaining butter in saucepan. Stir in flour, then add 2¹/₂ cups reduced stock and white wine. Bring to a boil, stirring constantly until smooth. Spoon sauce over turkey and serve hot.

Hunter's Turkey

Serves 4

3 tablespoons oil
1 onion, chopped
1 clove garlic, peeled and
 crushed
2 tablespoons flour
3 tablespoons tomato sauce
1/4 cup white wine
1 cup turkey stock
8 mushrooms, sliced
2 tablespoons butter
1 tablespoon chopped
 parsley
1/2 teaspoon oregano
Salt and pepper to taste
2 turkey legs, disjointed,
 or 8 slices turkey breast
3 tablespoons grated Cheddar
 cheese
2 tablespoons bread crumbs

1. Preheat oven to 350 degrees.
2. Heat oil in saucepan. Saute onion
and garlic until golden brown. Stir in
flour and saute for 1 minute to brown
lightly. Add tomato sauce, wine, and
stock. Bring to a boil, stirring frequently.
3. Saute mushrooms in butter for 3 to
4 minutes. Add mushrooms, parsley,
and oregano to sauce. Season with
salt and pepper. Simmer for 3 to 4
minutes.
4. Place turkey in ovenproof dish.
Spoon sauce over turkey. Bake for 15
minutes. Sprinkle with cheese and
bread crumbs, then broil until cheese
is melted and browned. Remove from
heat, and serve at once.

Turkey and Tomato Pancakes

Serves 6

1 cup flour
Salt and pepper to taste
2 eggs, beaten
About 1 cup milk
1 tablespoon melted butter
Oil
2 cups ground cooked turkey
1 (10³/₄-ounce) can condensed
 tomato soup
1/2 cup cooked vegetables,
 such as peas or corn,
 optional
1 teaspoon tomato paste
1/4 teaspoon onion powder
Pinch of garlic powder
Salt and pepper to taste
2 tablespoons butter
2 tablespoons grated Cheddar
 cheese

1. Sift flour with salt and pepper into
bowl. Make hollow in center of flour;
add beaten eggs and 1/4 cup milk. Mix
eggs and milk together with spoon
before gradually drawing in flour. Add
1/4 cup more milk as mixture thickens.
When mixture is smooth and
consistency of thick cream, beat for 5
minutes with electric mixer. Stir in
melted butter and another 1/4 cup milk.
Leave batter in covered bowl for 30
minutes.
2. Test thickness of batter, which
should just coat back of spoon. If too
thick, add more milk and stir well.
Grease griddle or frying pan with a
small amount of oil. When hot, pour in
enough batter to coat pan thinly. Cook
until golden brown on one side; turn
and cook on other side. Pile up and
keep warm. Allow 2 to 3 pancakes per
person.
3. Mix ground turkey with tomato
soup. Add cooked vegetables if available. Heat mixture and add tomato
paste. Sprinkle in onion and garlic
powders. Season with salt and pepper.
4. Preheat broiler.
5. Spoon filling onto pancakes, roll up,
and place in center of ovenproof dish.
Sprinkle with butter and cheese. Broil
until cheese is golden brown. Serve at
once.

Turkey Liver Pilaf

Serves 4

1 cup long-grain rice
3 cups water
1 teaspoon salt
2 tablespoons butter
1¼ pounds turkey livers,
 cut into ³/₄-inch cubes
1 large onion, finely diced
2 red peppers, seeded and
 chopped into small pieces
1/2 cup vegetable bouillon
1/4 cup white wine
Salt and pepper to taste
1/4 cup sour cream
1 tablespoon chopped parsley

1. Wash rice in colander. Bring water
and salt to a boil in saucepan. Add
rice, cover, and cook over low heat
about 20 minutes, until liquid is
absorbed.
2. Heat 1 tablespoon butter in heavy-
bottomed pan. Add turkey livers and
saute for 4 minutes. Remove from pan
and keep warm. Add remaining butter
to pan and saute diced onion until
translucent. Add chopped peppers and
saute for 10 minutes longer. Do not
allow to brown. Pour in vegetable
bouillon, cover, and cook over low
heat for 10 minutes.
3. Add rice, wine, and cooked livers to
vegetables. Season with salt and
pepper. Stir in sour cream and
parsley, and serve.

Turkey Liver and Tomato

Serves 4

1/4 cup butter
2 large onions, sliced into
 rings
1/2 cup dry white wine
3 ripe tomatoes, skinned and
 cut into chunks
1¼ pounds turkey livers
1 teaspoon flour
2 leaves sage, chopped, or
 1/2 teaspoon dried sage
1/2 teaspoon salt
1/8 teaspoon freshly ground
 black pepper

1. Melt 2 tablespoons butter in large frying pan. Add onions and saute until brown. Pour in white wine; cover and simmer for 5 minutes.
2. Add tomato pieces to onions and cook, uncovered, over medium heat for 5 minutes, until liquid becomes slightly thickened.
3. Remove any fat or skin from livers. Cut livers into strips and dust with flour. Melt remaining butter in separate frying pan and saute liver strips until browned.
4. Add cooked liver to tomato sauce, sprinkle with sage, and season with salt and pepper. Serve hot.

Turkey Brochettes

Serves 6

¹/₂ cup white wine
¹/₄ cup olive oil
1 clove garlic, peeled and
   crushed
¹/₂ teaspoon sage
2 pounds turkey cutlets,
   cut into 1¹/₂-inch cubes
1 pound Italian sweet sausage
   links
24 mushroom caps
2 green peppers, seeded and
   cut into chunks

1. Combine wine, oil, garlic, and sage in glass bowl; mix well. Add turkey, cover, and let marinate for 1 hour.
2. Prick sausages. Simmer in water to cover for 15 minutes. Drain; cool. Cut each sausage into 1¹/₂-inch pieces.
3. Preheat broiler or heat coals in outdoor grill.
4. Grease 6 skewers. Alternately thread turkey, sausage, and vegetables on skewers. Broil or grill brochettes about 8 inches from heat for 20 minutes, or until meats are thoroughly cooked. Baste occasionally with marinade.
5. Place brochettes on platter; discard leftover marinade. Serve with rice or noodles.

Barbecued Turkey and Stuffing

Serves 10

1 (5-pound) turkey
2¹/₂ cups barbecue sauce
¹/₃ cup shortening
¹/₃ cup chopped onion
8 cups fresh bread cubes
1 teaspoon salt
¹/₂ teaspoon sage
¹/₂ teaspoon thyme
¹/₂ teaspoon rosemary
1 egg, beaten

1. Have butcher cut turkey in half lengthwise.
2. Preheat oven to 325 degrees.
3. Place sheet of aluminum foil on rack in large, shallow baking pan. Place turkey halves on foil. Pour 1 cup barbecue sauce over turkey. Roast, uncovered, for 1 hour. Turn halves over and baste with more sauce. Roast for 1 hour longer.
4. Melt shortening in frying pan. Add onion and saute until translucent. Mix onion with bread cubes, salt, sage, thyme, rosemary, and egg.
5. Remove turkey from oven and turn halves onto their sides. Divide stuffing in half and form into 2 mounds on top of foil. Lay turkey halves down over stuffing and continue roasting until done, allowing 25 to 30 minutes per pound. Baste occasionally with barbecue sauce. Remove from oven and place turkey on platter; slice turkey. Spoon stuffing into serving dish, and serve with turkey slices.

Cranberry Tom

Serves 18

1 (16-pound) turkey
Salt and pepper to taste
1 pound fresh cranberries,
   chopped
1 cup sugar
16 cups small bread cubes
1 cup butter, melted
2 cups raisins
1 teaspoon cinnamon
2 teaspoons lemon rind
1 cup turkey broth

1. Preheat oven to 325 degrees.
2. Dust turkey cavity with salt and pepper.
3. Place cranberries in saucepan with sugar. Bring to a boil, then remove from heat. Moisten bread cubes with melted butter. Mix bread cubes with cranberries, raisins, seasonings, lemon rind, and broth. Stuff turkey with mixture; truss.
4. Place turkey, breast side up, on rack in shallow roasting pan. Place loose tent of aluminum foil over turkey. Roast for 4¹/₂ to 5 hours, until turkey is tender.

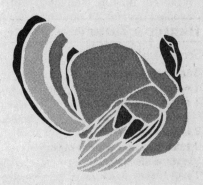

Braised Turkey Wings

Serves 4

¹/₃ cup flour
¹/₂ teaspoon salt
¹/₈ teaspoon paprika
4 large turkey wings
3 tablespoons butter
¹/₂ cup tomato juice
4 small onions
1 bay leaf
1 clove

1. Season flour with salt and paprika. Place in paper bag and add turkey wings, tossing until well coated with flour mixture. Melt butter in Dutch oven. Add turkey and brown well. Add tomato juice, onions, bay leaf, and clove. Cover tightly and simmer for 1¹/₂ hours, or until turkey is tender. Add more tomato juice as needed during cooking, and turn wings several times.
2. Serve turkey, onions, and pan juices on bed of cooked noodles.

Turkey Calvados

Serves 6

1 (4- to 5-pound) turkey breast
2 teaspoons salt
1/2 teaspoon pepper
1 teaspoon allspice
1/4 cup butter
2 medium onions, thinly sliced
2 carrots, finely diced
1 cup apple cider

1. Sprinkle turkey with salt, pepper, and allspice. Melt butter in heavy skillet. Add turkey and cook for 30 minutes, turning frequently until evenly browned. Remove from pan. Layer onions and carrots in skillet. Lay turkey on top of vegetables. Pour apple cider over turkey. Cover and cook over low heat for about 2 1/2 hours, or until turkey is fork-tender. Baste occasionally, adding more cider if needed. Remove turkey to warm serving dish.
2. Strain pan juices, mashing vegetables through sieve to make rich gravy. Season to taste. Serve gravy separately with turkey.

Turkey aux Claret

Serves 6

1/2 cup flour
2 teaspoons salt
1 teaspoon paprika
1/2 teaspoon pepper
1 (4- to 5-pound) turkey breast, cut into pieces
1/2 cup butter
1 clove garlic, peeled and minced
1/2 cup diced cooked ham
18 pearl onions
1 tablespoon minced parsley
1/2 teaspoon thyme
2 bay leaves
Salt and pepper to taste
1/2 pound mushrooms
2 tablespoons brandy
1 cup claret or other red wine

1. Preheat oven to 325 degrees.
2. Season flour with salt, paprika, and pepper. Dredge turkey in flour mixture. Melt butter in Dutch oven. Add turkey and garlic; cook, turning turkey frequently, for about 30 minutes, or until turkey is evenly browned all over. Add ham, onions, parsley, thyme, bay leaves, salt, and pepper. Cover tightly and bake for 1 1/2 hours, or until thickest part is fork-tender. Add mushrooms, brandy, and wine during last 30 minutes of cooking.
3. Refrigerate overnight and reheat when ready to serve.

Gala Stuffed Turkey

Serves 12 to 14

1 (16-pound) turkey
1/4 cup lemon juice
Salt and pepper to taste

Stuffing

1/2 cup butter
1 pound ground beef
1 turkey liver, chopped
1 clove garlic, peeled and minced
1 cup chopped celery
1 cup chopped onion
1/4 cup chopped parsley
1 teaspoon salt
1/2 teaspoon pepper
1/2 teaspoon cinnamon
1 cup long-grain rice
2 cups water
1 (8-ounce) can tomato sauce
1/2 cup currants
1/2 cup dry white wine
1/2 cup chopped walnuts
1/4 cup pine nuts
1/2 cup butter, melted

1. Remove giblets from turkey, reserving liver for stuffing. Sprinkle turkey inside and out with lemon juice, salt, and pepper.
2. To prepare stuffing, melt butter in large Dutch oven. Brown ground beef and turkey liver. Add vegetables and cook for 3 minutes. Add seasonings, rice, water, and tomato sauce. Cover and simmer for 20 to 25 minutes, or until rice is tender.
3. While rice cooks, soak currants in wine. When rice is done, add currants and nuts to stuffing, mixing well. Cool.
4. Preheat oven to 325 degrees.
5. Stuff turkey with prepared stuffing, and truss. Brush with melted butter. Roast, brushing frequently with butter, for 5 hours, or until meat thermometer inserted in thigh of turkey registers 185 degrees. Remove from oven and let stand 15 minutes before carving. Place turkey slices on platter and surround with stuffing.

Turkey with Leeks

Serves 4 to 6

5 tablespoons butter
1 pound leeks, white part and 2 inches of green stem, quartered lengthwise and sliced
1 pound boneless turkey breast cutlets, cut into 1 x 1/4-inch strips
Salt and pepper to taste
1/2 cup flour
2 tablespoons vegetable oil
1/2 pound rigatoni
1/4 cup white wine
3/4 cup half and half
1/3 cup blue cheese, crumbled
1 cup shredded Muenster cheese
1/4 cup chopped parsley

1. Melt 3 tablespoons butter in large skillet. Add leeks and cook over medium-high heat for 5 minutes, stirring frequently. Remove leeks from pan and set aside.
2. Season turkey strips with salt and pepper. Dredge with flour; shake off excess flour.
3. Heat oil and remaining butter in skillet. Saute turkey, stirring frequently, for 5 minutes or until golden. Remove from pan and set aside with leeks.
4. Cook rigatoni until just tender according to package directions; drain.
5. Add wine to pan drippings remaining in skillet. Cook over medium-high heat, scraping pan bottom to remove browned particles. Reduce heat and simmer for 1 minute. Add leeks, turkey, half and half, cheeses, and parsley. Season with salt and pepper.
6. To serve, place rigatoni in heated serving dish. Spoon turkey mixture on top; toss gently and serve at once.

ENTICING ENTREES: OTHER FOWL

Duck in Pineapple Sauce

Serves 4

1 (3¹/₄-pound) duckling,
   cut into serving pieces
1 tablespoon corn oil
¹/₃ cup pineapple juice
³/₄ cup dry red wine
¹/₂ teaspoon salt
¹/₈ teaspoon freshly ground
   black pepper
Juice of 1 lemon
1 tablespoon cornstarch
Juice and grated peel of
   1 orange
1³/₄ cups fresh pineapple,
   cut into wedges
1 tablespoon pineapple jam

1. Preheat oven to 400 degrees.
2. Brush duck with oil, arrange in casserole dish, and roast 20 minutes.
3. Combine pineapple juice with red wine, salt, pepper, and lemon juice, and pour over duck. Cook 40 minutes longer, frequently basting duck with juice mixture.
4. Mix cornstarch with orange juice.
5. After 1 hour of cooking, remove duck from oven and place in warm serving dish. Keep warm in switched-off oven.
5. Skim fat off roasting juices, then strain. Combine strained roasting juices with cornstarch mixture; bring to a boil and stir in grated orange peel. Add pineapple pieces and jam to sauce. Season well with salt and pepper. Pour sauce over duck, and serve.

Boned Duck with Orange Stuffing

Serves 8 to 10

1 (5-pound) duck, boned
Salt and pepper to taste
4 tablespoons butter
1 large onion, chopped
¹/₂ cup chopped celery
³/₄ pound sausage meat
¹/₄ teaspoon ground nutmeg
¹/₂ cup soft white bread crumbs
1 teaspoon finely grated
   orange rind
1 egg, beaten
1 orange, peeled and
   quartered
Watercress for garnish

1. Preheat oven to 375 degrees.
2. Season inside of duck with salt and pepper. Melt butter in saucepan and saute onion and celery until soft and golden. Stir in sausage, nutmeg, bread crumbs, grated orange rind, and just enough egg to bind mixture. Place one-third of stuffing in duck.
3. Arrange orange quarters evenly on top of duck. Cover with remaining stuffing. Arrange duck into neat parcel and sew opening together with fine string.
4. Place duck on rack in roasting pan and roast for 2 hours. Cover with foil if duck becomes too brown. Serve garnished with watercress.

Wild Ducks with Baked Oranges

Serves 4

2 onions, quartered
2 stalks celery, cut into large
   pieces
2 tablespoons lemon juice
Salt and pepper to taste

2 (1¹/₂-pound) wild ducks
7 tablespoons butter
2 tablespoons vegetable oil
4 small oranges
4 teaspoons sugar
¹/₂ cup chicken broth

1. Preheat oven to 400 degrees.
2. Put a quartered onion, some celery pieces, lemon juice, and seasonings into each duck. Rub breasts with 2 tablespoons butter each and sprinkle with salt.
3. Heat oil and 2 tablespoons butter in roasting pan. When hot, add ducks, basting well. Roast for 25 to 30 minutes, depending on size of birds; baste every 15 minutes.
4. Rub skins of oranges with butter. Arrange oranges around ducks for last 15 minutes of cooking time. The oranges should swell and burst.
5. Transfer ducks to serving platter and keep warm. Make a hole in each orange, fill with ¹/₂ teaspoon sugar, and arrange around ducks. Skim fat from pan drippings and add broth. Boil several minutes until slightly reduced, and season to taste. Serve separately with ducks.

Duck
with Cherries

Serves 4 to 6

2 onions, 1 finely chopped
4 stalks celery
1 (4- to 5-pound) duck
3 tablespoons butter
Salt and pepper to taste
2 tablespoons vegetable oil
2 small carrots
5 mushrooms
1$\frac{1}{2}$ tablespoons flour
2 teaspoons tomato paste
2 cups duck stock made with
    giblets or a chicken bouillon
3 sprigs parsley
1 bay leaf
1 cup red wine
1 orange
1 (16-ounce) can pitted cherries,
    drained
$\frac{1}{2}$ teaspoon sugar

1. Preheat oven to 400 degrees.
2. Put 1 onion and 2 celery stalks inside duck. Rub breast with 1 tablespoon butter and sprinkle with salt and pepper.
3. Heat 2 tablespoons butter in roasting pan. Add duck, basting well. Roast 15 minutes per pound, basting every 15 minutes. The duck should not be completely cooked, since it will cook longer in the sauce.
4. To prepare sauce, melt 2 tablespoons oil in saucepan. Add chopped onion, carrots, 2 celery stalks, and mushrooms. Saute for 7 to 10 minutes, until vegetables are lightly browned. Stir in flour and brown for 1 minute. Add tomato paste, stock,

parsley, and bay leaf. Bring to a boil, then simmer for 30 minutes. Strain, add seasoning to taste, and bring to a boil again. Skim as needed. Add $\frac{1}{2}$ cup wine and reheat.
5. Carve duck and arrange pieces in covered casserole. Pour sauce on top and cook at 400 degrees for 20 minutes.
6. Squeeze juice from orange and grate rind. Place cherries, orange juice, grated rind, $\frac{1}{2}$ cup red wine, and sugar in saucepan. Cook over low heat for 6 to 7 minutes.
7. Arrange duck pieces on serving platter, spoon sauce on top, and arrange cherries around edge of dish. Serve hot.

Duck Flambé

Serves 4

2 (10-ounce) boneless duck
    breasts
Salt and pepper to taste
1 tablespoon butter
1$\frac{1}{2}$ cups coarsely chopped
    plums
2 tablespoons brandy
1 cup sour cream
1 cup light cream
Pinch of ground cinnamon
Pinch of cayenne pepper

1. Remove duck skin and cut into fine strips. Put skin strips into frying pan without fat; cover and fry until crisp and brown. Remove from pan.
2. Using fat still in skillet, cook duck breasts for 3 minutes on each side. Season with salt and pepper. Remove from skillet and wrap in aluminum foil to keep warm. Clean frying pan.
3. Heat butter in frying pan and saute plums until juicy without losing their shape. Add duck and brandy; ignite. After 3 seconds, cover frying pan. Let sit 1 minute, then transfer duck and plums to serving dish.
4. Combine cooking juices with sour cream, light cream, cinnamon, and cayenne pepper, seasoning to taste with salt and pepper.
5. Carve duck in thin diagonal slices and sprinkle with crispy skin. Serve sauce separately.

Duck
with Olives

Serves 4 to 6

3 tablespoons olive oil
1 (3$\frac{1}{4}$-pound) duckling, cut
    into serving pieces
1 onion, finely chopped
1 clove garlic, peeled and
    finely chopped
$\frac{1}{2}$ cup chopped parsley
$\frac{1}{4}$ teaspoon basil
2 tablespoons small capers
1 teaspoon salt
$\frac{1}{4}$ teaspoon pepper
$\frac{1}{3}$ cup dry white wine
$\frac{1}{3}$ cup chicken bouillon
$\frac{1}{4}$ cup pitted green olives

1. Heat oil in heavy skillet. Brown duck pieces on all sides over high heat. Reduce heat to low and add onion, garlic, parsley, basil, and capers; cook gently for 10 minutes. Season with salt and pepper.
2. Pour in wine and continue to cook over low heat, stirring constantly, for 5 minutes. Add bouillon, cover pan, and simmer for 1 hour.
3. Add olives to duck 10 minutes before end of cooking time. Stir well before serving.

Duck with Tomatoes

Serves 4 to 6

1 (3$\frac{1}{4}$-pound) duckling, cut
    into serving pieces
2 sprigs fresh rosemary or
    $\frac{1}{2}$ teaspoon dried rosemary
6 peppercorns
$\frac{1}{3}$ cup dry white wine
$\frac{1}{3}$ cup wine vinegar
$\frac{1}{4}$ cup olive oil
1 large onion, thinly sliced
2$\frac{1}{2}$ cups ripe tomatoes,
    skinned and coarsely
    chopped
Pinch of powdered saffron
1 teaspoon salt
$\frac{1}{2}$ teaspoon pepper
5 tablespoons chicken
    bouillon

1. Place duck in bowl with rosemary, peppercorns, wine, and vinegar. Marinate for 3 hours, turning duck occasionally.

2. Heat oil in heavy skillet. Add onion and saute until golden brown. Add tomatoes and saffron. Season with salt and pepper, then cover and simmer for 15 minutes.

3. Remove duck pieces from marinade and drain. Add duck and bouillon to tomato sauce. Cover and simmer for 1 hour, adding more bouillon if needed. Adjust seasonings to taste and serve with boiled rice.

Duck Goulash

Serves 6

1 (3³/₄-pound) duckling, cut into 12 pieces
1 teaspoon salt
¹/₂ teaspoon pepper
1 teaspoon marjoram
6 tablespoons olive oil
2 onions, finely chopped
2 tablespoons tomato paste
1 teaspoon paprika
¹/₂ teaspoon tarragon
³/₄ cup dry red wine
¹/₃ cup chicken bouillon
¹/₄ cup halved mushrooms
16 pitted black olives
¹/₃ cup heavy whipping cream

1. Rub duck pieces well with salt, pepper, and marjoram.

2. Heat oil in heavy skillet. Brown duck over high heat, then remove from skillet. Add onions and tomato paste to oil remaining in skillet; saute until onions are translucent. Add paprika, tarragon, red wine, and chicken bouillon. Bring to a boil. Place duck pieces in sauce, cover, and cook over low heat for 1 hour. Add mushrooms and olives to duck after 30 minutes.

3. Remove duck from skillet. Boil cooking sauce, stirring constantly, until reduced by half. Stir in cream and heat gently; do not boil. Season to taste.

4. Return duck pieces to skillet and reheat in sauce. Transfer to serving dish, and serve hot.

Deviled Duck

Serves 6 to 8

2 (4-pound) ducklings, cut into serving pieces
Salt and pepper to taste
¹/₄ cup butter
¹/₄ cup flour
2 cups water
¹/₂ cup ketchup
1 teaspoon dry mustard
1 teaspoon salt
¹/₈ teaspoon Tabasco sauce
1 tablespoon steak sauce

1. Preheat oven to 350 degrees.

2. Season ducklings with salt and pepper. Melt butter in frying pan. Add ducklings and brown on all sides. Sprinkle with flour.

3. Transfer ducklings to large casserole dish. Mix remaining ingredients together and pour over ducklings. Cover and bake, stirring occasionally, for 1 to 1¹/₄ hours, or until ducklings are tender. Remove from oven, and serve.

Duck and Almonds

Serves 6 to 8

1 (4-pound) duck
1 clove garlic, peeled and quartered
2 cups water
¹/₂ teaspoon salt
1 cup dry sherry
¹/₂ cup oil
³/₄ cup blanched almonds
1 onion, thinly sliced
1 tablespoon cornstarch, mixed with enough cold water to form paste
Pinch of pepper
Pinch of sugar
¹/₄ cup soy sauce

1. Cut neck and wings off duck and place in pot with garlic, water, salt, sherry, and giblets. Bring to a boil. Cut duck into 4 pieces and place in boiling broth. Simmer for 1 hour. Strain broth, then boil over high heat until liquid is reduced to 1¹/₂ cups.

2. Remove duck from broth and let cool slightly. Remove meat from bone, retaining skin.

3. Heat oil in deep frying pan. Saute almonds and onion slices until evenly browned, then remove from pan. Place duck in frying pan, skin side down, and saute until browned. Remove to serving dish and keep warm.

4. Add cornstarch paste to stock, stirring until thickened. Season with pepper, sugar, and soy sauce. To serve, pour sauce over duck and garnish with onions and almonds.

Duckling California-Style

Serves 6

1 (6-pound) duckling
Salt and pepper to taste
¹/₄ cup salad oil
1 clove garlic, peeled and chopped
1 cup seedless raisins
1 cup crushed pineapple and juice
2 cups apricot juice
1 cup water
¹/₂ cup dry white wine

1. Preheat oven to 350 degrees.

2. Season duckling with salt and pepper. Heat oil in frying pan. Add duck and garlic; brown duck on all sides. Transfer duck to large casserole dish. Mix remaining ingredients together and add to duck. Cover and bake for 1¹/₄ to 1¹/₂ hours, or until duck is tender. Stir mixture occasionally to prevent sticking. Remove from oven, and serve.

Roast Duck
with Celery Stuffing

Serves 4

1 (4-pound) duck
Salt and pepper to taste
¼ pound fatty bacon, chopped
1 duck liver
2 onions, chopped
2 stalks celery, chopped
1 cup soft white bread crumbs
½ cup milk
2 tablespoons chopped parsley
¼ teaspoon sage
¼ teaspoon thyme
1 egg, beaten
Canned cherries for garnish
Watercress for garnish

1. Preheat oven to 375 degrees.
2. Sprinkle inside of duck with salt and pepper.
3. Fry bacon in saucepan until browned; add liver and cook for 3 minutes. Chop liver and return to pan. Add onions and celery; saute until soft. Stir in bread crumbs, milk, herbs, salt, and pepper. Add just enough beaten egg to bind stuffing together. Spoon stuffing into duck and truss. Roast for 15 minutes per pound plus 15 minutes more.
4. To serve, place duck on large serving platter.
Garnish with cherries and watercress.

Duck Stuffed with
Apricots

Serves 4 to 6

1 (4- to 5-pound) duck
1 pound fresh apricots, stones removed
3 strips orange peel
1 onion, finely chopped
Salt and pepper to taste
2 to 3 tablespoons oil
3 tablespoons honey, heated
Juice of 1 orange
1 to 1½ cups stock made from duck giblets or chicken bouillon
3 to 4 tablespoons apricot brandy

1. Preheat oven to 400 degrees.
2. Stuff duck with half the apricots, 3 strips orange peel, onion, and seasonings. Prick skin of duck several times to allow fat to run out while cooking.
3. Heat oil in baking pan. When very hot, add duck and baste all over with oil. Roast for 20 minutes per pound. Cover with honey and orange juice 30 minutes before end of cooking time. Add remaining apricots 10 minutes before end of cooking. Transfer duck to warm serving dish and spoon stuffing into bowl. Arrange apricots around duck.
4. Pour off fat from roasting pan; add stuffing and stock to pan; bring to a boil, stirring constantly. Strain or blend in blender or food processor. Return sauce to heat and add apricot brandy. Serve at once with duck and apricots.

Braised Duck

Serves 4

1 (3½- to 4-pound) duck
Salt and pepper to taste
3 onions, 1 whole and 2 sliced
Thinly pared rind of 1 orange
Thinly pared rind of 1 lemon
3 to 4 tablespoons oil
3 to 4 carrots, sliced
3 stalks celery, sliced
1 small white turnip, sliced
3 tablespoons flour
1 teaspoon tomato paste
2 cups brown sauce
1 cup cider or red wine
2 sprigs parsley
1 sprig fresh thyme or ¼ teaspoon dried thyme
1 small sage leaf or ⅛ teaspoon dried sage
1 bay leaf

1. Preheat oven to 350 degrees.
2. Prick duck breast all over with fork. Rub skin with salt and pepper. Put whole onion inside duck with few strips of orange and lemon rind. Heat oil in skillet and brown duck on all sides for 6 to 8 minutes. Remove from pan and keep warm.

3. Add sliced onions, carrots, celery, and turnip to same skillet and brown over low heat. Cool slightly, then add flour and cook, stirring, for 2 to 3 minutes. Add tomato sauce, brown sauce, and cider or wine. Boil for 1 minute. Add parsley, thyme, sage, bay leaf, and remaining orange and lemon rind.
4. Place duck in casserole dish, cover with sauce, and cook in oven for 2 hours, or until duck is tender.
5. Remove duck from oven and carve. Place duck pieces on hot serving dish. Strain sauce and boil until slightly reduced, skimming off any fat that rises to top. Season to taste. Spoon a little sauce over duck and serve rest separately.

Lancaster
Roast Duckling

Serves 6

1 (6-pound) duckling
Salt and pepper to taste
Pinch of powdered garlic
2 tart green apples, peeled, cored, and sliced
6 cups sauerkraut, drained
1 teaspoon caraway seeds
1 cup water
3 tablespoons brown sugar
1 teaspoon salt
¼ teaspoon pepper

1. Preheat oven to 350 degrees.
2. Prick duckling to allow fat to drain; season cavity with salt, pepper, and garlic. Bake uncovered in large baking dish for 45 minutes, turning occasionally to brown evenly. Pour off fat.
3. Combine remaining ingredients and arrange over duckling. Cover and bake for 2 hours more, stirring occasionally, until duckling is tender. Remove from oven, and serve.

Traditional Christmas Goose

Serves 12

3 cups chestnuts in shells
2 cups chicken broth
1 (11-pound) goose
3 teaspoons salt
1 teaspoon white pepper
2¼ cups peeled and sliced tart apples
½ cup raisins
1 cup boiling water
1 tablespoon flour
½ teaspoon sugar

1. Preheat oven to 325 degrees.
2. Cut cross on top of each chestnut and bake until shells split open. Peel chestnuts. Bring broth to a boil in saucepan. Add chestnuts and simmer for 10 minutes. Drain, reserving broth. Set chestnuts aside to cool.
3. Wash and dry goose, then rub well with salt and pepper. Combine apple slices, raisins, and chestnuts. Stuff goose with this mixture and truss.
4. Place goose, breast side down, in roasting pan. Pour boiling water over goose and bake about 4 hours. After 1 hour, turn goose over and prick legs well. Continue to bake 2½ hours longer, basting frequently with pan juices. After 3½ hours, brush goose several times with cold salted water to make skin crisp.
5. Remove goose from roasting pan and place on serving platter. Switch off oven and return goose to oven for 20 minutes.
6. Skim fat off pan juices; add boiling water to roasting pan, stirring to deglaze. Strain and add enough water to make 2 cups liquid. Thicken with flour mixed with enough cold water to form thin paste. Season to taste with salt, pepper, and sugar.
7. Remove goose from oven and serve with gravy.

Roast Goose with Sage and Onion Stuffing

Serves 6 to 8

6 to 8 tablespoons butter
2 pounds onions, sliced
8 to 9 fresh sage leaves or 2 teaspoons dried sage
2 large tart apples
3 cups fresh white bread crumbs
Grated rind of 1 lemon
1 egg, beaten
2 cups chicken bouillon or stock made from goose giblets
1 (8- to 10-pound) goose
Salt and pepper to taste
4 to 5 tablespoons hot oil
2 teaspoons flour
1 (25-ounce) jar apple sauce

1. Preheat oven to 400 degrees.
2. Melt butter in frying pan. Cook sliced onions over low heat for 10 to 15 minutes without browning, stirring frequently. If using fresh sage leaves, dip into boiling water for 1 to 2 minutes; drain and chop. Peel and chop 1 apple and mix with bread crumbs. Add sage and lemon rind. Stir in softened onions, egg, and a few spoonfuls of bouillon or stock. Season well with salt and pepper.
3. Fill goose cavity with stuffing. Sew up opening and prick breast several times to allow fat to run while cooking.
4. Place goose on rack over roasting pan. Baste well with hot oil and season with salt and pepper. Reduce heat to 350 degrees and roast for 20 to 25 minutes per pound, basting every 20 minutes. Place remaining apple in roasting pan during last 30 minutes of cooking time. Increase heat to 400 degrees for last 20 minutes of cooking to give goose brown, crisp skin. Remove bird from oven and keep warm.
5. Pour off all fat from roasting pan. Sprinkle flour into cooking juices. Add remaining bouillon or stock and bring to a boil. Mash roasted apple into sauce. Strain gravy into sauceboat and serve apple sauce separately.

Goose with Cranberry Sauce

Serves 6

1 (6½-pound) goose
2 teaspoons salt
1 teaspoon pepper
2 cups boiling water
1 cup cranberry jelly
½ cup dry red wine
¼ teaspoon cinnamon
¼ teaspoon nutmeg
1 teaspoon sugar

1. Preheat oven to 350 degrees.
2. Rub goose well with salt and pepper. Finely chop giblets. Truss goose and lay, breast side down, in roasting pan. Add giblets to roasting pan and 1 cup boiling water. Roast on bottom oven rack for 1 hour. Turn goose over and prick legs in several places to allow fat to run out. Roast for 1 hour longer, basting often with pan juices and adding more boiling water if necessary. Skim fat as needed.
3. After roasting goose for 2 hours, brush several times with cold, salted water. When goose is done, let set for 20 minutes in switched-off oven.
4. Combine cranberry jelly, red wine, cinnamon, nutmeg, and sugar in saucepan. Pour 1 cup boiling water into roasting pan and stir to deglaze; strain and combine with cranberry mixture. Bring to a boil, then pour into sauceboat. Serve separately with goose.

Goose Stuffed with Dried Fruit

Serves 8

1 (9-pound) goose
2 teaspoons salt
1 teaspoon pepper
½ cup raisins
1 cup pitted prunes
2 oranges, peeled and divided
    into sections
1 cup diced dried figs
1 cup boiling water

1. Preheat oven to 350 degrees. Rub goose well inside with salt and pepper.
2. Soak raisins and prunes in water to cover for 15 minutes; drain. Thinly slice orange peel. Combine raisins, prunes, figs, and orange peel. Stuff goose with mixture. Truss goose and lay on wire rack over roasting pan.
3. Pour boiling water over goose and place pan on bottom oven rack. Roast for 3½ hours, basting frequently with pan juices. After first hour, turn goose over and prick legs several times to allow fat to run out. During next 2½ hours, brush goose frequently with cold, salted water and skim fat off pan juices.
4. When goose is done, let sit in switched-off oven for 20 minutes.
5. Place goose on serving platter. Carve goose and garnish with orange sections.

Roast Goose with Apple-Sausage Stuffing

Serves 6

¾ pound sausage, hot or mild
5 tablespoons butter
1 medium onion, chopped
2 stalks celery, chopped
5 cups toasted white bread
    cubes
1 large apple, peeled, cored,
    and chopped
½ teaspoon marjoram
3 teaspoons salt
½ teaspoon pepper
1 (8-pound) goose
Juice of 1 lemon

Giblet Stock

Goose giblets and liver
4 cups water
2 celery tops
1 small onion
2 cloves
Salt and pepper to taste

Gravy

6 tablespoons goose drippings
6 tablespoons flour
Salt and pepper to taste
1 teaspoon brown gravy mix
4 cups giblet stock

1. Fry sausage in heavy skillet until well browned, breaking into bite-size pieces as sausage cooks. Drain well and set aside. Melt butter in skillet. Add onion and celery; saute for 5 minutes. Combine sausage, onion, celery, butter, bread cubes, apple, marjoram, 1 teaspoon salt, and pepper in mixing bowl. Set aside.
2. Remove giblet pack from goose; set aside. Remove and discard loose fat in body cavity.
3. Preheat oven to 325 degrees.
4. Rub goose inside and out with lemon juice and 2 teaspoons salt. Stuff neck cavity loosely and skewer shut. Spoon remaining stuffing into body cavity; truss. Tie wings and legs closely to bird. Place goose on rack, breast side up. Prick breast and thighs several times so fat will run out. Roast for 3 to 3½ hours, or until meat thermometer registers 185 degrees when inserted into breast.
5. While goose cooks, prepare stock. Combine giblets, water, celery, onion, and seasonings in small saucepan. Bring to a boil, then cover and simmer for 30 minutes. Remove liver and cook for 30 minutes more. Strain broth and let cool. Chop liver and giblets; set aside.
6. Transfer goose to serving platter. Cover with tent of aluminum foil while making gravy. Combine goose drippings from roasting pan and flour in medium saucepan. Cook over low heat, stirring constantly, until lightly browned. Add salt, pepper, and gravy mix. Slowly stir in giblet stock. Cook, stirring constantly, over low heat until

thickened. Add reserved giblets and heat thoroughly.
7. Carve goose and spoon stuffing into serving dish. Serve with gravy.

Herbed Game Hens

Serves 6

6 (1- to 1¼-pound) Cornish hens
2 cups herb-seasoned croutons
½ cup sliced pitted black olives
¼ cup lemon juice
¼ cup vinegar
¼ cup vegetable oil
1 clove garlic, peeled and crushed
½ teaspoon thyme
¼ teaspoon salt

1. Preheat oven to 350 degrees.
2. Dry cavities of hens, but do not rub cavities with salt. Mix croutons and olives together. Stuff each hen loosely with ⅓ cup crouton-olive stuffing. Fasten opening with skewers and lace shut with string. Place hens, breast side up, in ungreased, shallow baking pan.
3. Mix lemon juice, vinegar, oil, garlic, thyme, and salt; pour mixture over hens. Bake, uncovered, 2 hours, spooning lemon mixture onto hens every 20 minutes. Transfer hens to warm serving platter, and serve.

Roast Cornish Hens with Savory Stuffing

Serves 4

4 (1-pound) Cornish hens
8 thick slices home-style white
    bread, crusts removed and cut
    into ½-inch cubes
1½ tablespoons parsley flakes
¾ teaspoon salt
½ teaspoon poultry seasoning
¼ teaspoon freshly ground black
    pepper
¾ cup butter
1 cup onions, peeled and finely
    chopped
3 tablespoons melted butter

1. Preheat oven to 350 degrees.
2. Remove giblet packs from hens; reserve livers. Wash hens and pat dry.

3. Place bread cubes on baking sheet. Bake until golden, stirring occasionally. Remove from oven. Combine bread cubes with parsley, salt, poultry seasoning, and pepper; set aside.

4. Turn oven temperature up to 375 degrees.

5. Melt ³/₄ cup butter in heavy frying pan. Add onions and livers. Saute until livers are lightly browned and onions are soft. Remove livers from pan, and chop. Add chopped livers, onions, and butter from pan to bread-cube mixture, tossing until well mixed.

6. Lightly salt and pepper hens. Pack tightly with stuffing; truss. Place hens, breast side up, in ovenproof baking dish. Brush with melted butter. Roast for 45 to 60 minutes, turning every 15 minutes and basting with butter and pan juices. Remove from oven, and serve.

Roast Pheasant

Serves 4

3 slices fatty bacon
1 pheasant
1 onion, peeled
6 tablespoons butter
3 sprigs parsley
Salt and pepper to taste
1 cup chicken broth
1 cup red wine

1. Preheat oven to 400 degrees.

2. Tie bacon slices over pheasant breast. Put onion, 2 tablespoons butter, parsley, salt, and pepper inside pheasant.

3. Melt 4 tablespoons butter in roasting pan. Place pheasant on rack in roasting pan and baste well with butter. Pour ¹/₂ cup broth and ¹/₂ cup red wine over pheasant. Roast for 40 to 60 minutes, depending on size, basting every 15 minutes and turning bird over from side to side. For last 15 minutes, remove bacon and string, and allow breast to brown.

4. Transfer pheasant to serving platter and keep warm while making gravy. Pour off butter from roasting juices and add ¹/₂ cup broth and ¹/₂ cup red wine. Bring to a boil, stirring con-

stantly, for 3 to 4 minutes. Season to taste and strain into sauceboat.

5. Serve pheasant with sauce separately.

American Pheasant

Serves 4

1 pheasant
Salt and pepper to taste
1 cup butter
1¹/₂ to 2 cups fresh white bread crumbs
Pinch of cayenne pepper
4 tomatoes, halved
4 slices bacon
8 mushroom caps, filled with butter

1. Preheat broiler

2. Cut pheasant open along back with sharp knife. Open pheasant out and flatten with heavy rolling pin. Season with salt and pepper. Melt butter in large frying pan. Saute pheasant until brown on both sides. Remove from heat.

3. Coat pheasant with bread crumbs. Sprinkle with cayenne pepper. Broil pheasant until bird is cooked and crumbs are brown.

4. Broil halved tomatoes, bacon, and mushrooms. To serve, place pheasant on serving platter and surround with broiled accompaniments.

Pheasant and Apple Casserole

Serves 4

4 to 5 tablespoons butter
1 pheasant
2 onions, sliced
3 stalks celery, sliced
2 medium-size apples
4 cups chicken broth
¹/₂ cup white wine
Salt and pepper to taste
1 tablespoon fines herbes
1 bay leaf
2 teaspoons sugar
1 tablespoon chopped parsley

1. Preheat oven to 350 degrees.

2. Melt 2 to 3 tablespoons butter in Dutch oven. Add pheasant and cook

over low heat until brown on all sides. Remove pheasant from pan and keep warm. Add onions to pan and saute for 5 minutes. Add celery and saute for 2 to 3 minutes more. Slice 1 apple and add to pan.

3. Return pheasant to Dutch oven; cover with broth and wine. Sprinkle with salt, pepper, fines herbes, and bay leaf. Cover and cook in oven for 50 minutes, or until pheasant is tender. Transfer pheasant to serving dish and carve into portions.

4. Remove bay leaf from cooking juices, then put pan drippings and vegetables into blender or food processor; blend until smooth. Reheat, skimming off any surplus butter that rises to surface. Season to taste and pour over pheasant.

5. Peel and core remaining apple; cut into rings. Sprinkle apple rings with sugar. Melt 2 tablespoons butter in small frying pan and saute apple rings until golden brown. Serve pheasant topped with apple rings and sprinkled with parsley.

Stuffed Pheasant

Serves 2 to 4

1 (2³/₄-pound) pheasant
¹/₄ pound Parma ham, finely diced
3 ounces lean bacon, finely diced
¹/₄ teaspoon sage
1 teaspoon salt
¹/₂ teaspoon pepper
¹/₂ teaspoon grated lemon rind
¹/₄ cup olive oil
4 thin strips bacon
¹/₂ cup dry white wine

1. Preheat oven to 425 degrees.

2. Rub pheasant inside with salt. Combine ham, bacon, sage, salt, pepper, and lemon rind; stuff pheasant with mixture and sew up.

3. Heat oil in roasting pan. Brown pheasant well on all sides, lay on back in pan, and cover breast with bacon strips. Roast on lowest oven rack for 40 minutes, basting frequently with wine and pan juices. Remove bacon 10 minutes before end of roasting time to allow breast to brown. Remove from oven, and serve.

Squab
with Brown Rice

Serves 4

1 cup long-grain brown rice
2 cups water
4 (10-ounce) squabs
2 teaspoons sea salt
1 teaspoon pepper
¹/₄ cup softened butter
³/₄ cup heavy whipping cream
¹/₂ cup dry white wine
1 large onion, finely chopped
3 cups cucumber, cut into thin
 strips
2 tablespoons butter
¹/₄ teaspoon seasoning salt
¹/₈ teaspoon white pepper
Fresh dill for garnish

1. Place rice in saucepan with 2 cups water. Bring to a boil, then remove from heat and set aside.
2. Preheat oven to 425 degrees.
3. Rub squabs inside and out with salt and pepper. Spread with thick layer of softened butter. Place squabs, breast side down, in roasting pan; roast for 20 minutes.
4. Place pan of rice on bottom oven rack. Turn squabs over, pour cream on top, and cook for 10 minutes longer, basting frequently with cooking juices. Pour in white wine.
5. Switch off oven and let squabs and rice sit for 10 minutes.
6. Saute onion and cucumber gently in butter until onion is translucent. Season with salt and pepper. Continue to cook gently until cucumber is tender, about 15 minutes. Combine onion and cucumber mixture with rice and cooking juices. Spoon mixture onto warm serving dish. Arrange squabs on top, garnish with dill, and serve.

Squabs Stuffed
with Orange Rice

Serves 4

1 cup rice
3 oranges
¹/₂ cup seedless grapes
Salt and pepper to taste
Pinch of powdered onion
4 squabs
2 to 3 tablespoons oil
2 tablespoons flour
¹/₂ cup dry white wine
¹/₂ cup chicken bouillon

1. Preheat oven to 400 degrees.
2. To prepare stuffing, cook rice following package directions. Let cool. Grate rind of 1 orange and mix with ¹/₂ cup cooked rice. Remove pith and skin from 2 oranges with serrated knife and cut out sections; add orange sections to rice. Dip grapes into boiling water for a few seconds, then into cold water; peel and add to stuffing. Season with salt, pepper, and powdered onion. Fill squabs with stuffing.
3. Heat oil in roasting pan. Add squabs and baste well with hot oil. Roast for 35 to 40 minutes, basting and turning every 10 minutes.
4. Remove squabs from pan and keep warm. Pour off oil and sprinkle flour into roasting pan, stirring to blend with pan drippings. Add wine and bouillon. Bring to a boil, stirring constantly, then simmer for 1 minute. Add juice of 1 orange and a few strips of peel. Serve gravy separately with squabs.

Squabs
Stuffed with
Almonds and Raisins

Serves 4

1 cup rice
¹/₄ cup raisins
2 to 3 tablespoons sherry
2 onions, chopped
3 tablespoons butter
3 to 4 tablespoons flaked almonds
1 tablespoon chopped parsley
4 squabs
4 slices fatty bacon

2 to 3 tablespoons oil
2 tablespoons flour
¹/₂ cup red wine
¹/₂ cup chicken bouillon
Salt and pepper to taste

1. Preheat oven to 400 degrees.
2. To prepare stuffing, cook rice according to package directions. Let cool. While rice is cooking, soak raisins in sherry. Saute onions in butter until translucent. Add almonds and saute until golden brown. Add ¹/₂ cup rice to pan and cook for 1 minute. Remove from heat, then add parsley and raisins. Stuff squabs with mixture.
3. Tie bacon slice around breast of each squab. Heat oil in roasting pan. Add squabs and baste well with hot oil. Roast for 35 to 40 minutes, basting and turning every 10 minutes. Remove bacon for last 15 minutes to brown breast. Transfer squabs to serving dish and keep warm.
4. Pour off oil and sprinkle flour into roasting pan, blending well with pan drippings. Add wine and bouillon. Bring to a boil, stirring constantly until smooth. Add seasoning. Serve gravy separately with squabs.

Braised Partridge
with Lentils

Serves 4

1¹/₄ cups lentils
Water
1 leek, white part only, cut
 into julienne strips
³/₄ cup sliced carrots
2 cloves
1 bay leaf
2 (1-pound, 2-ounce) partridges
1 teaspoon salt
¹/₄ teaspoon pepper
³/₄ cup chopped bacon
3 small onions, sliced
¹/₄ cup dry white wine
³/₄ cup beef bouillon
1 cup sour cream

1. Place lentils in large bowl of water; pick over lentils, discarding any bad ones. Drain well, then place in saucepan. Cover with water and let soak for 30 minutes.

2. Add leek and carrots to lentils, cover, and simmer for 1½ hours. Add cloves and bay leaf after first 30 minutes.

3. Rub partridges inside with salt and outside with pepper.

4. Fry bacon in large frying pan until brown and crisp; drain on paper towels.

5. Preheat oven to 400 degrees.

6. Brown partridges on all sides in bacon fat. Remove from pan and place side by side in casserole dish. Surround with onions. Roast for 30 minutes in center of oven. Reduce temperature to 325 degrees. Pour wine and bouillon over partridges, cover, and continue to cook for 45 minutes more.

7. Remove bay leaf and cloves from lentils. Season lentils with salt and pepper, then arrange in deep serving dish and keep warm. Halve partridges and arrange on top of lentils.

8. Combine cooking juices from partridges with sour cream in small saucepan. Boil, stirring constantly, until sauce is slightly reduced, smooth, and creamy. Pour sauce over partridges. Sprinkle with bacon, and serve.

Stuffed Guinea Fowl

Serves 4

1 teaspoon butter
2 ounces lean bacon, diced
1 cup thinly sliced mushrooms
1 small onion, diced
7 ounces chicken livers, finely chopped
¼ cup brandy
1 teaspoon tarragon
1 teaspoon salt
1 teaspoon pepper
2 tablespoons bread crumbs
2 (1¾-pound) guinea fowl
¼ cup oil
1 carrot, chopped
1 stalk celery, chopped
1 cup dry red wine
1 small bay leaf
½ cup light cream

1. Melt butter in frying pan. Add bacon and mushrooms; saute until browned. Remove from pan and cool.

2. Combine onion, liver, brandy, tarragon, ½ teaspoon salt, ½ teaspoon pepper, and bread crumbs. Combine mixture with mushrooms and bacon. Stuff guinea fowl with mixture. Sew up openings.

3. Preheat oven to 400 degrees. Rub remaining salt and pepper well into guinea fowl. Heat oil in Dutch oven and saute guinea fowl for 10 minutes. Pour off oil. Lay birds on backs in Dutch oven, add carrot and celery, and roast for 10 minutes.

4. Add ½ cup red wine and bay leaf to guinea fowl. Return to oven for 30 minutes, then add remaining red wine and bay leaf. Cook for 10 minutes more, basting frequently with cooking juices.

5. Transfer guinea fowls to serving dish. Strain cooking juices, then combine with cream in saucepan. Boil until sauce is reduced by half. Serve sauce separately with guinea fowl.

Quail Stuffed with Morels

Serves 6

2 tablespoons dried morels or small mushrooms
¼ cup dry sherry
1 slice bread
1 cup plus 2 tablespoons light cream
6 (7-ounce) quails, boned
Salt and pepper to taste
1 shallot, peeled and chopped
1 cup chopped fresh chervil or ½ teaspoon dried chervil
9 ounces sausage meat
Pinch of nutmeg
1 tablespoon oil
2 tablespoons butter

1. Soak morels or mushrooms in sherry for 10 minutes; drain, reserving sherry. Cut crusts off bread, cube, and sprinkle with 2 tablespoons cream.

2. Rub each quail with salt and chopped shallot. Combine chervil, sausage, nutmeg, bread cubes, morels, salt, and pepper. Stuff quails with mixture and truss.

3. Preheat oven to 425 degrees.

4. Heat oil and butter in large frying pan. Brown quails on all sides. Transfer to roasting pan and pour on remaining fat, reserved sherry, and 1 cup cream. Cook on lowest oven rack for 30 minutes. Turn off oven and let quails sit for 5 minutes. Remove from oven, and serve.

Ducklings in Claret

Serves 6 to 8

2 (4- to 5-pound) ducklings, cut into serving pieces
2 cups claret
½ cup brandy
2 onions, chopped
1 clove garlic, peeled and slivered
8 sprigs parsley, minced
1 small bay leaf
Pinch of thyme
¼ cup oil
2 cups sliced mushrooms
Salt and pepper to taste

1. Place duckling pieces in deep dish. In separate bowl, combine claret, brandy, onions, garlic, parsley, bay leaf, and thyme; pour over ducklings. Marinate in refrigerator for 5 hours, turning pieces occasionally.

2. Drain ducklings, reserving marinade. Place marinade in blender or food processor container; process until smooth.

3. Heat oil in heavy kettle; add ducklings and cook until browned. Drain excess fat. Add marinade to kettle; bring to a boil. Cover and simmer for 1½ to 2 hours, or until ducklings are tender.

4. Add mushrooms to kettle; simmer for 15 minutes longer. Spoon off fat. Season with salt and pepper. Serve immediately.

Duckling
with Applekraut

Serves 4

2 tablespoons rendered duck
   fat or butter
1 (4-pound) duckling, quartered
1/2 cup chopped onion
1 pound sauerkraut, drained
1 teaspoon caraway seeds
3 tart apples, peeled, cored,
   and diced

1. Heat in fat in heavy skillet. Add
duck and cook over moderate heat
until well browned on all sides, about
40 minutes. Remove duck from pan;
pour off excess fat, leaving 3
tablespoons drippings in pan. Add
onion and saute until translucent. Stir
in sauerkraut, caraway seeds, and
apples.
2. Arrange duck, skin side down, on
top of mixture in skillet. Cover and
simmer for 30 minutes. Transfer to
serving dish, and serve with fluffy
mashed potatoes.

Squabs Mercedes

Serves 6

6 squabs
Salt and pepper to taste
3 tablespoons butter
1 small onion, chopped
1/2 cup chopped pitted prunes
1/2 cup minced apple
1 cup cooked rice
1 tablespoon minced parsley
1 tangerine, peeled and broken
   into sections
6 thin slices salt pork
1/2 cup sherry

1. Preheat oven to 325 degrees.
2. Rub squabs all over with salt and
pepper. Melt butter in small frying
pan. Saute onion until translucent.
Combine onion with prunes, apple,
rice, and parsley, mixing well.
3. Place 1 tangerine section in each
squab cavity, then fill with rice-fruit
stuffing. Tie legs together, and cover
each breast with slice of salt pork.
Roast for 45 minutes, basting with

sherry and pan juices frequently.
Roast remaining tangerine sections
beside squabs for last 15 minutes of
cooking.
4. Place squabs on platter, garnished
with tangerine sections. Spoon
stuffing into serving dish, and serve
with squabs.

Roast Guinea Hen
aux Garni

Serves 4 to 6

2 (2-pound) guinea hens
Salt to taste
1/2 lemon, optional
4 small onions
1/4 pound salt pork, cut into thin
   strips
2 cups garlic-flavored croutons
12 large mushroom caps, sauteed
   in butter
1 cup cooked peas
1/2 pimento, slivered

1. Preheat oven to 325 degrees.
2. Rub hens inside and out with salt
and cut lemon, if desired. Place 2
onions in each hen. Place, breast side
down, on rack in roasting pan. Lay
pork strips over each hen. Roast for
1 1/4 hours, or until tender. Turn hens
over halfway through roasting time;
rearrange pork strips over breast.
3. Place hens on hot platter. Garnish
with croutons, mushroom caps filled
with peas, and slivers of pimento.

Guinea Hen
Supreme

Serves 2

1 (2-pound) guinea hen
1/2 small onion, sliced
2 celery tops
1/2 small carrot, sliced
3 tablespoons flour
1/2 teaspoon salt
1/4 teaspoon white pepper
2 tablespoons butter
1 cup heavy whipping cream
1/4 cup white wine
4 mushroom caps, sauteed in
   butter

1. Disjoint guinea hen, taking care to
keep breasts intact. Reserve legs for
future use. Place neck, back, and
giblets in water to cover. Add onion,
celery tops, and carrot. Simmer for 1
hour. Strain broth and measure out 1/2
cup; set aside.
2. Season flour with salt and pepper.
Dredge breasts in flour mixture. Melt
butter in deep frying pan with lid.
Saute breasts until golden brown on
both sides. Add reserved 1/2 cup
strained broth. Cover and cook over
low heat for 15 minutes.
3. Combine cream and wine in
saucepan. Cook over low heat until hot
but not boiling. Pour cream sauce over
breasts, garnish with mushroom caps,
and serve.

Squabs with
White Grapes

Serves 4

4 squabs, cleaned and trussed
1/4 cup softened butter
1 teaspoon salt
1/3 cup chicken consomme
1/3 cup white wine
1 1/2 cups seedless white grapes

1. Preheat oven to 375 degrees.
2. Rub squabs with butter. Sprinkle
cavities with salt. Place in buttered
casserole dish. Cover tightly and bake
for 10 minutes.
3. Reduce heat to 325 degrees. Add
consomme and wine. Cover again and
continue to bake for 45 minutes, or
until tender. Add grapes 5 minutes
before end of cooking time. Remove
from oven, and serve.

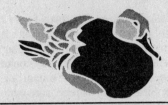

Sherry-Glazed Duckling

Serves 4

1 (4-pound) duckling
1 teaspoon salt
1 teaspoon celery salt
1 green pepper, seeded and
  chopped
2 scallions, chopped
4 sprigs parsley
¹/₂ cup sherry
¹/₄ cup honey
1 clove
Pinch of cayenne pepper
1 teaspoon cornstarch
1 (3-ounce) can mushrooms,
  drained

1. Preheat oven to 325 degrees.
2. Rub duckling with salt and sprinkle with celery salt inside and out. Insert green pepper, scallions, and parsley into cavity. Skewer neck skin to back; fold back wings. Place, breast side up, on rack in roasting pan. Roast, uncovered, for 1 hour.
3. Meanwhile, combine sherry, honey, clove, and cayenne pepper in saucepan. Bring to a boil, then remove from heat.
4. Pour excess fat from roasting pan. Continue to roast duck for 45 minutes, basting every 15 minutes with sherry sauce. Remove duck to warm platter.
5. Stir cornstarch into pan juices. Heat, stirring constantly, until gravy is smooth. Mix in drained mushrooms. Pour gravy into sauceboat and serve separately with duckling.

Sweet and Pungent Duckling

Serves 4

1 (4-pound) duckling
2 tablespoons soy sauce
2 tablespoons honey
2 tablespoons sherry
1 clove garlic, peeled and minced

¹/₂ teaspoon ginger
2 tablespoons rendered duck fat or
  butter
1 cup pineapple juice
1 large green pepper, diced
1 cup canned pineapple chunks,
  drained
1 tablespoon lemon juice
2 tablespoons cornstarch
¹/₄ cup cold water

1. Score duck skin from neck to vent; remove skin with sharp, pointed knife, leaving flesh intact. Cut duck into serving-size pieces.
2. Combine soy sauce, honey, sherry, garlic, and ginger; pour over duck. Set aside for 1 hour, turning pieces occasionally. Remove duck, reserving marinade.
3. Heat duck fat in heavy skillet. Add duck and brown on all sides. Drain off excess fat. Combine pineapple juice with marinade; pour over duck. Cover and simmer for 50 minutes.
4. Add green pepper, pineapple chunks, and lemon juice to skillet. Mix cornstarch with cold water to form paste. Add to skillet, stirring constantly, until sauce thickens. Simmer for 10 minutes.
5. Place duck in serving dish. Spoon sauce on top, and serve with boiled rice.

Roast Goose with Sweet Potato and Apple Dressing

Serves 8

1 (8-pound) goose
Salt to taste
2 tablespoons butter
1 cup finely chopped onions
3 cups finely chopped apples
2 cups mashed sweet potatoes
¹/₄ teaspoon thyme
¹/₄ teaspoon sage
1 teaspoon salt
¹/₂ teaspoon pepper
¹/₂ cup cider or orange juice
Orange slices for garnish

1. Preheat oven to 325 degrees.
2. Rub goose inside and out with salt. Melt butter in frying pan. Saute onions

and apples for 5 minutes. Stir in sweet potatoes and seasonings. Stuff mixture into cavity of goose; close with skewers. Fasten neck skin to back with skewer. Prick skin all over.
3. Place goose, breast side down, on rack in roasting pan. Roast, uncovered, for 2 hours. Pour off excess fat; baste goose with cider or orange juice. Continue to roast for 1¹/₂ hours, basting every 20 minutes.
4. Transfer goose to warm platter. Garnish with orange slices, and serve.

Rock Cornish Game Hen in Foil

Serves 1

¹/₄ cup butter
1 cup minced onion
¹/₂ cup minced celery
1 cup seedless grapes,
  quartered
¹/₄ cup sherry
1 teaspoon salt
2 cups cooked wild rice
1 Rock Cornish game hen
Melted butter for brushing

1. Preheat oven to 425 degrees.
2. Melt butter in frying pan. Saute onion and celery for 5 minutes. Add grapes, sherry, salt, and wild rice; blend well.
3. Stuff hen with wild rice stuffing. Tie legs to tail. Brush with melted butter and sprinkle with salt. Place in center of sheet of heavy-duty aluminum foil. Wrap foil around hen tightly, using double folds to seal top and sides. Place on rack in shallow roasting pan. Roast for 1¹/₄ hours. Open foil for last 15 minutes of cooking time, to brown hen.
4. Remove hen from oven, discard foil, and serve.

Duck
Braised in Red Wine

Serves 5

1 (5-pound) duckling
Salt to taste
Garlic powder to taste, optional
2 tablespoons butter
2 teaspoons flour
1 cup dry red wine
Lemon juice to taste
1 teaspoon lemon rind
Pinch of sugar

1. Two hours before cooking, rub duck with salt and garlic, if desired. Melt butter in Dutch oven until very hot. Brown duck quickly on all sides.
2. Brown flour lightly in dry frying pan, stirring to prevent sticking or burning. Remove from heat and add wine, a little at a time, stirring constantly to prevent lumps. Add to duck, cover tightly, and braise over low heat for 1½ hours, or until tender.
3. Add lemon juice, rind, and sugar at end of first hour of cooking. Cover and continue braising. Remove from heat, and serve.

Duck with Peas

Serves 4

1 (5-pound) duck, cut into
    serving pieces
Salt to taste
2 tablespoons butter
½ cup water
2 tablespoons diced bacon
10 small onions
1 pound fresh peas, shelled

1. Sprinkle duck pieces with salt. Melt butter in heavy skillet. Add duck and cook over low heat for 1 hour, until duck is almost tender. Add water as needed, when pan gets too dry.
2. Add bacon, onions, and peas. Cook for 20 minutes, or until vegetables are tender. Place duck on serving dish and spoon vegetables around it.
Serve at once.

Quails in Wine

Serves 6

6 quails, cleaned
Salt and freshly ground pepper
    to taste
¼ cup butter
1 carrot, diced
1 small onion, chopped
2 tablespoons chopped green
    pepper
½ cup chopped mushrooms
2 small slices orange rind,
    blanched in boiling water to
    cover for 1 minute
1 tablespoon flour
1 cup chicken broth
½ cup white wine

1. Preheat oven to 350 degrees.
2. Season quails with salt and pepper. Melt butter in large skillet. Add quails and brown lightly. Transfer quails to buttered casserole dish.
3. To make sauce, add carrot, onion, green pepper, mushrooms, and orange rind to same skillet. Cook over low heat for 5 minutes. Stir in flour. Gradually add chicken broth. Cook over medium heat, stirring constantly, until sauce thickens. Season with salt and pepper. Reduce heat and simmer for 10 minutes.
4. While sauce cooks, pour wine over quails in casserole dish; bake for 10 minutes. Pour sauce over quails, cover, and bake for 20 minutes longer, or until quails are tender. Serve immediately.

Rock Cornish Hens with
Mincemeat Stuffing

Serves 2

2 Rock Cornish game hens
¼ cup butter, melted
4 slices whole-wheat bread, cubed
¾ cup orange juice
½ cup prepared mincemeat,
    drained
¼ cup diced celery
½ teaspoon salt

1. Preheat oven to 375 degrees.
2. Remove giblets and necks from hens. Tuck neck skin under wings. Place hens, breast side up, on rack in open roasting pan. Roast hens,

brushing occasionally with melted butter, for 1 to 1½ hours, or until a leg can be moved up and down easily.
3. To make stuffing, combine bread cubes, orange juice, mincemeat, celery, and salt in 1-quart casserole dish; toss gently. Bake stuffing along with hens for the last 30 minutes of cooking time.
4. Transfer hens to serving platter. Serve with mincemeat stuffing.

Duck with Cornbread
Pecan Stuffing

Serves 4

2 cups enriched self-rising
    cornmeal
2 eggs, beaten
1 to 1¼ cups milk
¼ cup oil
¼ cup butter
½ cup chopped onion
½ cup chopped green pepper
½ cup chopped celery
1 cup chicken broth
1 teaspoon salt
½ teaspoon pepper
1 teaspoon basil
1 teaspoon thyme
1 cup coarsely chopped pecans
1 (4½-pound) duck

1. Preheat oven to 425 degrees.
2. To make cornbread, place cornmeal in medium-size bowl. In separate bowl, blend eggs, milk, and oil together. Add egg mixture to cornmeal; stir until smooth.
3. Pour cornmeal batter into greased, 8-inch square pan. Bake for 25 to 30 minutes, or until golden brown. Cool in pan; crumble. Reduce oven temperature to 350 degrees.
4. Melt butter in frying pan. Add onion, green pepper, and celery; saute until tender. Add chicken broth and simmer for 3 to 5 minutes.
5. Combine crumbled cornbread, salt, pepper, basil, thyme, and pecans in bowl. Pour sauteed onion mixture on top; toss lightly.
6. Stuff cornbread mixture into cavity of duck; fasten shut with skewers or string. Roast for 2 to 2½ hours, or until duck is tender. Transfer duck to heated platter and serve.

Duck à l'Orange

Serves 2

1 (3¼-pound) oven-ready duck
1 teaspoon salt
¼ teaspoon freshly ground
   black pepper
3 oranges
1 lemon
2 tablespoons vegetable oil
1 carrot, peeled and diced
1 medium onion, diced
½ cup diced celery
1½ cups hot chicken broth
⅓ cup sugar
¼ cup white wine vinegar
¼ cup orange liqueur
2 tablespoons cornstarch
2 tablespoons cold water
2 tablespoons orange marmalade
Shredded orange peel for garnish
Watercress sprigs for garnish

1. Rub inside of duck well with salt and pepper; truss.
2. Peel 1 orange, removing all white fibers; using a sharp knife, cut down between orange sections and separate pieces carefully. Peel second orange and lemon as thinly as possible and cut peel into julienne strips. Squeeze juice from lemon and 2 oranges, and set aside.
3. Preheat oven to 400 degrees.
4. Heat oil in roasting pan in oven. When oil is hot, place duck, breast side down, in pan and roast for 15 minutes. Arrange carrot, onion, and celery around duck. Roast duck for 15 minutes on each side. Turn duck over on back, pour hot broth over it, and bake for 25 minutes longer, until done.
5. While duck is roasting, melt sugar to a light brown in heavy-bottomed pan over low heat. Add orange and lemon rind and juice. Simmer gently for 30 minutes.
6. When duck is done, place on warm platter, switch off oven, and return duck to oven while preparing gravy.
8. Pour cooking juices from roasting pan into chilled metal bowl; put in freezer for 10 to 15 minutes until fat forms on top. Skim off fat. Stir vinegar into roasting pan to deglaze, then combine with citrus syrup and simmer gently for 1 minute. Remove saucepan from heat; stir in liqueur and de-fatted juices.
9. Mix cornstarch with cold water to form thin paste, then stir into sauce and bring to a boil again. Stir in marmalade. Season to taste with salt and pepper.
10. Remove trussing string from duck. Garnish platter with orange segments, grated orange rind, and watercress. Serve sauce separately.

Hungarian Turkey Ragout

Serves 4

1¼ cups thinly sliced
   mushrooms
1 tablespoon lemon juice
2 tablespoons vegetable oil
1¼ pounds boneless turkey
   breast, thinly sliced
1 tablespoon butter
1 onion, finely chopped
½ cup sour cream
1 teaspoon cornstarch
1 teaspoon paprika
½ cup dry white wine
½ teaspoon salt
½ teaspoon freshly ground
   white pepper

1. Sprinkle mushrooms with lemon juice and set aside.
2. Heat oil in large, heavy skillet. Add turkey and cook, stirring, until browned and cooked thoroughly; remove from pan.
3. Melt butter with oil remaining in skillet. Add onion and saute until transparent. Add mushrooms, cover, and simmer for 10 minutes.
4. Mix sour cream with cornstarch and paprika. Return turkey to skillet. Add cream mixture, then white wine. Simmer gently for 3 to 4 minutes.
5. Season with salt and pepper, and serve.

Braised Paprika Chicken

Serves 4

3 tablespoons butter
2 medium onions, finely chopped
3 pounds chicken pieces
2 red peppers, seeded and cut into
   strips
2 green peppers, seeded and cut
   into strips
6 tablespoons chicken broth
½ cup sour cream
1 tablespoon paprika
1 teaspoon salt
⅛ teaspoon freshly ground black
   pepper
1 tablespoon finely chopped
   parsley

1. Heat butter in large, heavy skillet. Saute onions until translucent, stirring constantly. Add chicken and brown on all sides. Add red and green pepper strips and chicken broth. Cover and cook over low heat for 30 minutes.
2. Stir sour cream, paprika, salt, and pepper together. Add mixture to chicken. Let stand for 5 minutes on warm oven top. Sprinkle with parsley, and serve.

Chicken Paprika

Serves 4

½ cup plus 2 tablespoons
  flour
Salt and pepper to taste
1 (3-pound) chicken, cut into
  serving pieces
¼ cup butter
1 medium onion, sliced
½ pound mushrooms,
  sliced
1 tablespoon Hungarian sweet
  paprika
1 cup chicken broth
½ cup dry white wine
½ cup sour cream

1. Combine ½ cup flour, salt, and pepper in paper bag. Add chicken pieces, a few at a time; shake to coat. Melt butter in Dutch oven over medium heat. Add chicken and brown well on all sides. Remove from pan.
2. Add onion to pan and saute until lightly browned. Remove from pan with slotted spoon and set aside. Add mushrooms to pan and saute for 5 minutes. Remove pan from heat, then add paprika. Stir in chicken broth and wine. Return chicken and onion to pan.
3. Bring pan to a boil over medium heat. Cover and simmer for 50 to 60 minutes, or until chicken is tender.
4. Combine 2 tablespoons flour and sour cream, blending well. Remove chicken from pan and keep warm. Stir sour-cream mixture into pan juices. Cook over very low heat until sauce thickens. Pour sauce over chicken, and serve.

Grilled Paprika Chicken

Serves 4

3 tablespoons lemon juice
3 tablespoons butter,
  melted
1 clove garlic, peeled and
  crushed
1 teaspoon salt
1 teaspoon Hungarian sweet
  paprika
Pepper to taste
1 (3-pound) chicken, cut into
  serving pieces

Sauce

3 tablespoons butter
1 small onion, diced
¼ cup chopped green pepper
¼ cup chopped mushrooms
1½ tablespoons flour
2 teaspoons Hungarian
  sweet paprika
1 cup chicken broth
½ cup tomato sauce
2 tablespoons dry sherry

1. Combine lemon juice, butter, garlic, salt, paprika, and pepper in dish. Place chicken in marinade, turning to coat well. Cover and refrigerate overnight.
2. Preheat broiler.
3. Drain chicken, discarding marinade. Arrange chicken on broiler pan, skin side down. Broil 6 inches from heat source, basting occasionally with melted butter. Turn and broil 15 minutes more.
4. To make sauce, melt butter in saucepan. Add onion and saute until translucent. Add green pepper and mushrooms; saute until tender. Add flour and cook, stirring constantly, until boiling. Remove from heat. Stir in paprika, then return to heat. Add chicken broth and tomato sauce. Cook, stirring constantly, until sauce thickens. Add sherry, stirring well.
5. Serve chicken accompanied by sauce, boiled rice, and a green salad.

Chicken Livers Paprikash

Serves 4

1 pound chicken livers
¼ cup butter
1 cup thinly sliced onions
1 clove garlic, peeled and crushed
1 tablespoon paprika
Salt and pepper to taste
1 cup chicken broth
¼ cup sour cream
1 tablespoon flour
Chopped parsley for garnish

1. Remove any fat or connective tissue from livers. Melt butter in large, heavy skillet with lid. Add onions and garlic, and saute over moderate heat until browned. Remove pan from heat. Add livers, paprika, salt, and pepper, stirring well.
2. Add chicken broth to livers and cover pan. Bring to a boil, then reduce heat to low. Simmer for 15 to 20 minutes, or until livers are done.
3. Mix sour cream and flour together well, then add slowly to liver mixture, whisking constantly. Cook over very low heat until sauce thickens. Garnish with chopped parsley, and serve.

Stuffed Chicken with Vegetables

Serves 4

1 stale slice bread
6 ounces boiled ham, trimmed of
  fat and diced
1 (3-pound) chicken
1 clove garlic, peeled and chopped
½ pound sausage meat
2 tablespoons chopped chives
4 cups water
1 teaspoon salt
1 sprig fresh thyme or ¼ teaspoon
  dried thyme
2 sprigs parsley
1 bay leaf
1 small onion, chopped
2 small carrots, chopped
¼ cup chopped celery
2 small leeks, white part only,
  chopped
1¾ cups savoy cabbage, cut into
  fine strips
1 cup string beans, broken into
  pieces

1. Soak bread in cold water for 5 minutes, then squeeze out water. Dice chicken giblets. Combine bread, ham, giblets, garlic, sausage, and chives.
2. Fill chicken with stuffing mixture; sew up opening. Bring 4 cups water to a boil in large, deep saucepan with salt, herbs, and bay leaf. Add chicken and simmer, covered, for 1 hour.
3. Add onion, carrots, celery, leeks, cabbage, and beans to chicken. Cover and cook for 30 minutes longer. To serve, place chicken on deep serving platter and surround with vegetables.

Bolivian Chicken

Serves 4 to 6

1/4 cup olive oil
3 large onions, cut into rings
3 1/4 pounds chicken pieces
1 1/2 cups hot chicken bouillon
1 teaspoon salt
1/4 teaspoon freshly ground black pepper
1 teaspoon hot paprika
1 3/4 cups tomatoes, skinned and chopped
1 red pepper, seeded and diced
1/2 teaspoon oregano
1 teaspoon caraway seeds
2 cloves garlic, peeled and finely chopped
5 tablespoons fresh bread crumbs
Sliced hard-boiled eggs for garnish
Green olives for garnish

1. Heat oil in large, heavy skillet. Add two-thirds of onions and saute until translucent. Add chicken pieces and brown well on all sides. Stir in 3/4 cup hot bouillon, salt, pepper, and paprika. Cover and simmer for 40 minutes.
2. Combine tomatoes, red pepper, remaining 3/4 cup bouillon, oregano, caraway seeds, remaining onions, and garlic in separate saucepan. Cover and simmer for 20 minutes.
3. Stir bread crumbs into tomato mixture. Serve chicken pieces with vegetables and sauce. Garnish with sliced eggs and green olives.

Chicken in Apricot Sauce

Serves 4

6 tablespoons corn oil
3 pounds chicken pieces
2 tablespoons flour
1 1/4 cups hot water
1 large onion, finely chopped
2 1/4 cups pitted apricots, halved
2 teaspoons brown sugar
1 teaspoon salt
1/4 teaspoons freshly ground black pepper

1. Heat oil in large, heavy skillet. Brown chicken pieces well over medium heat, then remove from pan.
2. Pour off all oil from pan; return 1 tablespoon oil to pan. Mix flour with enough water to form paste, then whisk into oil in pan. Add hot water, whisking constantly, until sauce thickens.
3. Stir in chopped onion and simmer for 3 or 4 minutes over low heat. Stir in apricot halves. Add sugar, salt, and pepper, then the chicken pieces. Cover and continue to simmer for 30 minutes longer. Remove from heat, and serve.

Basque Chicken

Serves 4

5 tablespoons olive oil
2 1/2 pounds chicken pieces
2 onions, finely chopped
3 cloves garlic, peeled and finely chopped
3 1/2 cups skinned and quartered tomatoes
2 green peppers, seeded and cut into strips
1/2 cup hot chicken bouillon
1 1/2 teaspoons salt
1/4 teaspoon freshly ground black pepper
1 1/4 cups long-grain rice
1 tablespoon paprika

1. Heat 3 tablespoons oil in large frying pan with lid. Brown chicken pieces well on all sides. Add onions and garlic; continue to saute, stirring frequently, until soft. Add tomato,

green pepper, bouillon, 1 teaspoon salt, and pepper. Cover and simmer for 30 minutes.
2. Saute rice in remaining oil until rice begins to brown. Pour in 2 1/2 cups water; add 1/2 teaspoon salt, cover, and cook over low heat for 20 minutes, or until rice is done. Stir in paprika.
3. To serve, place rice in serving dish, and arrange chicken and vegetables on top.

Chicken in a Roman Pot

Serves 4

2 1/2 pounds chicken pieces
1 tablespoon lemon juice
1 teaspoon salt
1/2 teaspoon freshly ground white pepper
3 thin slices bacon
2 cups chopped celery
2 cups chopped carrots
4 potatoes, peeled and quartered
1/4 cup dry white wine
1 sprig fresh rosemary or 1/4 teaspoon dried rosemary
2 fresh sage leaves or 1/4 teaspoon dried sage
1 tablespoon butter

1. Soak Roman pot and lid in cold water for 20 minutes.
2. Sprinkle chicken pieces with lemon juice. Season with salt and pepper, rubbing in well.
3. Remove pot from water and line with bacon slices. Arrange half the vegetables in the pot; season lightly with salt and pepper. Lay chicken pieces on top and finish with layer of remaining vegetables. Season lightly again.
4. Sprinkle wine over vegetables. Place herbs on top. Put lid on pot and place on bottom rack of cold oven. Turn heat to 425 degrees and cook for 1 1/2 hours. Remove lid 10 minutes before end of cooking time and dab small pieces of butter over vegetables.
5. To serve, transfer chicken to warm, deep platter, surround with vegetables, and pour cooking liquids over everything.

Southern-Style Chicken Stew

Serves 4

1 (2½-pounds) stewing
 chicken, cut into serving
 pieces (reserve giblets)
2 teaspoons salt
1 onion, cut into rings
3 medium potatoes, peeled and
 coarsely diced
1¾ cups tomatoes, skinned
 and cut into segments
1 (8-ounce) can kidney beans,
 drained
1 (8-ounce) can sweet corn
 kernels, drained
Sugar to taste
1 teaspoon salt
¼ teaspoon freshly ground
 black pepper
2 tablespoons finely chopped
 chives

1. Place chicken and giblets in large saucepan with boiling water to cover. Simmer, uncovered, for 45 minutes, skimming as needed. Add salt, cover pan with lid, and simmer for 45 minutes longer.
2. Add onion and potatoes to chicken for final 20 minutes of cooking time. Add tomatoes, drained kidney beans, and corn to chicken for last 10 minutes of cooking time.
3. Remove chicken from stew. Separate meat from skin and bones. Cut meat into pieces and return to stew. Season with sugar, salt, and pepper. Serve piping hot, sprinkled with chopped chives.

Creamy Chicken Stew

Serves 4

½ teaspoon salt
½ teaspoon paprika
⅛ teaspoon freshly ground black
 pepper
¼ cup vegetable oil
3 pounds chicken pieces
1 small onion, cut into pieces
1 cup chopped celery
1 carrot, cut into pieces
1 cup long-grain rice

1 bay leaf
⅛ teaspoon ground fennel seed
4 cups water
¾ cup cucumber, peeled and cut
 into pieces
¾ cup zucchini, peeled and cut
 into pieces
1 sweet gherkin, finely chopped
¼ cup sour cream

1. Mix salt, paprika, and pepper with 1 tablespoon oil. Coat chicken pieces with this mixture and marinate for 10 minutes.
2. Heat remaining oil in large pan. Saute chicken until browned. Add onion, celery, and carrot to pan; saute for 5 minutes. Add rice, bay leaf, and fennel. Stir in water, cover, and simmer for 30 minutes. Transfer to ovenproof casserole dish.
3. Preheat oven to 375 degrees.
4. Add cucumber and zucchini to chicken and rice mixture. Place dish, uncovered, in middle of oven and bake for 15 minutes.
5. To serve, stir chopped gherkin into sour cream, and spoon into center of casserole dish.

Chicken with Mozzarella

Serves 4

2 boneless chicken breasts,
 skinned and halved
1 tablespoon chopped chives
1 tablespoon chopped parsley
½ clove garlic, peeled and
 minced
¼ teaspoon salt
⅛ teaspoon pepper
½ cup grated, low-fat mozzarella
 cheese
2 tablespoons vegetable oil
1 tablespoon flour
¼ cup sherry
1 cup chicken broth

1. Pound each chicken breast half with flat side of meat mallet to ¼-inch thickness. Sprinkle herbs and seasonings evenly over chicken pieces. Cover with grated cheese and roll up each breast half, completely enclosing cheese. Secure with wooden toothpicks.
2. Heat oil in large frying pan. Saute chicken rolls until golden brown, about 8 minutes. Place in shallow baking dish.
3. Preheat oven to 350 degrees.
4. To make sauce, stir flour into drippings left in frying pan. Stir until smooth. Remove from heat. Add sherry and broth, then return to heat. Bring to a boil, stirring constantly. Boil until sauce is slightly reduced and thickened. Spoon sauce over chicken, cover, and bake for 30 minutes. Remove toothpicks before serving.

Chicken Tourangelle

Serves 6

1 (4-pound) stewing chicken
2 large onions, quartered
2 cups chicken stock
6 to 8 medium mushrooms
½ cup dry white wine
½ cup heavy whipping cream
Salt and pepper to taste
Grated rind of ½ orange
2 cups mashed potatoes
2 tablespoons toasted sliced
 almonds

1. Preheat oven to 325 degrees.
2. Place chicken, onions, and stock in roasting pan. Cover and bake for 2 hours, or until chicken is tender. Remove chicken from pan; cool until easily handled. Remove skin and bones from chicken; cut chicken into serving pieces. Arrange on heated platter and keep warm.
3. Cut stems from mushrooms; cut caps in half. Add mushrooms caps and stems to liquid in roasting pan. Bring to a boil over high heat. Boil until liquid is reduced to 2 cups. Stir in wine and cream. Cook, stirring constantly, until sauce is thick and smooth. Season with salt and pepper. Stir in orange rind. Pour sauce over chicken.

4. Place mashed potatoes in pastry bag with large writing tube affixed. Pipe potatoes around chicken mixture. Sprinkle potatoes with almonds, and serve.

Chicken Vol-au-Vent

Serves 4

2 whole chicken breasts
¼ cup butter
3 tablespoons flour
1 cup chicken stock
¾ cup heavy whipping
  cream
Salt and pepper to taste
2 ounces grated Cheddar cheese
1 (7-ounce) can small
  mushrooms, drained and
  sliced
3 shallots, peeled and chopped
1 tablespoon chopped parsley
2 teaspoons dry sherry
1½ teaspoons prepared
  mustard
4 patty-shell cases (vol-au-vents)

1. Cook chicken breasts in boiling water to cover until meat is tender. Reserve stock. Remove bones and skin from chicken; cut meat into 1-inch pieces.
2. Melt butter in saucepan. Stir in flour, blending well. Remove from heat. Gradually add chicken stock and cream, stirring until well mixed. Return to heat and cook, stirring constantly, until sauce thickens. Season with salt and pepper; simmer for 2 minutes more. Add cheese, mushrooms, shallots, parsley, sherry, and mustard. Stir until cheese melts. Add chicken and cook over low heat until thoroughly heated.
3. Preheat oven to 350 degrees.
4. Place patty shells on baking sheet and bake just until hot. Spoon chicken mixture into patty shells, and serve hot.

French Roast Chicken

4 to 6 servings

1 (3- to 4-pound) chicken
1 onion
Salt and pepper to taste
1½ cups water
6 tablespoons butter
3 sprigs parsley
Watercress for garnish

1. Preheat oven to 375 degrees.
2. Make stock by placing giblets, onion, seasoning, and water in saucepan. Cook over low heat for 15 minutes; strain.
3. Put 3 tablespoons butter, parsley, salt, and pepper inside chicken. Spread remaining 3 tablespoons butter over chicken. Place chicken into roasting pan, and pour half the giblet stock on top. Refrigerate remaining stock.
4. Roast chicken 20 minutes per pound, basting with stock every 15 minutes and turning chicken from side to side. During last 20 minutes of cooking time, turn chicken breast up to brown.
5. Transfer chicken to hot dish and keep warm in oven. Skim butter from top of pan drippings. Add remaining stock to roasting pan; bring to a boil, stirring constantly and scraping pan well. Serve as gravy.
6. Serve chicken hot or cold, garnished with watercress.

Circassian Chicken

Serves 4 to 6

1 (3- to 4-pound) chicken
3 cloves
5 onions, 3 whole and 2
  chopped
1 cup chopped celery
3 sprigs parsley
1 bay leaf
8 black peppercorns
⅛ teaspoon salt
2 cups shelled walnuts

½ cup bread crumbs
2 tablespoons butter
1 clove garlic, peeled and
  crushed
Pepper to taste
2 teaspoons paprika
⅛ teaspoon cayenne pepper
3 tablespoons vegetable oil

1. Place chicken in stock pot and just cover with cold water. Stick 1 clove in each of the whole onions, and add to chicken along with celery, herbs, peppercorns, and salt. Bring to a boil, then simmer for 1 hour, or until chicken is tender. Skim as needed. Remove chicken from pan and keep warm, reserving stock for sauce.
2. Grind walnuts finely in blender or food processor. Mix ground nuts with bread crumbs.
3. Melt butter in frying pan. Add chopped onions and garlic; saute until golden brown and soft. Add onions, garlic, and 1 cup reserved stock to walnut mixture, blending carefully. When smooth, cook over medium heat until sauce reaches boiling point, adding more stock if sauce becomes too thick. Season with salt and pepper.
4. Mix paprika, cayenne pepper, and oil together. Gradually add about 1 tablespoon of paprika-oil mixture to walnut sauce until sauce is a delicate pink.
5. Cut chicken into serving pieces. Spoon layer of sauce into bottom of ovenproof dish. Lay chicken pieces on top. Spoon remaining sauce on top of chicken, and reheat thoroughly. Sprinkle remaining red oil over dish, and serve with plain boiled rice.

Chicken Curry

Serves 4

5 tablespoons butter
4 large chicken pieces
2 medium onions, thinly
  sliced
1 tablespoon curry powder
1 teaspoon curry paste
1 tablespoon flour
1¹/₂ cups chicken stock
1 apple, peeled, cored, and
  chopped
2 tablespoons raisins
2 tablespoons chutney
1 bay leaf
Salt
¹/₄ cup boiling water
3 tablespoons finely shredded
  coconut
Juice of ¹/₂ lemon
2 teaspoons red currant jelly
2 teaspoons turmeric powder
2 cups cooked long-grain rice
1 lemon, thinly sliced
¹/₂ teaspoon paprika

1. Preheat oven to 350 degrees.
2. Melt butter in large frying pan. Add chicken and brown on all sides. Transfer chicken to ovenproof casserole dish and keep warm.
3. Add onions to butter in frying pan and saute until golden. Add curry powder and paste; saute for 3 to 4 minutes. Sprinkle in flour and brown slightly. Add stock and bring to a boil, stirring constantly. Reduce heat and simmer for 4 to 5 minutes. Add chopped apple, raisins, chutney, bay leaf, and salt. Cook together for 1 minute. Pour mixture over chicken pieces in casserole dish. Bake for 35 to 40 minutes, until chicken is nearly tender.
4. Pour ¹/₄ cup boiling water over shredded coconut. Let stand for 30 minutes. Strain coconut liquid onto chicken; stir in lemon juice and jelly. Cook for 15 minutes longer.
5. Heat turmeric in butter remaining in frying pan in which chicken was browned. Stir turmeric into cooked rice. Arrange cooked rice in ring on serving platter. Place chicken pieces in center of ring.

6. Boil sauce left in casserole dish, puree in blender or food processor, and spoon over chicken. To serve, garnish chicken with thin lemon slices and sprinkle with paprika.

Danish Curried Chicken

Serves 6 to 8

¹/₃ cup butter
1 medium onion, chopped
2 (3-pound) chickens, cut into
  serving pieces
1 tablespoon curry powder
3 cups boiling water
2 teaspoons salt
¹/₄ cup flour

1. Melt butter in Dutch oven. Add onion and saute until browned. Remove onion and brown chicken pieces in same fat. Return onion to pan; add curry powder. Pour boiling water over chickens; season with salt. Simmer for 1 hour, or until chickens are tender. Transfer chicken pieces to serving platter.
2. Mix flour with a small amount of water to make paste. Add flour mixture to chicken cooking liquid, stirring until sauce is thick and smooth. Serve sauce separately with chicken.

Mediterranean Chicken

Serves 8

4 pounds fresh tomatoes,
  skinned, seeded, and chopped
¹/₄ cup plus 2 tablespoons
  vegetable oil
2 tablespoons butter
¹/₂ teaspoon salt
¹/₈ teaspoon freshly ground
  black pepper
8 boneless chicken breasts,
  skinned
2 medium onions, thinly sliced
2 cloves garlic, peeled and
  crushed
¹/₂ teaspoon thyme
2 bay leaves
2 tablespoons tomato paste

1 cup dry white wine
¹/₂ teaspoon sugar
Parsley sprigs for garnish
Pitted black olives for garnish

1. Cook tomatoes in 2 tablespoons oil and butter for 5 minutes. Add salt and pepper.
2. In separate large frying pan, brown chicken on both sides in ¹/₄ cup hot oil. Add onions, garlic, thyme, bay leaves, and tomato paste. Saute until onions are translucent. Add wine and boil rapidly until reduced by half.
3. Add cooked tomatoes and sugar. Cover and simmer for 15 minutes. Remove from heat, and serve garnished with parsley sprigs and olives.

Stuffed Chicken Breast Athenian

Serves 4

4 split chicken breasts, skinned
  and boned
2 tablespoons crumbled feta
  cheese
1 tablespoon chopped walnuts
1 tablespoon chopped parsley
³/₄ cup flour
¹/₂ teaspoon salt
¹/₄ teaspoon pepper
1 egg
2 tablespoons milk
2 tablespoons olive oil
2 tablespoons butter

Kima Sauce

3 tablespoons olive oil
¹/₄ cup chopped onion
¹/₄ cup chopped carrots
¹/₄ cup chopped celery
1 clove garlic, peeled and
  chopped
1 (8-ounce) can tomatoes,
  drained and chopped
2 tablespoons chopped parsley
¹/₄ cup white wine
¹/₄ teaspoon sugar
¹/₄ teaspoon oregano

1. Cut small pocket in each chicken breast by partially slicing through each cutlet. Mix feta cheese, walnuts, and parsley together. Put 1 tablespoon

stuffing in each cutlet; seal edges by pressing them together.

2. Season flour with salt and pepper. Dredge cutlets in flour mixture. Mix egg and milk together. Dip cutlets in egg-milk mixture, then dredge again in flour mixture.

3. Heat olive oil and butter over medium heat in large, heavy frying pan until foam subsides. Cook chicken over medium-high heat until brown on bottom. Turn chicken over and reduce heat. Cook until brown on all sides and cooked thoroughly. Do not cover, or chicken will lose its crispness and cheese will begin to ooze out of pocket.

4. To make Kima sauce, heat olive oil in small, heavy frying pan. Saute onion, carrots, celery, and garlic until limp. Add drained tomatoes, parsley, wine, sugar, and oregano. Simmer for 20 minutes, until thick.

5. Serve chicken cutlets topped with Kima sauce.

Chicken Seville

Serves 4

¼ cup olive oil
4 chicken legs and thighs
1 Spanish onion, sliced
½ cup diced smoked ham
1 tablespoon tomato paste
2 (16-ounce) cans stewed tomatoes
1 large clove garlic, peeled and crushed
1 teaspoon salt
¼ teaspoon pepper
¼ teaspoon thyme
¼ cup sliced pitted black olives
¼ cup sliced stuffed Spanish olives

1. In large, deep skillet, heat oil until haze forms above skillet; reduce heat. Add chicken pieces and brown evenly on all sides. Remove chicken from pan.

2. Add onion and ham to pan and saute about 5 minutes, until onions slices wilt and ham begins to brown. Drain oil from skillet.

3. Add chicken, tomato paste, tomatoes, garlic, and spices; bring to a boil. Reduce heat to simmer, cover,

and cook for 30 minutes, until chicken is tender. Add olives and simmer for 5 minutes longer. Serve chicken directly from skillet.

Moroccan Chicken

Serves 4 to 6

¼ cup olive oil
4 pounds chicken pieces, skinned
1 medium onion, sliced into thin rings
2 cloves garlic, peeled and crushed
1 teaspoon salt
1 teaspoon pepper
½ teaspoon oregano
1 bay leaf
2 tablespoons lemon juice
1¼ cups chicken stock
1 teaspoon cornstarch

1. Heat oil over moderate heat. Add chicken pieces, a few at a time, and brown on all sides. Drain on paper towels.

2. Measure out 2 tablespoons oil, discarding remaining oil. Return the 2 tablespoons oil to pan and heat. Add onion and garlic; saute until onion is golden. Add remaining seasonings and chicken stock. Bring to a boil.

3. Return chicken to pan. Cover and simmer for 1½ hours, or until chicken is tender. Transfer chicken to heated platter.

4. Strain remaining liquid into small saucepan, pressing liquid through strainer to extract as much liquid as possible. Dissolve cornstarch in ¼ cup of the liquid and add to saucepan. Stir constantly until sauce thickens.

5. Pour sauce over chicken pieces, and serve.

Chicken Papillotes

Serves 4

1 pound boneless chicken meat, sliced very thin
2 tablespoons soy sauce
1 tablespoon dry sherry
½ teaspoon brown sugar
½ teaspoon salt
1 scallion, thinly sliced
1 teaspoon grated fresh ginger
Vegetable oil for deep-frying

1. Combine chicken slices, soy sauce, sherry, brown sugar, salt, scallion, and ginger. Marinate for 30 minutes.

2. Divide chicken mixture into 16 portions. Wrap each portion in piece of cooking parchment or aluminum foil, about 4 inches square; fasten well.

3. Heat oil in wok to 375 degrees. Deep-fry packages a few at a time for 3 minutes each. Drain on paper towels and keep warm. Serve wrapped to keep in juices.

Sour-Cream Chicken Enchiladas

Serves 6

Enchilada Sauce

1 clove garlic, peeled and minced
2 small onions, chopped
3 tablespoons vegetable oil
2 tablespoons flour
1¾ cups chicken bouillon
2 (5-ounce) cans green chilies, drained and chopped
2 cups canned tomatoes, drained and chopped

Enchiladas

1 pint sour cream
½ pound sharp white Cheddar cheese, shredded
4 cups cooked and shredded chicken
12 flour tortillas

1. To make sauce, saute garlic and onions in hot oil. Add enough bouillon to flour to form paste, then whisk into oil. Whisk in remaining bouillon. Cook, whisking constantly, for 5 minutes, until thickened. Add chilies and tomatoes. Simmer for 5 to 10 minutes.

2. Preheat oven to 350 degrees.

3. To assemble enchiladas, mix sour cream, shredded cheese, and chicken together. Place about ½ cup of filling in center of each tortilla. Roll up tortillas and place, side by side, in large baking dish. Pour sauce over enchiladas and bake for 30 minutes, until bubbling and hot.

Pomegranate Chicken

Serves 6

¹/₄ cup oil
1 (6-pound) stewing chicken,
   cut into serving pieces
1 (16-ounce) can tomatoes
1 cup chicken broth
1 teaspoon ground cloves
¹/₄ teaspoon pepper
¹/₄ teaspoon cinnamon
Pinch of saffron
¹/₄ cup blanched almonds
¹/₄ cup raisins
1 cup Malaga wine
Seeds of 1 pomegranate
1 avocado, sliced and sprinkled
   with lemon juice, optional

1. Heat oil in Dutch oven. Add chicken and cook over medium heat for about 30 minutes, until browned on all sides. Add tomatoes, broth, spices, almonds, and raisins. Cover and boil gently until meat is tender and sauce thickened, about 25 minutes. Add wine and simmer for 5 minutes more.
2. Transfer chicken to platter. Pour sauce on top and sprinkle with pomegranate seeds. Garnish with avocado slices, if desired.

Fiesta Turkey in Mole Sauce

Serves 8 to 10

¹/₄ cup oil
1 (10- to 12-pound) turkey,
   disjointed
1 teaspoon salt
Water

Mole Sauce

6 dried red chilies
Boiling water
2 tablespoons vegetable oil
1 medium onion, chopped
2 cloves garlic, peeled and minced
¹/₂ teaspoon crushed chilies
1 cup chopped canned Italian plum
   tomatoes
³/₄ teaspoon ground cinnamon
¹/₂ teaspoon ground cloves
¹/₄ teaspoon ground coriander
¹/₄ teaspoon anise
¹/₄ teaspoon cumin
1 dry tortilla, cut into pieces
¹/₄ cup sesame seeds
¹/₄ cup raisins
2 cups chicken broth
2 (1-ounce) squares semisweet
   chocolate, grated

1. Heat oil in Dutch oven. Brown turkey well on all sides, adding more oil if necessary to keep turkey from sticking. Add salt and enough water to cover. Bring to a boil. Cover and cook over low heat for 1 hour, or until turkey is tender. Remove from heat and set aside.
2. To prepare sauce, stem and seed dried chilies under cold running water. Tear chilies into pieces, then soak in boiling water to cover for 30 minutes. Drain, reserving ¹/₄ cup soaking liquid.
3. Heat oil in frying pan. Add onion and garlic, and saute until limp. Pour onion, garlic, dried chilies, reserved liquid, crushed chilies, tomatoes, and spices into food processor or blender. Add tortilla pieces, sesame seeds, and raisins; puree, scraping container frequently.
4. Heat frying pan in which onion was cooked over moderate heat for several minutes. Pour pureed mixture into pan. Add chicken broth, stirring well. Simmer for 10 minutes. Remove from heat and add chocolate. Stir until chocolate melts.
5. Drain broth from turkey. Pour sauce over turkey and cook gently until heated through. Remove from heat, and serve.

Mexican-Style Chicken

Serves 4

3 pounds chicken pieces
3 to 4 tablespoons flour
1 teaspoon salt
¹/₄ teaspoon garlic powder
¹/₂ teaspoon freshly ground
   black pepper
2 medium onions, sliced
5 tablespoons butter
2 tomatoes, skinned and
   chopped
¹/₄ cup white wine
³/₄ cup chicken broth
³/₄ cup raisins
¹/₂ cup pimento-stuffed olives
Salt and pepper to taste
¹/₂ teaspoon cinnamon
3 tablespoons browned, slivered
   almonds

1. Roll chicken pieces in flour seasoned with salt, garlic powder, and pepper. Set chicken aside and toss onion slices in same flour.
2. Melt butter in large frying pan. Add chicken pieces and cook until golden brown on all sides, about 7 to 10 minutes. Transfer chicken to ovenproof casserole dish.
3. Preheat oven to 350 degrees.
4. Add onion slices and chopped tomatoes to butter remaining in frying pan; saute for 4 to 5 minutes. Add wine, broth, raisins, and olives to onions; season with salt and pepper. Bring to a boil and pour over chicken pieces. Bake for 35 minutes, or until chicken is tender.
5. Sprinkle with cinnamon and stir until well mixed. Sprinkle with browned almonds, and serve immediately.

Mexican Chicken with Corn

Serves 4

¹/₄ cup butter
1 (2¹/₂- to 3-pound) chicken,
   quartered
Salt and pepper to taste
1 (16¹/₂-ounce) can whole kernel
   corn, drained and liquid
   reserved
¹/₂ cup chopped green chilies,
   optional

Sauce

5 tablespoons butter
2 tablespoons flour
1 cup half-and-half
2 eggs, separated
Salt and white pepper to taste
¹/₄ teaspoons nutmeg
2 tablespoons bread crumbs

1. Melt butter in heavy skillet. Brown chicken on all sides. Transfer to ovenproof casserole. Season chicken with salt and pepper. Add corn and chilies, if desired, to pan juices, along with ¼ cup reserved corn liquid. Stir well, then pour over chicken.

2. To make sauce, melt 3 tablespoons butter in saucepan. Add flour and cook until lightly browned, stirring constantly. Add half-and-half all at once; cook over medium heat, stirring constantly, until slightly thickened.

3. Preheat oven to 350 degrees.

4. Beat egg yolks, salt, pepper, and nutmeg together. Add 2 tablespoons hot sauce to egg yolks and beat well. Pour egg yolk mixture into saucepan and mix well with remaining sauce. Remove from heat. Beat egg whites until stiff but not dry; fold into sauce.

5. Pour sauce over chicken, sprinkle with bread crumbs, and dot with remaining butter. Bake for 45 minutes. Remove from oven, and serve hot

Mexican Tablecloth Stainer

Serves 6

2 tablespoons butter
2 tablespoons oil
1 pound boneless pork, cut into 1-inch chunks
1 (4- to 5-pound) roasting chicken, cut into serving pieces
½ cup flour

Sauce

1 tablespoon blanched, slivered almonds
2 teaspoons sesame seeds
1 medium onion, chopped
1 green pepper, seeded and chopped
1 (16-ounce) can tomatoes, broken up with fork
2 cups chicken stock
½ cup white wine
¼ cup sugar
1½ teaspoons cinnamon
1 tablespoon chili powder
3 cloves
1 bay leaf

1 sweet potato, peeled and cut into cubes
1 medium apple, peeled, cored, and diced
1 cup pineapple chunks, drained
2 medium bananas, optional

1. Heat butter and oil together in Dutch oven. Saute pork until well browned. Remove from pan. Dredge chicken in flour, then cook until browned. Remove from pan.

2. Saute almonds, sesame seeds, onion, and green pepper until lightly browned in fat remaining in Dutch oven; add 1 tablespoon oil if needed. Add tomatoes and simmer for 10 minutes. Puree sauce in blender or food processor.

3. Combine pureed sauce, chicken stock, wine, sugar, cinnamon, chili powder, cloves, and bay leaf in Dutch oven. Add pork and chicken. Bring to a boil, then reduce heat to low. Simmer for 30 minutes. Add sweet potato and simmer for 15 minutes longer.

4. Add apple and pineapple to stew and simmer until hot. Serve in soup bowls. Peel and slice bananas into individual bowls as stew is served, if desired.

Mexican Chicken Livers

Serves 4

1 pound chicken livers
½ cup flour, seasoned with salt and pepper
6 tablespoons butter
5 scallions, sliced
½ pound fresh mushrooms, sliced
¼ cup sherry

1. Coat chicken livers with seasoned flour. Melt butter in frying pan. Saute chicken livers until golden brown. Add scallions and mushrooms; saute for 6 to 7 minutes.

2. Add sherry and simmer for 5 minutes longer. Serve livers on toast or boiled rice.

Braised Duck in Green Mole Sauce

Serves 4 to 6

1 (5- to 6-pound) duckling
1 clove garlic, peeled and crushed
¾ teaspoon salt
½ teaspoon pepper
3 tablespoons butter

Green Mole Sauce

3 tablespoons olive oil
1 slice white bread
½ cup raw shelled pumpkin seeds (raw pepitas)
¼ cup blanched, slivered almonds
1 (10-ounce) can Mexican green tomatoes (tomatillos), drained
1 (4-ounce) can peeled green chilies, seeded and chopped
3 tablespoons chopped cilantro
1½ cups chicken broth
Salt and pepper to taste

1. Rub duck with garlic, salt, and pepper. Melt butter in Dutch oven over moderate heat. Brown duck well on all sides, pricking several times so fat will run out. Cover, reduce heat to low, and cook without liquid for 25 to 35 minutes, or until tender.

2. While duck is cooking, prepare sauce. Heat 2 tablespoons oil in frying pan. Add bread and fry until golden brown on both sides. Drain on paper towels, then tear into pieces. Add remaining oil to skillet, then brown pumpkin seeds and almonds. Drain. Combine green tomatoes, green chilies, bread pieces, pumpkin seeds, almonds, cilantro, ½ cup chicken broth, salt, and pepper. Puree mixture in blender or food processor.

3. Heat frying pan over moderate heat. Pour sauce into pan; stir in remaining chicken broth. Simmer for 5 to 10 minutes. Carve duck and serve topped with sauce.

Stewed Chicken with Tomatoes and Green Peppers

Serves 6

1 (3¹/₂-pound) stewing chicken
Salt to taste
2 quarts water
1 carrot
1 celery stalk
1 tablespoon vegetable oil
4 medium onions, diced
2 green peppers, seeded and cut
  into strips
2 tablespoons paprika
2 tomatoes, skinned and cut into
  pieces
¹/₈ teaspoon freshly ground black
  pepper

1. Place chicken and giblets, except liver, in large saucepan with salt and water. Bring to a boil, skimming as needed. Add carrot and celery and simmer for 1¹/₂ hours.
2. Strain chicken broth and measure out 2 cups. Divide chicken into serving portions and remove giblets.
3. Heat oil in large frying pan. Brown chicken pieces on all sides. Add onions and green peppers, and saute briefly. Stir in paprika, then chicken broth. Simmer for 10 minutes.
4. Chop liver and add to pan along with tomatoes. Simmer for 10 minutes longer. Season with salt and pepper, and serve.

Chicken Provençale

Serves 5 to 6

1 (5-pound) stewing chicken,
  cut into serving pieces
1 tablespoon cornstarch
Salt and pepper to taste
¹/₄ cup butter
3 small onions, halved
4 small carrots, quartered
1 clove garlic,
  peeled and crushed
¹/₄ cup red wine
1 cup chicken stock
¹/₂ cup pitted black olives

1. Preheat oven to 325 degrees.
2. Dredge chicken in cornstarch

seasoned with salt and pepper. Heat butter in frying pan. Brown chicken, then transfer to casserole dish.
3. Add onions, carrots, and garlic to butter remaining in frying pan. Saute for 5 minutes, then add wine and stock. Stir until boiling, then pour over chicken.
4. Cover casserole dish tightly and bake for 2 hours. Before serving, adjust seasonings and stir in olives.

Coq au Vin

Serves 4

3 pounds chicken pieces
¹/₂ teaspoon salt
¹/₈ teaspoon freshly ground
  black pepper
2 tablespoons butter
¹/₄ pound bacon, finely diced
8 small onions, chopped
1 clove garlic, peeled and
  chopped
2 carrots, diced
2 tablespoons brandy
1 bay leaf
1 sprig fresh thyme or
  ¹/₄ teaspoon dried thyme
2 sprigs parsley
3 cups dry red wine
³/₄ cup diced mushrooms
1 teaspoon flour
Chopped parsley for garnish

1. Season chicken pieces with salt and pepper. Heat butter in heavy skillet, and brown chicken pieces and bacon. Add onions, garlic, and carrots, continuing to saute for 4 to 5 minutes. Add brandy and ignite.
2. Add bay leaf, thyme, parsley sprigs, and red wine. Cover and simmer for 40 minutes.
3. Remove chicken from pan to heated serving dish and keep warm. Puree vegetables and cooking juices together in food processor, then simmer mushrooms in this sauce for 10 minutes.
4. Mix flour with a small amount of cold water to form paste. Add to sauce, whisking constantly until sauce thickens. Season to taste with salt. Pour sauce over chicken and sprinkle with parsley.

Greek Chicken

Serves 6

1 (5-pound) roasting chicken
3 teaspoons oregano
2 large cloves garlic, peeled and
  crushed
³/₄ teaspoon salt
¹/₂ teaspoon pepper

1. With sharp knife, slash chicken at 1-inch intervals on all skin surfaces, down to bone if possible. Combine oregano, garlic, salt, and pepper. Rub chicken cavity and skin with herb mixture, using all of it.
2. Preheat oven to 400 degrees.
3. Place chicken in center of 30-inch piece of heavy-duty aluminum foil. Bring 2 ends of foil together over chicken. Fold together and seal ends of foil. Do not fold foil too tightly around chicken, as juice will accumulate in package. Place foil package in roasting pan. Roast for 1¹/₂ hours.
4. Remove chicken from oven and carefully open corner of foil. Pour juices into sauceboat. Remove foil and slice chicken. Serve chicken with cooking juices and boiled rice.

Chicken Kampama

Serves 4 to 5

2 tablespoons butter
2 tablespoons olive oil
1 (3-pound) chicken, cut into
  serving pieces
2 medium onions, chopped
2 cloves garlic, peeled and minced
1 cup canned tomatoes
1 (3-ounce) can tomato paste
2 sticks cinnamon
¹/₄ teaspoon ground allspice
¹/₂ teaspoon sugar
¹/₄ cup red wine

1. Heat butter and olive oil in Dutch oven. Add chicken and brown on all sides, then remove from pan.
2. Add onions and garlic to pan and saute until browned. Add tomatoes, tomato paste, seasonings, and wine. Bring to a boil, then add chicken. Reduce heat to simmer and cook for 1 to 1¹/₂ hours, or until chicken is tender.

Irish
Chicken 'n Cabbage

Serves 4

1 (2½- to 3-pound) chicken,
  cut into serving pieces
Juice of ½ lemon
3 tablespoons butter
Salt and pepper to taste
¾ cup white wine
3 tablespoons bacon fat
1 medium onion, finely chopped
3 cups shredded cabbage
1 cup diced celery
¼ cup diced green pepper
2 cups diced tomatoes
¼ teaspoon garlic powder

1. Sprinkle chicken pieces with lemon juice. Heat butter in heavy skillet. Brown chicken well on all sides. Season with salt and pepper. Add wine, cover, and simmer for 45 minutes, or until chicken is tender.
2. Melt bacon fat in separate frying pan over moderate heat. Add onion and saute for 3 minutes, stirring constantly. Add cabbage, celery, green pepper, and tomatoes; mix well. Season with garlic powder, salt, and pepper. Cover and cook over low heat for 10 minutes, until vegetables are crisp-tender.
3. Place cabbage in serving dish; top with chicken. Serve immediately.

Goose with
Potato Stuffing

Serves 6

1 (8- to 9-pound) goose

Potato Stuffing

3 medium potatoes, peeled
1½ teaspoons salt
¼ pound lean salt pork, diced
¼ cup finely chopped onion
¼ pound bulk sausage
¼ cup butter, melted
1 egg
½ teaspoon pepper
1 teaspoon sage

1. Remove giblets from goose. Salt goose lightly inside and out.
2. Place potatoes in medium saucepan. Cover with cold water; add ½ teaspoon salt. Bring to a boil over moderate heat. Cover and cook over low heat for 20 to 30 minutes, until potatoes are tender. Drain.
3. Cook salt pork in heavy skillet over moderate heat until lightly browned. Remove with slotted spoon and set aside. Add onion to skillet and saute until translucent. Remove with slotted spoon and add to salt pork. Add sausage to skillet and cook until lightly browned, breaking into small chunks as sausage cooks. Remove with slotted spoon and add to salt-pork mixture.
4. Mash potatoes. Combine salt-pork mixture, potatoes, and remaining stuffing ingredients; mix well. Let cool.
5. Preheat oven to 325 degrees.
6. Stuff goose with potato mixture; truss. Place on rack in roasting pan, breast side up. Prick goose well on legs and wing joints to let fat run out. Roast for 2 to 2½ hours, or until leg joint moves easily. Remove from oven and let stand for 15 to 20 minutes before carving.
7. Carve goose. Place stuffing in serving dish. Serve with applesauce.

Baked Chicken
with Marinara Sauce

Serves 4

½ cup flour
1 teaspoon salt
¼ teaspoon pepper
1 (2½- to 3-pound) chicken, cut
  into serving pieces
3 tablespoons butter
1 (15½-ounce) can marinara
  sauce
1 teaspoon dill weed
2 tablespoons grated Parmesan
  cheese

1. Preheat oven to 450 degrees.
2. Combine flour, salt, and pepper in paper bag. Add chicken, a few pieces at a time, and shake until coated with flour mixture. Place chicken in single layer in shallow baking dish. Dot with butter. Bake for 25 minutes. Remove from oven.
3. Pour marinara sauce over chicken. Sprinkle with dill weed and cheese. Reduce heat to 350 degrees and bake for 25 minutes. Remove from oven, and serve hot or cold.

Lake Como
Chicken

Serves 4

1 (3-pound) chicken
1 tablespoon olive oil
1 clove garlic, peeled
½ teaspoon salt
½ teaspoon sage
2 thin slices salt pork
Juice of 1 lemon
¼ teaspoon freshly ground
  pepper

1. Preheat oven to 350 degrees.
2. With kitchen string, tie chicken legs together. Place another piece of string around chicken and tie wings so they stay close to sides of bird. Rub outside of chicken with olive oil. Place chicken in shallow baking dish, breast side up.
3. Sprinkle garlic clove with salt; crush. Rub chicken with garlic and sage. Lay salt pork over chicken. Roast for 1 hour. Remove from oven.
4. Combine lemon juice and pepper; pour over chicken. Return chicken to oven and roast for 30 minutes more, basting occasionally. Chicken is done when skin is well browned and leg joint moves easily when pulled. Transfer chicken to serving platter, remove strings, and carve. Serve with pan juices.

Chicken Florence

Serves 4

2 tablespoons olive oil
1 (2½- to 3-pound) chicken,
   quartered
1 medium onion, chopped
1 clove garlic, peeled and
   minced
4 large fresh tomatoes, skinned
   and chopped
4 large pitted green olives,
   chopped
½ teaspoon basil
½ teaspoon oregano
½ teaspoon celery salt
¼ teaspoon pepper
4 bay leaves

1. Preheat oven to 425 degrees.
2. Cut 4, 10-inch pieces of aluminum foil and grease with olive oil. Place chicken piece in center of each piece of foil. Combine onion, garlic, tomatoes, olives, basil, oregano, celery salt, and pepper. Mix well. Spoon mixture over each piece of chicken. Add 1 bay leaf to each package. Fold up foil and place on cookie sheet. Bake for 40 minutes.
3. Remove packages from oven and place on individual plates. Serve from packages, with a green salad and garlic bread.

Italian-Style Fried Chicken

Serves 4

⅓ cup flour
½ teaspoon seasoned salt
¼ teaspoon pepper
2½ pounds chicken pieces
2 eggs
2 tablespoons milk
⅔ cup bread crumbs
⅓ cup grated Parmesan cheese
Oil for frying
½ cup chopped parsley
Lemon slices for garnish

1. Combine flour, seasoned salt, and pepper in paper bag. Add chicken, a few pieces at a time, and shake until lightly coated with flour mixture. Beat eggs and milk together in shallow bowl. On piece of wax paper, combine bread crumbs and Parmesan cheese. Dip floured chicken pieces in egg, then in bread crumbs, coating well.
2. Preheat oven to 350 degrees.
3. Heat 1½ inches of oil in heavy skillet over moderate heat. Fry chicken a few pieces at a time until golden brown. Drain on paper towels.
4. Place chicken on baking sheet and bake for 15 or 20 minutes, or until juices run clear when pierced with knife. Transfer to platter, sprinkle with parsley, and garnish with lemon slices.

Piedmont-Style Chicken Breasts

Serves 4

2 boneless chicken breasts,
   skinned and halved
2 tablespoons flour
¾ teaspoon salt
¼ teaspoon pepper
3 tablespoons butter
½ cup sliced mushrooms
4 thin slices Fontina or Swiss
   cheese

1. Place chicken breasts between sheets of wax paper and pound until thin. Combine flour, salt, and pepper and coat chicken with mixture. Heat 2 tablespoons butter in heavy skillet. Saute chicken in butter for 5 to 6 minutes on each side, or until golden and thoroughly cooked.
2. Preheat broiler.
3. Melt 1 tablespoon butter in small skillet. Add mushrooms and saute for 5 minutes. Place chicken in single layer in small ovenproof casserole. Top with mushrooms, and then with cheese. Broil just until cheese is melted, then serve.

Chicken Breasts with Italian Ham

Serves 4

4 boneless chicken breasts,
   skinned
Salt and pepper to taste
1 teaspoon sage
¼ pound prosciutto, thinly sliced
¼ cup butter
1 small onion, minced
1 clove garlic, peeled and
   minced
½ pound mushrooms, sliced
¼ cup chicken broth
¼ cup white wine
2 tablespoons chopped parsley

1. Place chicken between sheets of wax paper; pound until thin. Season chicken with salt, pepper, and sage. Evenly distribute prosciutto on top of each breast. Fold in half and secure with wooden toothpicks.
2. Melt butter in heavy skillet. Add chicken and cook over moderate heat until lightly browned on all sides. Remove from pan. Add onion and garlic to pan and saute for 1 minute. Add mushrooms and cook until mushroom liquid evaporates. Return chicken to skillet; spoon mushrooms over chicken. Add broth and wine. Cover and simmer for 20 minutes.
3. Transfer chicken and mushrooms to platter. Pour pan juices over chicken, sprinkle with parsley, and serve.

Chicken with Rosemary and White Wine

Serves 4

2 tablespoons butter
2 tablespoons vegetable oil
2 or 3 cloves garlic, peeled
1 (2½-pound) chicken,
   quartered
1 sprig fresh rosemary, halved,
   or ½ teaspoon dried rosemary
Salt and pepper to taste
½ cup dry white wine
3 tablespoons water

1. Heat butter and oil over medium heat in large skillet. When butter foam subsides, add garlic and chicken quarters. Brown chicken on all sides. Add rosemary; remove garlic. Add salt, pepper, and wine. Continue cooking over moderate heat until wine bubbles. Reduce heat to simmer, cover, and cook for 30 minutes, or until chicken is fork-tender. Remove chicken to serving platter and keep warm.

2. Remove all but 3 tablespoons fat from skillet. Over high heat, add 3 tablespoons water, stirring to mix with cooking juices. Pour sauce over chicken, and serve at once.

Chicken Parmesan with Mushroom Marsala Sauce

Serves 6

1 cup seasoned bread crumbs
1 cup grated Parmesan cheese
1 tablespoon herbes d'Provence
6 boneless chicken breasts
1 cup flour seasoned with salt
  and pepper
2 eggs, beaten
2 to 3 tablespoons olive oil
2 tablespoons butter

Sauce

1 pound fresh mushrooms, sliced
3 to 4 tablespoons butter
$^1/_3$ cup marsala wine

1. Combine bread crumbs, cheese, and herbs on plate. Dredge chicken in seasoned flour, then dip in eggs. Coat with bread crumb mixture. Set aside on wax paper until all pieces are coated. Refrigerate for 2 to 3 hours.
2. Pour oil in center of 12-inch frying pan. Place pats of butter around oil. Heat slowly until butter melts and oil is hot. Place chicken in frying pan and fry until golden brown. Remove from pan and keep warm.
3. Saute mushrooms in butter for 5 minutes. Add wine; stir until sauce is hot but not boiling. Pour sauce over chicken just before serving.

Spanish Bread Pies

Serves 6

3 tablespoons olive oil
$^1/_2$ cup chopped onion
$^1/_2$ cup chopped green pepper
$^1/_2$ cup chopped Italian ham
$1^1/_2$ cups chopped tomatoes
1 cup chopped cooked chicken
$^1/_2$ teaspoon garlic powder
$^1/_2$ teaspoon salt

Pinch of cayenne pepper
1 box packaged roll mix
1 cup warm water
1 egg, beaten
1 egg white, unbeaten

1. Heat oil in frying pan. Add onion and green pepper; saute for 3 minutes. Add ham, tomatoes, garlic powder, salt, and cayenne pepper. Simmer until mixture thickens and is heated thoroughly.
2. Dissolve yeast from roll package in warm water as directed on package. Add beaten egg; blend well. Add flour mixture from package to yeast mixture, blending well. Cover and let rise in warm place until double in bulk.
3. Preheat oven to 350 degrees.
4. Punch down dough and place on well-floured surface. Roll out to 16 x 20-inch rectangle. Cut into 4-inch squares. Fill each square with heaping tablespoon of chicken mixture. Bring corners together; pinch edges together. Place on greased cookie sheet, pinched edges down. Let rise for 30 minutes.
5. Brush dough with egg white and bake for 30 minutes. Remove from oven, cool slightly, and serve.

Chicken Akbar

Serves 4

4 sheets phyllo pastry
$^1/_2$ pound boneless chicken
  breasts, shredded
2 scallions, chopped
1 small clove garlic, peeled and
  crushed
Salt and pepper to taste
$^1/_2$ cup butter
1 tablespoon pine nuts
1 tablespoon slivered almonds
2 tablespoons raisins
1 teaspoon curry powder
1 tablespoon flour
$3^1/_2$ tablespoons chicken stock
$3^1/_2$ tablespoons heavy whipping
  cream
Mixture of butter and oil for frying

1. Cover pastry with paper towel until needed. Mix shredded chicken with scallions and garlic. Season with salt and pepper.

2. Melt 3 tablespoons butter in saucepan. Add nuts, raisins, and chicken mixture; saute until chicken is lightly browned. Sprinkle on curry powder, then add flour and saute for 1 minute. Add chicken stock and bring almost to a boil, while stirring constantly. Add cream, salt and pepper. Simmer for about 2 minutes, stirring constantly, until sauce thickens. Remove from heat and cool slightly.
3. Fold each sheet of pastry in half in give rectangular shapes about 8 x 7 inches. Melt remaining butter and brush over pastry. Place $^1/_4$ of filling on each pastry piece. Fold in sides, then fold pastry over to completely enclose filling. Press edges to seal.
4. Heat about $^1/_3$ inch of mixed butter and oil in frying pan. Fry pastries, 2 at a time, until golden brown. Drain and arrange on serving plate. Serve hot.

Indonesian Chicken with Soy Sauce

Serves 4

1 (3-pound) chicken
Salt
2 tablespoons dark soy sauce
2 shallots, peeled and finely sliced
2 cloves garlic, peeled and crushed
$^1/_2$ teaspoon chili powder
Juice of $^1/_2$ lemon or lime
2 teaspoons sesame oil
Oil for basting

1. Preheat oven to 375 degrees.
2. Gently rub outside of chicken with salt. Place chicken in roasting pan and roast for 45 minutes, or until chicken is golden brown and tender. Remove from oven and cool.
3. Divide chicken into quarters. Use mallet to beat chicken meat and loosen fibers. Mix soy sauce, shallots, garlic, chili powder, lemon or lime juice, and sesame oil together. Pour over chicken and marinate for 1 hour.
4. Preheat broiler.
5. Remove chicken from marinade; discard marinade. Brush each chicken piece with oil and broil until heated thoroughly. Remove to platter, and serve.

Sweet and Sour Chicken Drumsticks

Serves 3 to 4

6 chicken drumsticks
2 teaspoons light soy sauce
2 teaspoons dry sherry
1 teaspoon sugar
Oil
1 cup cornstarch
1/2 medium onion, thinly sliced
1/2 stalk celery, thinly sliced
1 small carrot, thinly sliced
1/2 red pepper, seeded and diced
1 (8-ounce) can sliced bamboo
   shoots, drained
3 slices fresh ginger, shredded, or
   1 teaspoon powdered ginger

Sauce

3 1/2 tablespoons chicken stock
3 1/2 tablespoons white vinegar
1/4 cup sugar
1/2 teaspoon salt
1 teaspoon chili sauce
1 tablespoon cornstarch

1. Prick drumsticks all over and place in bowl. Combine soy sauce, sherry, and sugar; rub mixture all over drumsticks. Let sit for 20 minutes.
2. Heat about 2 inches oil in large skillet to moderately hot. Drain drumsticks and coat thickly with cornstarch, shaking off excess. Fry until golden brown and thoroughly cooked, about 5 minutes. Turn occasionally using tongs. Remove and drain on paper towels.
3. Pour off oil and rinse out pan. Place 2 tablespoons oil back in pan. Add onion, celery, carrot, red pepper, bamboo shoots, and ginger; stir-fry for 2 1/2 minutes.
4. Combine sauce ingredients and pour over vegetables. Bring to a boil. Reduce heat and simmer, stirring constantly, for 2 to 3 minutes. Add drumstick and reheat in sauce. Serve at once.

Lebanese Orange Duck

Serves 6 to 8

3 1/2 tablespoons butter
1 large onion, chopped
1 (4 1/2-pound) duck, cleaned
   and dressed
3 large oranges
1/2 lemon
Salt and pepper to taste
1 tablespoon flour
1 tablespoon toasted almonds

1. Melt butter in large frying pan. Add onion and saute until lightly browned. Push onion to one side of pan and add duck. Brown lightly all over, turning duck with 2 wooden spoons to avoid breaking skin. Pour off fat.
2. Squeeze juice from 2 oranges and lemon half; pour over duck. Add salt and pepper. Cover pan and cook over low heat for 1 1/2 hours, or until duck is very tender and pan juices have been reduced to rich, dark glaze. Turn duck several times to ensure even cooking.
3. Remove duck from pan and arrange on platter. Pour off most of fat from pan. Sprinkle flour into pan and add juice of remaining orange. Bring to a boil, stirring constantly, until sauce thickens
4. Serve duck whole, or cut into serving pieces; sprinkled with almonds.

Thai Chicken Ginger

Serves 4 to 6

5 scallions, cut into 1/2-inch
   pieces
1 1/4 cups shredded fresh
   ginger
2 tablespoons vegetable oil
3 boneless chicken breasts,
   skinned and cut into bite-size
   pieces
3 chicken livers, chopped
1 onion, sliced
1 clove garlic, peeled and finely
   chopped
2 tablespoons tree ear mushrooms,
   soaked in warm water for 20
   minutes
2 tablespoons soy sauce
1 tablespoon honey

1. Cover scallions with cold water and let soak until needed. Rinse ginger under cold running water; drain.
2. Heat oil in large frying pan. Add chicken and liver; cook for 5 minutes. Remove from pan and drain on paper towels. Add onion, garlic, and tree ears to pan; stir-fry for 1 minute. Return chicken to pan.
3. Mix soy sauce and honey together well. Pour over chicken. Add ginger and cook over moderate heat for 2 to 3 minutes. Drain scallions and add to pan. Transfer chicken mixture to bowl, cover, and refrigerate overnight.
4. When ready to serve, reheat until dish is heated thoroughly.

Szechuan Chicken

Serves 4

2 1/4 pounds boneless chicken
   breasts, cut into thin,
   2-inch-long strips
3 tablespoons light soy sauce
2 teaspoons cornstarch
1/4 cup peanut oil
3 carrots, finely shredded
4 scallions, finely chopped
1 fresh, hot red chili pepper,
   seeded and cut into fine
   rings

1. Place chicken strips in bowl and sprinkle with soy sauce and cornstarch. Mix well, cover, and marinate for 30 minutes.
2. Heat 2 tablespoons oil in wok or large skillet. Stir-fry chicken strips for 5 minutes, then remove from pan.
3. Heat remaining oil in wok or skillet; stir-fry carrots, scallion, and chili pepper for 6 minutes, stirring constantly. Add meat and stir-fry together for 2 minutes longer. Serve at once with rice and soy sauce.

Chicken Cantonese

Serves 3 to 4

¼ cup peanut oil
½ pound boneless white chicken
  meat, sliced into strips
  about 1½ inches long
  and ½ inch wide
½ pound snow peas, strings
  removed
¼ cup bamboo shoots
1 cup thinly sliced bok choy,
  drained if canned
1 cup thinly sliced mushrooms
1 cup thinly sliced celery
¼ cup sliced water chestnuts,
  drained if canned
4 cups chicken stock
2 tablespoons cornstarch
½ cup cold water

1. Heat oil in wok or frying pan. Add chicken and stir-fry about 10 seconds, until chicken changes color. Add snow peas, bamboo shoots, bok choy, mushrooms, celery, and water chestnuts; stir-fry for 10 seconds longer.
2. Add chicken stock and bring to a boil. Cover and simmer about 1 minute.
3. Mix cornstarch with cold water. Stir cornstarch mixture into chicken mixture, stirring constantly until sauce thickens. Serve immediately with white rice.

Chicken Teriyaki

Serves 4

¾ cup soy sauce
¼ cup sugar
¼ cup sherry
2 teaspoons grated fresh ginger
  or ¼ teaspoon powdered
  ginger
1 large clove garlic, peeled and
  crushed
3 pounds chicken pieces

1. Mix soy sauce, sugar, sherry, ginger, and garlic together; pour over chicken. Cover and refrigerate for several hours, turning occasionally.
2. Preheat oven to 450 degrees.

3. Drain chicken, reserving marinade. Place chicken, skin side down, in greased baking pan. Bake for 15 minutes. Turn chicken over and bake for 15 minutes longer.
4. Place reserved marinade in saucepan and bring to a boil; boil for several minutes.
5. Reduce oven temperature to 350 degrees. Pour off and reserve liquid in pan. Continue baking for approximately 30 minutes, or until chicken is tender, brushing occasionally with marinade.
6. Broil, if desired, about 6 inches from heat until well browned. Serve immediately.

Egg Foo Yung

Serves 4

1 small onion, cut into strips
½ cup sliced cooked chicken
¼ cup sliced canned water
  chestnuts, drained
3 scallions, thinly sliced
2 tablespoons soy sauce
3 large mushrooms, sliced
2 eggs, slightly beaten
2 tablespoons vegetable oil
1 cup bean sprouts
1 tomato, sliced
2 teaspoons sugar
1½ teaspoons cornstarch
¾ cup water

1. Combine onion, chicken, water chestnuts, scallions, 1 tablespoon soy sauce, mushrooms, and eggs in bowl; mix together lightly.

2. Heat 1 tablespoon oil in small, heavy frying pan. Spoon about ¼ of egg mixture into pan. Spread ¼ of sprouts and tomato slices over egg mixture. Sprinkle with ⅛ teaspoon sugar. Cook until nicely browned on underside, about 3 minutes. Carefully turn with spatula and brown on other side. Cook until edges are a little crisp. Remove from pan and keep warm while cooking other egg cakes.
3. Adding more oil to pan as needed, cook remaining 3 cakes, following above instructions.
4. While egg foo yung is cooking, mix cornstarch and 1½ teaspoons sugar together in small saucepan. Gradually add water, blending until smooth. Heat to boiling. Add 1 tablespoon soy sauce and simmer for 1 minute. Serve hot sauce on egg foo yung.

Chicken Balls in Oyster Sauce

Serves 4

2 boneless chicken breasts,
  skinned and finely chopped
2 scallions, finely chopped
1 teaspoon salt
1 tablespoon cornstarch
1 tablespoon sherry
2 tablespoons water
Oil for deep-frying
½ cup thinly sliced onions
1 teaspoon sugar
½ teaspoon chopped fresh ginger
  or ⅛ teaspoon powdered ginger
2 tablespoons oyster sauce
¼ cup chicken broth
Freshly ground black pepper to
  taste

1. Mix chicken, scallions, salt, cornstarch, sherry, and water together. Shape into small balls. Heat oil in frying pan; fry balls until well browned on all sides. Drain on paper towels. Pour off oil.
2. Place onion, sugar, ginger, oyster sauce, and chicken broth in saucepan. Cook, stirring constantly, over low heat for 5 minutes. Sprinkle with pepper.
3. Place chicken balls in serving dish, and serve with oyster sauce.

Chinese Lemon Chicken

Serves 4

1 (3-pound) chicken
1½ teaspoons salt
2 tablespoons soy sauce
2 tablespoons brandy
5 tablespoons safflower oil
½ teaspoon powdered ginger
1 cup chicken broth
¼ cup lemon juice
½ teaspoon sugar

1. Rub inside of chicken with 1 teaspoon salt. Rub outside with soy sauce. Place in deep bowl and pour brandy on top. Marinate, refrigerated, for 6 hours, turning chicken frequently.
2. Drain chicken. Place marinade in saucepan and bring to a boil; set aside. Heat oil and ginger in wok over medium-high heat. Brown chicken on all sides. Reduce heat to low and add marinade, chicken broth, lemon juice, sugar, and remaining salt. Cover and simmer for 25 minutes, or until chicken is tender.
3. Place chicken on serving platter, cut into pieces, and pour cooking juices over chicken.

Oriental Chicken

Serves 4

½ cup slivered almonds
3 tablespoons peanut oil
¾ cup chopped onion
4 boneless chicken breasts, thinly sliced
2 (6-ounce) cans sliced bamboo shoots, drained
1 cup sliced water chestnuts, drained
1 cucumber, unpeeled and thinly sliced
½ cup chicken stock
2 teaspoons sherry
¼ teaspoon ground ginger
1 teaspoon soy sauce
½ teaspoon cornstarch
1 tablespoon cold water
Salt and pepper to taste

1. Preheat oven to 400 degrees. Place almonds on baking sheet and toast for 10 minutes, or until browned. Watch closely to avoid burning. Set aside.
2. Pour oil into large frying pan or wok; heat to medium-high heat. Add onion and cook until translucent. Remove onion from pan. Add chicken to pan and toss gently for 1 minute. Add bamboo shoots and water chestnuts; toss gently for 1 minute. Add cucumber; cook for 1 minute. Combine stock, sherry, ginger, and soy sauce. Add to pan and cook for 1 minute.
3. Combine cornstarch and water in small dish. Stir slowly into hot mixture. Season with salt and pepper. Cook, stirring constantly, until liquid thickens. Return onions to pan and reheat. Sprinkle chicken with almonds.

Oriental Chicken with Vegetables

Serves 4

¼ cup soy sauce
¼ cup chicken broth
2 whole boneless chicken breasts, skinned and cut into bite-size pieces
¼ cup peanut oil
1 clove garlic, peeled and minced
2 small yellow squash, thinly sliced
1 medium zucchini, thinly sliced
1½ cups snow-pea pods, fresh or frozen
½ pound sliced mushrooms

1. Mix soy sauce with chicken broth in shallow bowl. Pour over chicken and marinate for at least 1 hour. Heat 2 tablespoons oil in wok until sizzling. Add garlic and stir-fry for 2 minutes. Drain chicken. Add to wok and cook, stirring constantly, for 2 minutes. Remove from wok and keep warm.
2. Add 2 tablespoons oil to wok; heat. Add squash and zucchini. Stir-fry for 1 minute, then push to one side. Add pea pods and mushrooms; stir-fry for 1 minute. Add chicken and soy sauce mixture. Cover and simmer for 5 minutes, or until vegetables are crisp-tender. Serve with boiled rice.

Bean Sprouts with Chicken

Serves 5 to 6

1½ pounds boneless chicken breasts, shredded
2½ teaspoons rice wine or sherry
1½ teaspoons salt
1 egg white
1 tablespoon cornstarch
Oil for deep-frying
1 cup fresh bean sprouts
½ teaspoon sesame oil
1 teaspoon cornstarch
1 teaspoon water

1. Mix chicken with 1½ teaspoons wine or sherry, salt, and egg white. Coat with 1 tablespoon cornstarch. Deep-fry chicken in hot oil in wok or deep skillet. Remove from oil; drain.
2. Discard all but 1 tablespoon oil in pan. Stir-fry bean sprouts for 1 minute. Add chicken, remaining wine or sherry, and sesame oil. Mix cornstarch with water to form paste. Add to pan, stirring constantly, until sauce thickens. Continue stirring until all ingredients are thoroughly heated. Remove from heat, and serve.

Chicken with Dates

Serves 4

1 (3-pound) chicken, cut into serving pieces
Salt and pepper to taste
Pinch of curry powder
2 tablespoons oil
1 medium onion, chopped
2 green pepper, seeded and cut into thin strips
1 cup beef bouillon
½ pound rice
1 teaspoon cornstarch
12 dates, pitted and cut into halves
1 cup plain yogurt
3 tablespoons toasted sliced almonds

1. Remove all bones from chicken except wing and leg bones. Rub chicken with salt, pepper, and curry powder. Heat oil in heavy skillet. Add

chicken and cook until golden brown on all sides. Add onion and cook until golden brown. Add green pepper and bouillon. Simmer for 30 minutes.

2. Cook rice following package directions, until just tender.

3. Remove chicken from sauce; keep warm. Strain sauce. Blend cornstarch with small amount of cold water to form paste. Slowly stir cornstarch mixture into sauce. Cook, stirring constantly, until sauce is thick and bubbling. Add dates.

4. Beat yogurt with fork, then stir into sauce. Heat thoroughly, but do not boil. Spoon rice onto platter; arrange chicken on top. Pour sauce over chicken and top with almonds.

Chicken Velvet

Serves 2

2 boneless chicken breasts, skinned and minced
2 teaspoons cornstarch
¼ cup cold water
Pinch of salt
3 egg whites, beaten until stiff peaks form
Oil for deep-frying
½ cup halved snow-pea pods
1 tablespoon oil

Sauce

1 teaspoon cornstarch
1 teaspoon cold water
½ cup chicken broth
1 tablespoon sherry
1 tablespoon vegetable oil

1. Mix chicken with cornstarch, water, and salt. Fold egg whites into mixture. Drop by teaspoonfuls into hot oil; cook until lightly browned. Drain on paper towels.

2. Saute pea pods in 1 tablespoon oil for 1 minute.

3. To make sauce, mix cornstarch with cold water in small saucepan until smooth. Add chicken broth, sherry, and oil. Bring to a boil. Add chicken and pea pods. Bring to a boil again, then remove from heat and serve.

Chicken with Walnuts

Serves 4

1 pound boneless chicken breasts, skinned and cut into 1-inch cubes
1 teaspoon salt
1 teaspoon sugar
1 tablespoon soy sauce
3 tablespoons sherry
2 tablespoons cornstarch
1 egg, beaten
½ cup peanut oil
1 cup walnuts
2 teaspoons minced fresh ginger or ⅛ teaspoon powdered ginger
3 cloves garlic, peeled and minced
½ cup boiling water
1 cup sliced bamboo shoots, drained

1. Combine chicken, salt, sugar, soy sauce, and sherry in bowl; mix well. Let stand for 30 minutes, then drain, reserving marinade. Dip chicken pieces into cornstarch, then into egg.

2. Heat oil in wok or deep skillet; brown walnuts. Remove walnuts from pan and pour off all but 2 tablespoons oil. Brown chicken, ginger, and garlic. Add water, bamboo shoots, and marinade. Cover and cook over low heat for 10 minutes. Add walnuts, stirring until well mixed. Reheat briefly, then serve.

Kang Pao Chicken

Serves 2 or 3

12 ounces boneless chicken breast, skinned and cut into ½-inch squares
1 egg white
2 teaspoons cornstarch
2 tablespoons brown bean sauce
1 tablespoon hoisin sauce
2 teaspoons sherry
1 teaspoon sugar
1 tablespoon white rice-wine vinegar
2 tablespoons water
2 teaspoons garlic, peeled and minced
1 cup peanut oil
1½ teaspoons crushed red pepper
½ cup roasted peanuts

1. Combine chicken with egg white and cornstarch in bowl. Mash bean sauce in separate bowl. Add hoisin sauce, sherry, sugar, vinegar, water, and garlic to bean sauce.

2. Heat wok over high heat. Add oil. When oil is very hot, add chicken and stir-fry fro 30 seconds, or until chicken changes color. Remove from wok and set aside. Drain off all but 2 tablespoons oil

3. Reheat wok. When oil is very hot, add red pepper. Stir for 25 seconds, or until pepper darkens. Add chicken, bean-sauce mixture, and peanuts to wok. Stir-fry for 1 minute, or until heated thoroughly.

Cashew Chicken

Serves 4

2 tablespoons oil
½ teaspoon salt
1 cup sliced uncooked chicken breast meat
¾ cup snow-pea pods
½ cup bamboo shoots, drained
½ cup sliced mushrooms
1 cup chicken broth
½ cup cashews
¼ teaspoon sugar
½ teaspoon cornstarch
1 teaspoon water

1. Heat wok over high heat. Add oil and swirl around until wok is coated. Sprinkle in salt. Add chicken and stir-fry for 2 minutes. Add pea pods, bamboo shoots, mushrooms, and chicken broth. Cover and cook for 2 minutes.

2. Carefully stir in nuts and sugar. Mix cornstarch with water to form paste. Add cornstarch mixture to chicken and cook, stirring constantly, until sauce thickens. Remove from heat, and serve.

Chicken Go Wan

Serves 4 to 6

2 boneless chicken breasts,
  skinned and cut into
  ¹/₂-inch cubes
³/₄ cup soy sauce
2 cups long-grain rice
4¹/₂ cups chicken stock
1 cup sliced mushrooms

1. Combine chicken and soy sauce in mixing bowl; let stand for 1 to 2 hours.
2. Combine rice, stock, and mushrooms in Dutch oven; mix lightly. Spoon chicken and soy sauce on top. Cover and cook over low heat for 30 minutes, or until chicken and rice are tender. Remove from heat, and serve.

Oven Barbecued Chicken

Serves 4

¹/₄ cup soy sauce
2 cloves garlic, peeled and
  minced
2 teaspoons salt
¹/₄ teaspoon freshly ground
  black pepper
1 teaspoon five spices powder
1 teaspoon sugar
2 tablespoons oil
1 (4-pound) roasting chicken

1. Mix soy sauce, garlic, salt, pepper, five-spice, sugar, and oil together. Rub chicken inside and out with mixture. Let stand 1 hour.
2. Preheat oven to 425 degrees.
3. Place chicken on rack in shallow roasting pan. Roast for 2¹/₂ hours, or until chicken is tender and browned. Turn and baste often.
4. To serve, chicken can be cut into serving pieces, or meat can be taken off bones and cut into 1-inch s square pieces.

Japanese Fried Chicken

Serves 4

¹/₄ cup soy sauce
2 teaspoons mirin (or sherry
  mixed with 1 teaspoon sugar)
Juice of 1 lemon
Salt to taste
Paprika to taste
¹/₄ cup cornstarch
Oil for deep-frying
1 (2¹/₂- to 3-pound) chicken,
  cut into pieces

1. Mix soy sauce, mirin, lemon juice, salt, and paprika. Pour over chicken and marinate for at least 2 hours. Remove chicken from marinade; discard marinade. Sprinkle chicken with cornstarch until well coated.
2. Heat oil in wok or deep skillet over medium-high heat. Fry chicken for 15 to 20 minutes, or until chicken is nicely browned. Drain on paper towels, and serve.

Chicken Sukiyaki

Serves 3 to 4

2 cups chicken stock
1 cup sugar
1 cup soy sauce
1 pound boneless chicken breasts,
  skinned and cut into bite-size
  pieces
8 large mushrooms, sliced
3 carrots, sliced diagonally and
  parboiled
6 scallions, cut into 2-inch
  lengths

1. Place chicken stock, sugar, and soy sauce in wok or saucepan. Bring to a boil. Add chicken, then simmer for 12 minutes. Add remaining ingredients and simmer for 3 minutes longer.
2. Remove from heat, and serve with boiled rice.

Chicken with Fresh Coconut

Serves 4

¹/₂ cup ghee
1 large onion, sliced
2 cloves garlic, peeled and sliced
4 whole cardamoms
4 whole cloves
1-inch piece cinnamon stick
2 teaspoons garam masala
1 teaspoon turmeric
1 teaspoon chili powder
1 teaspoon salt
1 (3-pound) chicken, skinned,
  boned, and cut into 8 pieces
1 cup thinly sliced fresh coconut
1 tablespoon tomato paste
1¹/₄ cups water

1. Melt ghee in large skillet. Add onions and garlic; stir-fry until both are soft. Add spices and salt; stir-fry for 3 minutes more. Add chicken pieces and brown on both sides, about 10 minutes. Add coconut, tomato paste, and water.
2. Bring to a boil, stirring constantly. Lower heat, cover, and simmer for 45 minutes. When chicken is fork-tender, serve at once.

Fried Rice with Chicken

Serves 4 to 6

3 tablespoons vegetable oil
1 cup finely chopped cooked
  chicken
2 scallions, sliced
2 to 3 cups cold boiled rice
1 tablespoon soy sauce
¹/₄ teaspoon salt
2 eggs, beaten
2 tablespoons cooked peas

1. Heat oil in wok or frying pan. Add chicken and stir-fry for 2 minutes. Add scallions and rice; continue to stir-fry until rice is hot and golden brown. Add soy sauce and salt.
2. Make a well in rice; pour in eggs. Cook over high heat until eggs are set. Stir, then add peas; heat for 1 minute longer. Transfer to serving dish, and serve.

Sweet-and-Sour Chicken

Serves 4

2 tablespoons soy sauce
1 tablespoon sugar
¹/₂ teaspoon salt
1 tablespoon dry sherry
3 pounds boneless chicken
  breasts, cubed
1 egg yolk
2 tablespoons oil
2 onions, sliced
2 scallions, chopped
1 red pepper, seeded and sliced
¹/₂ cup sliced mushrooms
1 medium cucumber; cut into
  strips
1 (15-ounce) can pineapple
  chunks, drained, liquid
  reserved
Oil for shallow frying
1 tablespoon cornstarch
¹/₄ cup vinegar
1 tablespoon tomato sauce
Salt and pepper to taste

1. Combine soy sauce, sugar, salt, sherry, and egg yolk in large bowl. Add chicken cubes and marinate for 1 hour.
2. Heat 2 tablespoons oil in wok or frying pan. Add onions and cook until translucent. Add scallions, red pepper, and mushrooms; stir-fry for 5 minutes more. Add cucumber strips and pineapple chunks. Stir-fry for 2 minutes. Remove from heat.
3. Drain chicken, reserving marinade. Heat oil in wok or frying pan to depth of ¹/₂ inch. Add chicken and fry until golden brown. Drain well, then add chicken to vegetables.
4. Blend cornstarch with reserved pineapple liquid. Add vinegar and tomato sauce. Combine mixture and reserved marinade in saucepan. Bring to a boil, stirring constantly. Continue to boil for 5 minutes, stirring. Season with salt and pepper.
5. Pour sauce over chicken and vegetables; stir to coat evenly. Reheat gently, then serve.

Sherried Orange Chicken

Serves 4

2 tablespoons flour
¹/₂ teaspoon paprika
¹/₂ teaspoon salt
¹/₂ teaspoon ginger
4 chicken breasts, halved
¹/₄ cup butter
2 tablespoons oil
1 cup orange juice
¹/₃ cup dry sherry
1 tablespoon cornstarch
1 tablespoon water
4 scallions, chopped
¹/₄ cup slivered almonds,
  optional

1. Combine flour, paprika, ¹/₂ teaspoon salt, and ¹/₄ teaspoon ginger. Coat chicken lightly with mixture. Heat 2 tablespoons butter and oil in large frying pan. Add chicken and saute until golden brown. Add orange juice, sherry, and remaining ginger to pan. Cover and simmer for 25 to 30 minutes, or until chicken is tender. Remove chicken to heated serving plate.
2. Combine cornstarch and water; add to pan. Heat, stirring constantly, until sauce thickens slightly. Add scallions, then pour sauce over chicken.
3. If desired, saute almonds in remaining butter until lightly browned; drain. Sprinkle almonds over chicken, and serve at once.

Tomato-Pineapple Chicken

Serves 4 to 6

2 (3-pound) chickens, cut into
  serving pieces
¹/₃ cup flour, seasoned with salt
  and pepper
¹/₄ cup butter
1 green pepper, seeded and
  thinly sliced
1 onion, chopped
2 (10¹/₂-ounce) cans condensed
  tomato soup

1 (3-ounce) can tomato paste
1 (15-ounce) can pineapple
  chunks, undrained
³/₄ cup water or chicken stock
1 tablespoon soy sauce

1. Dredge chicken pieces in seasoned flour. Heat butter in large frying pan. Brown chicken, a few pieces at a time. Add green pepper, onion, tomato soup, tomato paste, pineapple and its liquid, water, and soy sauce. Blend well. Bring to a boil, then cover and simmer for 40 to 45 minutes, or until chicken is tender.
2. Place chicken pieces and sauce in serving dish. Serve at once.

Chicken with Chinese Mushrooms

Serves 4

4 dried black Chinese mushrooms
2 tablespoons soy sauce
1 tablespoon cornstarch
4 boneless chicken breasts,
  skinned and cubed
1 tablespoon vegetable oil
1 clove garlic, peeled and halved
  lengthwise
3 (¹/₈-inch thick) slices fresh
  ginger or ¹/₂ teaspoon powdered
  ginger
¹/₂ pound fresh mushrooms,
  quartered
2 tablespoons hoisin sauce

1. Soak Chinese mushrooms in warm water to cover for 30 minutes. Drain and dice. Set aside.
2. Combine soy sauce and cornstarch. Pour mixture over chicken and marinate for ¹/₂ hour.
3. Heat oil in wok or frying pan. Brown garlic and ginger in hot oil for 2 to 3 minutes. Remove from pan, and discard. Add both types of mushrooms to pan; stir-fry for 2 minutes. Remove mushrooms and set aside.
4. Stir-fry chicken cubes for 3 to 4 minutes, or until cooked thoroughly. Stir in hoisin sauce. Return mushrooms to pan and cook until all ingredients are hot. Remove from pan, and serve.

Japanese Chicken with Sesame Seeds

Serves 2

2 boneless chicken breasts,
  cut into pieces
2 tablespoons rice wine or
  sherry
¹/₂ teaspoon salt
¹/₂ teaspoon oil
2 teaspoons sesame seeds

1. Sprinkle chicken with rice wine or sherry and salt. Marinate for 30 minutes. Drain; discard marinade.
2. Heat oil in frying pan. Cook chicken until browned on both sides and thoroughly cooked. Transfer chicken to heated platter.
3. Add sesame seeds to frying pan and cook, stirring, just until heated. Sprinkle sesame seeds over chicken, and serve.

Teriyaki Chicken Breasts

Serves 2 to 3

2 boneless chicken breasts,
  skinned and halved
¹/₄ cup oil
¹/₄ cup soy sauce
¹/₄ cup sugar
¹/₂ teaspoon grated fresh ginger
  or ¹/₄ teaspoon powdered
  ginger

1. Place chicken breasts in boiling water to cover and parboil for 30 seconds. Drain.
2. Heat oil in frying pan over medium-high heat. Add chicken and cook until browned on both sides. Pour off oil. Add soy sauce, sugar, and ginger to pan with chicken. Cover and simmer until sauce has consistency of syrup. Serve chicken with rice; spoon sauce on top.

Japanese Chicken in Cream Sauce

Serves 4

1¹/₂ cups flour
Salt and pepper to taste
1 (2¹/₂- to 3-pound) chicken,
  cut into serving pieces
2 eggs, beaten
2 tablespoons milk
¹/₂ cup sesame seeds
Peanut oil for deep-frying

Cream Sauce

¹/₄ cup butter, melted
¹/₄ cup flour
¹/₂ cup half-and-half
1 cup chicken stock
¹/₂ cup heavy whipping cream
¹/₂ teaspoon salt, optional

1. Season ¹/₂ cup flour with salt and pepper. Lightly coat chicken with flour mixture. Beat eggs with milk.
2. Mix 1 cup flour, sesame seeds, salt, and pepper together. Dip chicken in egg mixture, then roll in sesame-seed mixture. Heat oil in frying pan. Fry chicken until browned and cooked thoroughly.
3. To prepare sauce, blend butter and flour together over low heat, stirring constantly. Mix half-and-half, stock, and cream together. Gradually add cream mixture to butter and flour; cook, stirring constantly, until sauce is smooth. Stir in salt, if desired. Serve sauce separately with chicken.

Chicken Sate

Serves 4

1 tablespoon dark soy sauce
2 shallots, peeled and finely
  sliced
1 clove garlic, peeled and
  crushed
Pinch of chili powder
1 tablespoon lemon juice
2 pounds boneless chicken
  breasts, skinned and cut into
  1-inch cubes

1. Mix soy sauce, shallots, garlic, chili powder, and lemon juice together in large bowl. Add chicken cubes and

marinate for at least 1 hour.
2. Preheat broiler or heat coals in outdoor grill.
3. Divide chicken cubes onto skewers. Broil or grill for 5 to 8 minutes; turn skewers so chicken is cooked on all sides.
Remove from heat, and serve hot.

Chicken Tarts

Serves 4

¹/₄ cup butter
1 medium onion, chopped
1 clove garlic, peeled and crushed
1 tart apple, peeled, cored, and
  diced
1 teaspoon tomato paste
1 heaping tablespoon flour
1 cup chicken broth
1 tablespoon grated coconut
1 teaspoon curry
Salt to taste
¹/₄ cup oil
4 boneless chicken breasts,
  skinned and cut into bite-size
  pieces
2 tablespoons mango chutney
12 small puff pastry shells
1 sweet apple, peeled, cored,
  and cut into 8 slices

1. Heat 3 tablespoons butter in frying pan. Add onion and garlic; saute for 5 minutes. Add diced apple, then stir in tomato paste. Sprinkle with flour. Cook, stirring constantly, for 3 minutes. Gradually add broth, stirring constantly until well mixed. Simmer gently for 20 minutes. Add coconut, curry, and salt.
2. While sauce is simmering, heat oil in frying pan over medium-high heat. Add chicken and cook for 6 minutes, until chicken is golden brown. Add chicken and chutney to sauce. Remove from heat and keep warm.
3. Preheat oven to 350 degrees.
4. Place pastry tarts on baking sheet; bake for 5 minutes, until hot and crisp. Fry apple slices in remaining butter for 2 minutes on each side, until golden brown.
5. Fill baked tarts with chicken mixture. Cover with apple slices, and serve immediately.

Chicken with Coconut Milk Gravy

Serves 4

2¹/₂ teaspoons grated fresh ginger
    or 1 teaspoon powdered ginger
2 medium onions, chopped
Rind of 1 lemon, grated
6 fresh red chilies, seeded
1 (3-pound) chicken, cut into
    serving pieces
1 teaspoon turmeric
3 tablespoons oil
3 cups coconut milk
3 fresh basil leaves,
    optional
2 teaspoons salt

1. Mix ginger, onions, lemon rind, and chilies together to make paste; add a little oil if needed. Thoroughly coat chicken with turmeric.
2. Heat oil in heavy skillet. Add paste and cook over medium heat for 15 minutes, stirring constantly. Add chicken and fry for 10 minutes more. Add coconut milk, basil leaves if desired, and salt. Simmer, uncovered, for 20 minutes, or until chicken is tender. Serve at once.

Korean Chicken Stew

Serves 4 to 6

1 (3-pound) chicken, cut into
    small serving pieces
¹/₄ cup light soy sauce
2 tablespoons sesame oil
1 tablespoon finely chopped
    garlic
¹/₂ teaspoon chili powder or
    cayenne pepper
3 scallions, finely chopped
¹/₄ teaspoon salt

1. Place chicken in heavy pan with all other ingredients. Mix well so that chicken is covered with seasonings. Let stand for 2 hours at room temperature.
2. Place chicken and marinating mixture in saucepan. Cover and cook over low heat for 20 minutes, or until chicken is tender. Serve with boiled rice.

Korean Chicken with Vegetables

Serves 4

1 cup flour
2 eggs, well beaten
About 2 tablespoons water
1 pound boneless chicken breasts,
    cut into 1-inch cubes
Vegetable oil for deep-frying
2 medium carrots, sliced
2 medium potatoes, peeled and
    cubed
¹/₂ small red pepper, seeded and
    thinly sliced
1 medium onion, chopped
¹/₂ small green pepper, seeded
    and thinly sliced

Sauce

2 tablespoons soy sauce
2 tablespoons water
1 tablespoon sugar
2 teaspoons crushed fresh
    ginger or 1 teaspoon
    powdered ginger
2 teaspoons garlic, peeled and
    crushed
2 tablespoons sake
1 tablespoon sesame oil
2 scallions, sliced
¹/₂ teaspoon salt

1. Combine flour and egg in bowl. Add water, stirring constantly until batter is smooth. Coat each piece of chicken in batter. Heat oil in deep frying pan; fry chicken until golden brown. Drain on paper towels.
2. Place carrots and potatoes in boiling water to cover and cook for 3 minutes. Drain and dry thoroughly. Add carrots and potatoes to oil and fry for 5 minutes. Drain on paper towels.
3. Place all sauce ingredients in saucepan; bring to a boil, then remove from heat.
4. Transfer 2 tablespoons oil to different frying pan; heat over low heat. Add chicken, carrots, potatoes, peppers, and onions. Stir-fry for 1 minute. Increase heat to medium; add sauce, stirring constantly. When all ingredients are well covered with sauce, remove from heat and serve at once.

Chicken with Ginger

Serves 4

4 boneless chicken breasts,
    cut into small pieces
Salt to taste
2 tablespoons oil
¹/₂ cup hot water
1 slice fresh ginger
1 clove garlic, peeled and
    minced
1 medium onion, sliced

1. Sprinkle chicken liberally with salt. Heat 1 tablespoon oil in frying pan. Add chicken and cook until browned. Add ¹/₄ cup hot water and simmer until chicken is tender.
2. Heat 1 tablespoon oil in separate pan. Add ginger and stir-fry for 1 minute. Remove from pan and set aside. Add garlic and onion to pan; stir-fry for 1 minute more. Remove from pan and add to ginger.
3. Place ginger, garlic, and onion in pan with chicken. Add ¹/₄ cup hot water and simmer for 10 minutes. Remove from heat, and serve hot.

Chicken Tinola

Serves 4 to 6

1 tablespoon butter
1 onion, sliced
2 cloves garlic, peeled and crushed
1 tablespoon grated fresh ginger
    or 1 teaspoon powdered ginger
1 (3-pound) chicken, cut into
    serving pieces
2 cups water
1 papaya, peeled and sliced
Pepper to taste

1. Melt butter in heavy skillet. Add onion, garlic, and ginger; saute for 5 minutes. Add chicken and brown on all sides. Add water; cover pan and simmer gently until chicken is tender, about 40 minutes.
2. Add papaya; simmer for 10 minutes more. Season with pepper, and serve.

Chicken Fritada

Serves 4 to 6

2 tablespoons butter
5 cloves garlic, peeled and
 crushed
1 large onion, finely sliced
1 (3-pound) chicken, cut into
 serving pieces
2 ripe tomatoes, diced
1½ teaspoons salt
½ teaspoon pepper
1½ cups hot chicken stock
1 pound new potatoes
1 red pepper, seeded and cut
 into strips
1 green pepper, seeded and cut
 into strips

1. Heat butter in large skillet. Add
garlic and onion; saute for 5 minutes.
Add chicken pieces and brown on both
sides. Add tomatoes, salt, pepper, and
stock. Cover and cook over medium
heat for 20 minutes.
2. Add potatoes and peppers;
continue to cook over medium heat for
25 minutes, until potatoes are soft.
Serve at once, piping hot.

Burmese Chicken Curry

Serves 4 to 6

2 teaspoons curry powder
2 tablespoons soy sauce
Pinch of saffron
2 (2½-pound) chickens, cut into
 serving pieces
2 large onions, finely chopped
½ teaspoons ground dried chili
 peppers
3 cloves garlic, peeled
¼ cup oil
2½ cups water
1 teaspoon cinnamon
1 teaspoon salt
3 bay leaves

1. Combine curry powder, soy sauce,
and saffron. Rub chicken with curry
mixture. Set aside.
2. Pound onions, chili pepper, and
garlic together. Heat oil in large skillet;
brown onion mixture. Add chicken,

turning to ensure that each piece is
seasoned with onion mixture.
3. Add remaining ingredients. Cover
and simmer for 1 hour. When chicken
is tender, remove from heat and
serve.

Garlic Chicken

Serves 4

4 boneless chicken breasts,
 skinned
3 cloves garlic, peeled and crushed
1 tablespoon pepper
2 tablespoons soy sauce
1 teaspoon sugar
1 teaspoon salt
1 teaspoon sesame oil
About 5 tablespoons vegetable oil

1. With sharp knife, make cuts in
surface of chicken breasts on both
sides. Mix garlic, pepper, soy sauce,
sugar, salt, and sesame oil in bowl.
Rub mixture into chicken breasts;
marinate for at least 2 hours.
2. Heat about 5 tablespoons oil in wok
or frying pan. When hot, add 2 pieces
of chicken; cook for 4 minutes per
side, until both sides are golden
brown. Remove from pan and drain on
paper towels. Follow same procedure
with remaining chicken. Add more oil
if needed.
3. Cut each piece of cooked chicken in
half with sharp knife. Return to skillet
and cook until cut edges are no longer
pink. Serve at once.

Indonesian Skewered Chicken

Serves 6

½ cup chopped walnuts
Juice of 1 lemon
1 cup hot chicken broth
1 teaspoon salt
Pinch of pepper
1 onion, diced
1 clove garlic, peeled and crushed
2 tablespoons oil
4 boneless chicken breasts,
 skinned and cut into ½-inch
 wide strips
Parsley sprigs for garnish

1. Mix walnuts, lemon juice, chicken
broth, salt, and pepper in bowl. Add
onion, garlic, and oil, blending well.
Set aside ⅓ of marinade for later use.
Place chicken strips in remaining
marinade; marinate for at least 3
hours.
2. Preheat broiler.
3. Drain chicken and place meat on 4
skewers. Put skewers on flat pan.
Broil for 20 minutes, turning once.
Remove chicken from skewers and
place on heated platter. Garnish with
parsley, and serve hot.

Chicken Kai Yang

Serves 4 to 6

6 cloves garlic, peeled
2 teaspoons salt
2 tablespoons peppercorns
1 tablespoon coriander
2 tablespoons lemon juice
1 (3-pound) chicken, cut into
 serving pieces

1. Crush garlic with salt. Coarsely
crush peppercorns using mortar and
pestle or blender. Mix coriander and
lemon juice together; rub into chicken
pieces. Let stand for at least 1 hour;
refrigerate overnight if possible.
2. Preheat broiler or heat coals on
outside grill. Broil or grill chicken
pieces for 30 minutes, or until chicken
is tender and skin crisp.

Chicken in Nectar

Serves 4

1 package French onion soup
 mix
2 cups canned apricot nectar
1 teaspoon salt
Pinch of pepper
3 pounds chicken pieces

1. Preheat oven to 400 degrees.
2. Combine onion soup mix, apricot
nectar, salt, and pepper in bowl. Stir
until well blended. Place chicken in
casserole dish. Pour sauce on top.
Cover and bake for 1 hour. Remove
cover and bake for 30 minutes more,
or until chicken is very tender.

Chicken Florentine au Gratin

Serves 4

1 package frozen spinach leaves, thawed and well drained
2 boneless chicken breasts, skinned and cut into pieces
1/2 teaspoon salt
Pinch of nutmeg
1 1/2 tablespoons butter
3 tablespoons wheat flour
1 2/3 cups chicken bouillon
Freshly ground pepper to taste
1 egg yolk
2/3 cup light cream
3/4 cup grated Parmesan cheese

1. Preheat oven to 425 degrees.
2. Line ovenproof dish with spinach leaves. Place breast pieces on top of spinach. Season with salt and nutmeg.
3. Melt butter in saucepan over low heat. Add flour, blending well. Add bouillon; cook, stirring constantly, over medium-high heat until sauce boils. Reduce heat to low and simmer for 3 minutes. Season with pepper. Remove saucepan from heat.
4. Stir egg yolk into cream, then stir into saucepan. Add cheese; pour sauce over chicken and spinach. Bake for 15 minutes. Serve with boiled rice or potatoes.

Chicken and Shrimp Marengo

Serves 8 to 10

1/2 cup olive oil
2 pounds boneless chicken breasts, cut into bite-size pieces
1 onion, sliced
1 clove garlic, peeled and crushed
2 cups chicken broth
2 (16-ounce) cans Italian-style tomatoes
3/4 cup diced celery
1 bay leaf
2 tablespoons minced parsley
3/4 teaspoon thyme
3/4 teaspoon basil
3/4 teaspoon tarragon
1/4 cup dry sherry
Salt and pepper to taste
2 cups sliced mushrooms
1 cup pearl onions
1 pound cooked shrimp, shelled and deveined
2 tablespoons brandy

1. Heat olive oil in heavy skillet. Add chicken, sliced onion, and garlic; saute until browned. Remove from pan and set aside.
2. Combine broth, tomatoes, celery, and bay leaf in saucepan. Bring to a boil; cover and simmer for 30 minutes. Add parsley, herbs, sherry, salt, and pepper. Simmer for 5 minutes more. Add mushrooms, pearl onions, chicken mixture, shrimp, and brandy. Simmer until thickened.
3. Preheat oven to 350 degrees.
4. Transfer chicken and shrimp mixture to casserole dish. Bake for 20 to 30 minutes. Serve over boiled rice. This tastes even better if refrigerated overnight and reheated the next day.

Chicken Piccata

Serves 4

4 boneless chicken breasts, skinned and halved
1/2 cup flour, seasoned with pepper
2 tablespoons butter
1/4 cup olive oil
6 tablespoons fresh lemon juice
1 large lemon, very thinly sliced
3 tablespoons finely chopped parsley

1. Dust chicken breasts lightly with seasoned flour. Heat butter and oil in 2 large frying pans. Add half the chicken breasts to each pan. Cook quickly over high heat for 4 to 5 minutes, until chicken is golden brown on both sides. Transfer chicken to warm platter.
2. Add lemon juice to one of the frying pans. Stir to deglaze pan and remove bits from bottom. Pour sauce over chicken breasts. Garnish with lemon slices, and serve.

Parmesan Chicken

Serves 4

2 boneless chicken breasts, skinned and halved
2/3 cup flour
1 egg, lightly beaten
2/3 cup seasoned bread crumbs
1 1/2 tablespoons olive oil
1/2 cup marinara sauce
4 slices mozzarella cheese
1 tablespoon grated Parmesan cheese
1/2 teaspoon oregano

1. Roll chicken breasts in flour. Dip in egg, then coat with bread crumbs. Heat oil in large frying pan over medium-high heat. Add chicken to pan; cook for 3 minutes per side, or until golden brown and cooked thoroughly. Remove from heat.
2. Preheat broiler.
3. Place cooked chicken in shallow baking pan. Spoon 2 tablespoons marinara sauce over each chicken piece. Cover with slice of mozzarella cheese, then sprinkle each chicken piece with Parmesan cheese and 1/8 teaspoon oregano.
4. Broil chicken for 2 minutes, or until cheese starts bubbling. Remove from heat, and serve.

Soy Sauce Duck

Serves 3 to 4

1 (3-pound) duck
1/2 teaspoon five spices
1/2 teaspoon salt
3 scallions, sliced
4 slices fresh ginger or 1 teaspoon powdered ginger
1/4 cup soy sauce
2 tablespoons sherry

1. Place duck in Dutch oven, adding enough water to half cover. Cover pan and simmer for 1 hour. Remove duck from pot, reserving broth. Skim grease from top of broth.
2. Rub five spices and salt over duck. Combine scallions and ginger; place in cavity of duck. Return duck to Dutch oven.
3. Add soy sauce, sherry, and 4 cups reserved broth to duck. Boil for 30 minutes, or until duck is tender. Remove from pot, slice, and serve.

Roasted Duck with Orange Peel

Serves 4

2 to 3 slices orange peel, very finely chopped
1 tablespoon yellow bean sauce, mashed
5 slices fresh ginger, finely chopped, or 1 teaspoon powdered ginger
1 clove garlic, peeled and finely chopped
2 tablespoons soy sauce
1 teaspoon sugar
2 tablespoons whiskey
1 teaspoon salt
1 (4-pound) duck

1. Mix orange peel, bean sauce, ginger, garlic, soy sauce, sugar, whiskey, and salt together with fork. Rub duck thoroughly with mixture, inside and out.
2. Place duck in Dutch oven; cook for 2 minutes on each side.
3. Preheat oven to 450 degrees.
4. Line roasting pan with foil. Place duck in pan and roast for 20 minutes. Turn over and roast for 20 minutes longer. Reduce heat to 325 degrees. Roast each side for 30 minutes more. Transfer hot duck to platter, slice, and serve.

Kung Bao Chicken Ding

Serves 4

2 boneless chicken breasts, skinned and diced
1 egg white
2 teaspoons cornstarch
1 tablespoon soy bean sauce
1 teaspoon sugar
2 teaspoons light soy sauce
2 teaspoons sherry
2 teaspoons vinegar
¼ teaspoon sesame oil
¼ cup peanut oil
1 to 2 scallions, chopped
3 slices fresh ginger, chopped, or ½ teaspoon powdered ginger
2 to 3 dried hot red peppers or ¼ teaspoon red pepper flakes
½ cup water chestnuts, optional

1. Mix chicken with egg white and cornstarch. Combine soy bean sauce, sugar, soy sauce, sherry, vinegar, and sesame oil.
2. Heat oil in frying pan or wok. Stir-fry chicken for 2 minutes; remove from pan. Add scallions, ginger, red peppers, and water chestnuts to pan. Stir-fry for 1 minute. Return chicken to pan and stir-fry for 1 minute longer.
3. Add soy sauce mixture and cook, stirring, until well mixed and hot. Season with salt. Serve at once, with boiled rice.

Spicy Smoked Chicken

Serves 4

2 tablespoons sherry
2 teaspoons salt
1 (3-pound) roasting chicken
2 scallions, sliced
¼ teaspoon cinnamon
2 star anise
½ cup sugar
1 tablespoon molasses
3 tablespoons soy sauce
¼ teaspoon sesame oil
7 drops Tabasco sauce

1. Combine sherry and salt; rub chicken with mixture. Stuff cavity of chicken with scallions. Cover and refrigerate overnight.
2. Place chicken in steamer; steam over boiling water for 30 minutes. Remove from heat and let stand in steamer for 15 minutes longer.
3. Mix cinnamon, star anise, sugar, and molasses together.
4. Line Dutch oven with aluminum foil. Spread molasses mixture evenly over foil. Place rack in pan above molasses mixture. Put steamed chicken on rack, cover, and cook over low heat for 10 to 15 minutes. Remove from heat; let cool. Cut chicken into bite-size pieces.
5. Mix soy sauce, sesame oil, and Tabasco sauce together. Brush chicken with mixture. Serve hot or cold.

Chicken in Oyster Sauce

Serves 4

3 tablespoons peanut oil
1 (2½-pound) chicken, cut into small serving pieces
1 scallion, cut into 1-inch pieces
4 slices fresh ginger or 1 teaspoon powdered ginger
¼ cup oyster sauce
Salt to taste

1. Heat oil in heavy skillet. Add chicken pieces, scallion, and ginger. Saute until golden brown.
2. Add oyster sauce to skillet. Cover and cook over low heat for 25 minutes, or until chicken is tender. Season with salt. Serve hot or cold.

Curried Chicken Cantonese

Serves 4

1 cup milk
½ cup shredded coconut
1 tablespoon flour
3 tablespoons peanut oil
1 medium onion, chopped
2 slices fresh ginger or ¼ teaspoon powdered ginger
2 teaspoons curry powder
2 cups chicken broth
1½ teaspoons salt
2 pounds boneless chicken breasts, cut into bite-size pieces

1. Combine milk and coconut in saucepan. Cook for 30 minutes over low heat, stirring occasionally; do not boil. Strain milk, then mix with flour, stirring until well blended.
2. Heat oil in frying pan. Add onion and ginger; stir-fry for 1 minute. Add curry powder and stir-fry for 2 minutes more. Add chicken broth and salt. Bring to a boil, then simmer for 5 minutes. Remove onion and ginger; discard.
3. Add chicken to pan and simmer for 30 minutes. Stir in milk-flour mixture. Cook, stirring constantly, until sauce thickens. Serve hot with boiled rice.

Chicken and Rice Medley

Serves 4

¼ cup butter
1 onion, finely chopped
½ cup chopped mushrooms
1 green pepper, seeded and
    chopped
1 (10½-ounce) can condensed
    chicken or mushroom soup
1 cup diced cooked chicken
Salt and pepper to taste
1 cup long-grain rice
1 tablespoon chopped parsley

1. Melt 3 tablespoons butter in frying pan. Add onion and saute until translucent. Add mushrooms and green pepper. Saute, stirring, for 2 to 3 minutes. Stir in soup and chicken. Bring to a boil, then simmer for 10 to 15 minutes. Season with salt and pepper.
2. While chicken is heating, cook rice according to package directions. Drain well, then stir in parsley and remaining tablespoon of butter.
3. To serve, arrange rice on serving platter; pile chicken mixture on top.

Chicken in Potato Nest

Serves 4

2 cups mashed potatoes
2 tablespoons butter
2 tablespoons flour
½ teaspoon freshly ground black
    pepper
1 cup chicken broth
¼ cup heavy whipping cream or
    half-and-half
1 (3-ounce) can sliced mushrooms,
    drained
2 cups diced cooked chicken
2 tablespoons grated Parmesan
    cheese

1. Preheat oven to 400 degrees.
2. Line greased 9-inch pie plate with mashed potatoes.
3. Melt butter in saucepan. Stir in flour and pepper. Add broth gradually, whisking until boiling. Add cream or half-and-half and mushrooms, whisking constantly; simmer for 3 or 4 minutes.
4. Put chicken into prepared pie plate. Pour sauce over chicken and sprinkle with Parmesan cheese. Bake 25 to 30 minutes.

Chicken and Ham Risotto

Serves 4

1 onion, finely chopped
3 tablespoons vegetable oil
1 cup long-grain rice
2 cups hot chicken broth
¼ teaspoon black pepper
¼ cup seedless raisins
1 stalk celery, chopped
1 cup diced cooked chicken
½ cup diced cooked ham
Salt to taste

1. Saute onion in oil until translucent. Add rice and cook over low heat for 5 minutes, stirring constantly.
2. Add hot chicken broth, pepper, raisins, and celery. Stir until boiling. Cover and simmer until rice is tender and most of the liquid absorbed, about 20 minutes.
3. Stir in chicken and ham, adjust seasonings, and heat through. Serve on heated platter.

Chicken Crisps

Serves 4

Cream Sauce

3 tablespoons butter
2 tablespoons flour
1 cup milk

Chicken

¼ cup chicken broth
8 mushrooms, sliced
2 cups chopped or diced
    cooked chicken
½ cup cooked peas
    or corn

Bread Squares

5 thick slices white bread
1 cup safflower oil
1 tablespoon butter
1 tablespoon chopped parsley

1. To make cream sauce, melt butter in saucepan. Whisk in flour. Gradually whisk in milk; when smooth, bring to a boil, stirring constantly. Boil 3 minutes, then cool slightly.
2. Heat broth in separate saucepan. Add mushrooms and cook for 3 to 4 minutes. Add chicken and cooked peas or corn. Add chicken mixture to cream sauce, season well, and heat thoroughly. Keep warm while preparing bread squares.
3. Remove crusts from bread slices. With small cookie cutter, cut 4 crescent-shaped pieces from fifth slice. Heat oil and 1 tablespoon butter in frying pan. When foaming, fry bread slices until golden brown on both sides. Also fry 4 small crescents. Drain on paper towels.
4. To serve, arrange fried squares on serving dish. Spoon hot chicken mixture onto squares and garnish with crescents and chopped parsley.

Deluxe Chicken Sandwich

Serves 3

1 tablespoon butter
1 tablespoon flour
¹/₂ cup chicken broth
¹/₄ cup light cream
1 cup cooked diced chicken
¹/₄ cup chopped walnuts
1 teaspoon onion juice
Pinch of paprika
Salt and pepper to taste
3 slices hot toast
Pimento-stuffed green olives,
  cut into rings

1. Melt butter in saucepan. Whisk in flour. Gradually whisk in broth. Add cream, chicken, and walnuts. Season with onion juice, paprika, salt, and pepper. Simmer until well heated.
2. Pile chicken mixture onto slices of toast. Garnish with olive rings. Serve immediately.

Chicken Club Sandwich

Serves 1

3 slices bread
Mayonnaise
Lettuce
Slices of chicken breast
Prepared mustard
2 slices bacon, fried until crisp
2 slices tomato
Sliced sweet gherkins for garnish

1. Remove crusts from bread. Toast bread, then spread first slice with a little mayonnaise. Cover with 1 or 2 lettuce leaves and slices of chicken. Spread a little more mayonnaise on the chicken and cover with second slice of toast.
2. Spread a very small amount of mustard on the toast, then a little mayonnaise. Cover with bacon and tomato slices.
3. Place third slice of toast on top and press down firmly. Serve at once, garnished with gherkin slices.

Chicken Casserole with Biscuit Topping

Serves 4

Filling

2 tablespoons vegetable oil
1 small onion, chopped
¹/₂ green pepper, seeded and finely
  chopped
²/₃ cup sliced mushrooms
2 tablespoons cornstarch
1¹/₂ cups milk
2 cups diced cooked chicken
Salt and pepper to taste

Biscuits

2 cups flour
1 teaspoon salt
2¹/₂ teaspoons baking powder
¹/₃ cup shortening
²/₃ cup milk

1. Heat oil in frying pan. Add onion, green pepper, and mushrooms; saute for 4 or 5 minutes. Whisk cornstarch and milk together. Gradually add to frying pan, whisking until boiling. Add chicken, salt, and pepper. Transfer to deep 8-inch pie plate.
2. To make biscuits, sift flour, salt, and baking powder together. Cut in shortening with pastry blender until mixture resembles coarse bread crumbs. With fork, stir in enough milk to make a soft but not sticky dough.
3. Preheat oven to 450 degrees.
4. Knead dough lightly on floured board. Roll out about ¹/₂ inch thick and cut into 1¹/₂-inch rounds with cookie cutter.
5. Place biscuit rounds on top of chicken mixture. Brush with milk and bake for 10 to 15 minutes, or until biscuit topping is brown. Serve hot.

Chicken and Corn Croquettes

Serves 4

5 tablespoons butter
¹/₂ cup plus 2 tablespoons flour
1 cup milk
1 teaspoon finely chopped onion
¹/₂ cup canned whole kernel corn
2 cups finely chopped cooked
  chicken
2 teaspoons chopped parsley
1 teaspoon lemon juice
Pinch of ground mace
1 egg yolk
Salt and pepper to taste
2 eggs, beaten with
  1 teaspoon oil
1¹/₂ cups bread crumbs
Oil for deep frying
1 lemon, quartered

1. Melt 3 tablespoons butter in saucepan. Stir in ¹/₄ cup flour. Add milk and bring to a boil, stirring constantly. Boil for 3 to 4 minutes, until liquid is slightly reduced.
2. Melt 1 tablespoon butter in frying pan. Saute onion and corn for 3 to 4 minutes. Add chicken, parsley, lemon juice, and mace, mixing well. Stir in ³/₄ cup of reduced sauce. Remove from heat and let cool. Stir in 1 egg yolk, then spread mixture out on plate to cool and thicken for 15 minutes.
3. Divide chicken mixture into 8 equal portions and roll into balls. Season remaining flour with salt and pepper, then roll balls in flour mixture until well covered. Brush all over with eggs beaten with oil. Coat with bread crumbs.
4. Heat oil in deep frying pan until gently smoking. Fry 3 or 4 croquettes at a time until golden brown and crisp. Drain on paper towels, and serve at once with lemon quarters.

Chicken Cream

Serves 4

4 cups cooked chicken
2 cups soft bread crumbs
¹/₄ cup butter
2 tablespoons flour
1 cup milk
¹/₄ teaspoon ground mace or
  nutmeg
1 tablespoon chopped parsley
1 egg, beaten
Salt and pepper to taste

1. Preheat oven to 350 degrees.
2. Grind chicken and mix with bread crumbs.
3. Melt 2 tablespoons butter in sauce-

pan. Stir in flour, blending well. Gradually add milk, stirring until smooth. Boil for 2 to 3 minutes, stirring constantly, then add mace or nutmeg and parsley. Remove from heat and cool slightly.

4. Add sauce to chicken mixture, mixing well. Melt remaining butter and add to chicken with beaten egg. Season with salt and pepper. Place in buttered, ovenproof dish, allowing room for chicken cream to rise slightly. Bake for 30 to 35 minutes. Remove from oven, and serve hot.

Creamed Chicken and Ham

Serves 4

1½ tablespoons butter
1½ tablespoons flour
¾ cup chicken stock
¼ cup heavy whipping cream
½ cup diced cooked chicken
½ cup diced cooked ham
¼ cup chopped celery
1 tablespoon parsley
1 egg, beaten
1 or 2 tablespoons sherry, optional

1. Melt butter in saucepan. Add flour, stirring until well blended. Gradually stir in stock, then cream. Bring to a boil, stirring constantly. Add chicken, ham, celery, and parsley.
2. Mix 2 tablespoons hot sauce with egg. Reduce heat to low, then add egg mixture to saucepan. Stir constantly until sauce thickens. Before serving, add sherry if desired.

Popovers with Creamed Chicken

Serves 6

1 cup plus 2 tablespoons flour
½ teaspoon salt
2 eggs
1 cup milk
3 tablespoons butter
¾ cup chicken broth
1 cup cubed cooked chicken
⅓ cup chopped mushrooms
½ teaspoons salt
Pinch of nutmeg
1 egg
¼ cup heavy whipping cream
1 tablespoon sherry

1. Preheat oven to 425 degrees.
2. Sift 1 cup flour; measure and sift again with salt. Beat eggs until thick and lemon colored; gradually add milk and 1 tablespoon melted butter. Stir in salted flour. Beat until mixture is smooth. Fill buttered custard cups a little less than half full with batter. Bake for 40 minutes.
3. Meanwhile, melt remaining butter in saucepan. Stir in 2 tablespoons flour. Gradually add broth and cook, stirring constantly, until sauce thickens. Add chicken, mushrooms, salt, and nutmeg. Cook over low heat until hot.
4. Beat egg, cream, and sherry together. Add to chicken mixture, stirring until sauce is smooth; do not boil.
5. To serve, split sides of hot popovers and fill with creamed chicken.

Chicken Barley Casserole

Serves 4 to 6

2 cups chicken broth
½ pound barley
3 tablespoons butter
1 small onion, chopped
½ pound mushrooms, sliced
1 cup diced cooked chicken
½ cup plain yogurt
¾ cup shredded Monterey Jack cheese
2 tablespoons chopped parsley

1. Heat broth to boiling in large saucepan. Add barley, cover, and simmer for 45 minutes.
2. Melt butter in frying pan. Add onion and saute until translucent. Add mushrooms and saute just until juices appear. Remove from heat and set aside.
3. Preheat oven to 350 degrees.
4. Combine mushrooms, chicken, yogurt, and ½ cup shredded cheese. Add cooked barley. Spoon mixture into large, greased casserole dish. Sprinkle with remaining cheese and parsley. Bake for 50 minutes, and serve.

Chicken and Taco-Chips Casserole

Serves 4 to 6

9 taco shells or 1 (12-ounce) bag taco chips
2 whole cooked chicken breasts, chopped
1 (10½-ounce) can condensed chicken and rice soup
2 cups grated sharp Cheddar cheese
1 (10-ounce) can tomatoes and green chilies

1. Preheat oven to 350 degrees.
2. Crush taco shells or chips in bowl. Place layer of crushed tacos in bottom of greased 1-quart casserole. Sprinkle layer of chopped chicken on top. Pour several spoonfuls soup over chicken layer. Sprinkle with layer of cheese. Add several spoonfuls tomato and green chili mixture over cheese layer. Repeat layers until all ingredients have been used. Top with grated cheese.
3. Bake for 25 minutes, until hot. Remove from oven, and serve. This freezes well before and after baking.

Chicken in Crumb Baskets

Serves 6

Crumb Baskets

5 cups soft bread crumbs
1/4 cup minced onion
1 teaspoon celery salt
1/8 teaspoon pepper
1/2 cup melted butter

Chicken Filling

1/3 cup melted butter
1/3 cup flour
1/2 cup light cream
1 1/2 cups chicken broth
1/2 teaspoon salt
1/8 teaspoon pepper
1 teaspoon Worcestershire
   sauce
1 cup cooked peas
3 cups chopped cooked
   chicken

1. Preheat oven to 375 degrees.
2. Mix bread crumbs with onion, celery salt, pepper, and melted butter. Grease 6 individual casseroles and line with crumb mixture; press into place. Bake for 15 minutes, or until crumbs are brown.
3. To make filling, blend melted butter and flour together. Stir in cream, broth, salt, pepper, and Worcestershire sauce. Cook, stirring constantly, until sauce thickens. Add peas and chicken.
4. To serve, spoon chicken mixture into baked crumb baskets.

Chicken and Cheesy Rice Rings

Serves 4 to 6

6 tablespoons butter
2 onions, finely chopped
2 cups cooked rice
1 egg
1 cup milk
1 cup grated Cheddar cheese
Salt and pepper to taste
1/2 teaspoon dry mustard
1 teaspoon paprika
6 large mushrooms, sliced
2 tablespoons flour

1 cup chicken broth
3 cups diced cooked chicken
1/8 teaspoon nutmeg
1/4 cup bread or cornflake crumbs

1. Melt 5 tablespoons butter in frying pan. Add onions and saute for 4 to 5 minutes, until soft but not brown. Remove pan from heat and transfer half the onions to mixing bowl, leaving remainder in frying pan.
2. Add rice to onions in bowl. Beat egg with milk and add to rice with 3/4 cup grated cheese, salt, pepper, dry mustard, and 1/2 teaspoon paprika.
3. Preheat oven to 350 degrees.
4. Butter 7-inch ring mold and fill it with rice mixture, packing rice in well. Bake about 20 minutes, or until firm. Remove from oven and unmold onto serving platter. Turn oven to 400 degrees.
5. To prepare chicken sauce, add mushrooms to onions remaining in frying pan. Saute for 2 minutes. Remove from heat and add flour, mixing well. Whisk in broth. Bring to a boil, then simmer for 3 to 4 minutes. Add chicken, nutmeg, salt, and pepper. Spoon hot sauce into center of rice ring. Any extra sauce can be reheated and served separately.
6. Sprinkle top with mixture of remaining cheese and crumbs. Dot with remaining butter. Brown in hot oven or under broiler for a few minutes. Sprinkle with remaining paprika and serve hot.

Spicy Turkey Casserole

Serves 4

1 tablespoon vegetable oil
2 tablespoons finely chopped onion
1 (10 3/4-ounce) can condensed
   mushroom soup
1 hot green chili pepper, seeded
   and finely chopped
1 cup cooked diced turkey
2 1/2 cups cooked egg noodles
Salt and pepper to taste
1/2 cup grated sharp cheese

1. Preheat oven to 350 degrees.
2. Heat oil in frying pan. Saute onion until lightly browned. Add soup and chili pepper.

3. Arrange a layer of turkey, noodles, and soup mixture in a casserole dish. Sprinkle lightly with salt, pepper, and grated cheese. Repeat layers. Sprinkle remaining cheese on top and bake for 30 to 40 minutes. Serve with green vegetable or salad.

Quick Turkey Hash

Serves 4

1 (10 3/4-ounce) can condensed
   mushroom soup
1 (12-ounce) can evaporated milk
1/2 cup sliced mushrooms
3 cups chopped cooked turkey
1/2 cup cooked peas, beans,
   or corn
2 tablespoons grated cheese

1. Empty can of condensed soup into saucepan and heat with enough milk to thin soup to sauce consistency. Add sliced mushrooms and simmer for 5 minutes. Add chopped turkey and any available cooked vegetables.
2. Simmer hash until thoroughly heated. Sprinkle grated cheese on top. Serve hot with boiled rice or mashed potatoes.

Turkey Cottage Pie

Serves 4

1 pound potatoes, peeled
3 peeled onions, 1 whole and
   2 chopped
6 tablespoons butter
1/2 cup warm milk
Salt and pepper to taste
1/2 cup chopped mushrooms
1 tablespoon flour
1 1/4 cups turkey or chicken
   stock
1 tablespoon chopped parsley
3 cups diced cooked turkey
2 tablespoons milk

1. Preheat oven to 400 degrees.
2. Boil potatoes in salted water with 1 whole onion. Cook for 15 to 20

minutes, until potatoes are tender. Remove onion; drain potatoes and mash them. Beat in 2 tablespoons butter and enough warm milk to make a soft mixture without being too runny. Season with salt and pepper, and set aside.

3. Melt 2 to 3 tablespoon butter in saucepan and saute chopped onions for 3 minutes. Add mushrooms and saute for 1 minute longer. Whisk in flour. When mixture is blended, whisk in stock and parsley. Season with salt and pepper. Bring mixture to a boil, then simmer for 3 or 4 minutes. Add diced turkey. Add 2 tablespoons milk and transfer mixture to ovenproof dish.

4. Spread mashed potatoes carefully over top of dish and smooth with knife. Score potatoes with fork and dot with remaining butter. Bake for 20 to 30 minutes, or until potatoes are golden brown and crisp.

Curried Turkey

Serves 4

1½ cups diced cooked turkey
Juice of ½ lemon
¼ cup butter
1 clove garlic, peeled and crushed
½ teaspoon ginger powder
1 onion, chopped
1 tablespoon flour
1 tablespoon curry powder
1 cup chicken stock
1 tablespoon tomato paste
1 small, sweet apple, peeled, cored, and chopped
1 tablespoon raisins
Pinch of sugar
Salt and pepper to taste

1. Combine turkey and lemon juice in bowl.
2. Melt butter in saucepan. Add garlic, ginger, onion, flour, and curry powder. Saute, stirring constantly, for 3 to 4 minutes. Stir in chicken stock and bring to a boil. Add tomato paste, apple, raisins, sugar, salt, and pepper. Cover and simmer for 15 minutes.
3. Stir turkey into saucepan. Simmer for 10 minutes longer. Remove from heat, and serve.

Turkey Loaf

Serves 4

2 eggs
½ pound bacon
2 tablespoons butter
2 tablespoons flour
1 cup milk
Salt and pepper to taste
1 cup diced cooked turkey
¼ cup leftover stuffing, crumbled
Watercress sprigs for garnish

1. Cover eggs with water. Bring to a boil and cook for 10 minutes. Cool in cold water; remove shells and slice eggs.
2. With back of knife, stretch bacon strips until doubled in length. Arrange bacon over bottom and sides of loaf pan. Reserve some bacon strips for top.
3. Preheat oven to 350 degrees.
4. Melt butter in saucepan. Add flour and saute over low heat, stirring, for 2 to 3 minutes. Blend in milk. Bring to a boil, stirring constantly. Season with salt and pepper. Stir in turkey and stuffing.
5. Put half of turkey mixture into loaf pan. Place eggs on top, then cover with remaining turkey mixture. Press down firmly. Cover with reserved bacon slices. Cover pan with foil and place in larger pan filled with just enough water to come halfway up sides of loaf pan. Bake for 1 hour. Leave loaf in pan to cool, then refrigerate until well chilled. Turn loaf out onto serving plate and garnish with watercress.

Fried Turkey Crisps

Serves 4 to 6

3 tablespoons butter
1 tablespoon chopped onion
3 slices bacon
½ cup chopped mushrooms
3 tablespoons flour
1 cup chicken broth
3 egg yolks, beaten
Salt and pepper to taste
2 tablespoons grated Parmesan cheese

1 cup finely chopped cooked turkey
1½ cups plus 2 tablespoons bread crumbs
5 to 6 tablespoons flour, seasoned with salt, pepper, and paprika
2 eggs, beaten
Oil for deep-frying

1. Melt butter in saucepan. Add onion and bacon; saute for 3 to 4 minutes. Add mushrooms and saute for 2 minutes. Stir in flour, blending until smooth. Add broth and bring to a boil, stirring constantly. Simmer for 2 minutes, then let cool slightly. Add egg yolks, salt, pepper, cheese, turkey, and 2 tablespoons bread crumbs. Refrigerate until chilled.
2. Form tablespoonfuls of chilled mixture into balls. Roll in seasoned flour. Brush thoroughly with beaten eggs, then shake in bag of remaining bread crumbs until completely coated.
3. Heat oil in deep frying pan to 350 degrees. Cook balls until brown all over. Drain on paper towels. Serve at once.

Smothered Turkey

Serves 4

1½ cups rice
8 large slices cooked turkey
3 tablespoons butter
1 onion, finely chopped 1½ cups sour cream
Salt and pepper to taste
Pinch of nutmeg
2 tablespoons chopped chives

1. Preheat oven to 350 degrees.
2. Cook rice in boiling, salted water according to package directions. Drain and place in bottom of serving dish.
3. Place turkey slices on top of rice. Cover with buttered parchment paper or foil and bake for 15 to 20 minutes.
4. Melt butter in frying pan and saute onion until translucent. Add sour cream and blend well. Add salt, pepper, and nutmeg.
5. To serve, spoon sour cream sauce over turkey and rice, and sprinkle with chopped chives.

Baked Turkey Hash

Serves 2

1½ cups diced turkey
1 medium onion, diced
1 medium potato, diced
2 medium carrots, coarsely
 grated
1 teaspoon salt
2 teaspoons minced parsley
½ teaspoon poultry
 seasoning
½ cup turkey gravy

1. Combine all ingredients except gravy. Mix lightly. Blend in gravy and stir until all ingredients are moistened.
2. Preheat oven to 350 degrees.
3. Spoon turkey mixture into greased, 1-quart casserole. Cover and bake for 45 minutes. Remove cover and continue to bake for 15 minutes. Remove from oven, and serve.

Turkey Gratin

Serves 4

1½ tablespoons butter
1½ tablespoons flour
¼ teaspoon dry mustard
1 cup milk
Salt and pepper to taste
3 cups grated
 Cheddar or
 Parmesan cheese
1 teaspoon Worcestershire
 sauce
4 slices toast
8 thick slices turkey
Paprika

1. Melt butter in saucepan. Stir in flour and mustard. Cook, stirring constantly, for 2 minutes. Gradually add milk and stir until boiling. Add salt and pepper. Add cheese and Worcestershire sauce; stir over low heat until cheese melts.
2. Preheat broiler.
3. Arrange toast in shallow baking pan. Place turkey slices on top and cover with cheese sauce. Brown under hot broiler. Remove from heat, sprinkle with paprika, and serve.

Hot Game Cutlets

Serves 4

2 tablespoons butter
1 onion, chopped
1 cup chopped cooked partridge,
 pigeon, or pheasant
1 cup mashed potatoes
¼ teaspoon marjoram
2 tablespoons chutney
2 eggs, beaten
3 to 4 tablespoons flour,
 seasoned with salt and pepper
1 teaspoon oil
1 cup bread crumbs
Oil for deep frying
1 (8-ounce) can tomato sauce

1. Melt butter in frying pan. Add onion and saute until translucent. Add to chopped game with enough mashed potatoes to make a firm mixture. Add marjoram, chutney, 1 egg, and seasonings. Mold into cutlet shapes; roll in seasoned flour.
2. Beat second egg with 1 teaspoon oil. Brush cutlets with egg-oil mixture and coat with bread crumbs.
3. Heat oil in frying pan. Add cutlets and fry for 3 to 4 minutes, or until golden brown. Drain and serve with warmed tomato sauce.

Turkey and Spinach Pancakes

Serves 6

1 cup flour
Salt and pepper to taste
2 eggs, beaten
1 cup milk
1 tablespoon melted butter
Oil

Filling

2 cups ground cooked turkey
1 (10¾-ounce) can condensed
 cream of chicken soup
1 cup chopped cooked spinach,
 well trained
1 teaspoon tomato paste
¼ teaspoon onion powder
Pinch of garlic powder
Salt and pepper to taste
2 tablespoons butter
2 tablespoons grated Parmesan
 cheese

1. Sift flour with salt and pepper into bowl. Make hollow in center of flour and add beaten eggs and ¼ cup milk. Mix eggs and milk together with spoon before gradually drawing in flour. Add ¼ cup more milk as mixture thickens. When mixture is smooth and consistency of thick cream, beat for 5 minutes with electric beater. Stir in melted butter and another ¼ cup milk. Leave batter in covered bowl for 30 minutes.
2. Test thickness of batter, which should just coat back of spoon. If too thick, add more milk and stir well. Grease griddle or frying pan with small amount of oil. When hot, pour in enough batter to coat pan thinly. Cook until golden brown on one side; turn and cook on other side. Pile up and keep warm. Allow 2 to 3 pancakes per person.
3. Mix ground turkey with chicken soup. Add cooked spinach; mix thoroughly. Heat mixture and add tomato paste. Sprinkle in onion and garlic powders. Season with salt and pepper.
4. Preheat broiler.
5. Spoon filling onto pancakes, roll up, and place in center of ovenproof dish. Sprinkle with butter and cheese. Broil until cheese is golden brown. Serve at once.

Turkey and Mushroom Croquettes

Serves 4 to 6

5 tablespoons butter
¼ cup flour
½ cup turkey or chicken stock
½ cup milk
Salt and pepper to taste
Pinch of mace
Pinch of cayenne pepper
1 tablespoon chopped parsley
3 to 4 tablespoons chopped
 mushrooms, sprinkled with
 lemon juice

2 cups chopped cooked turkey
1 egg yolk, beaten
1/2 cup flour, seasoned with salt
   and pepper
2 eggs, beaten with 1 teaspoon
   oil
1 to 1 1/2 cups bread crumbs
Oil for deep-frying

1. Melt 4 tablespoons butter in saucepan. Stir in flour, then add stock and milk. Bring to a boil, stirring constantly until thick and smooth. Add seasonings and chopped parsley. Let cool.
2. Melt 1 tablespoon butter in frying pan. Add mushrooms and saute for 3 minutes. Add turkey, then the sauce. Stir well and remove from heat. When almost cooled, add egg yolk; place mixture in refrigerator to chill and set.
3. Divide mixture into 12 equal portions. Shape each into a small roll with floured fingers. Roll in seasoned flour, coating ends carefully. Brush all over with eggs beaten with oil. Cover thickly with bread crumbs.
4. Heat oil in deep skillet to 400 degrees. Fry 4 croquettes at a time until well browned. Drain on paper towels, and serve at once.

Turkey and Vegetables

Serves 4 to 6

3 tablespoons butter
1 onion, chopped
3 large mushrooms, chopped
2 tablespoons flour
1 1/2 cups turkey or chicken stock
2 to 3 cups chopped cooked turkey
1 cup cooked vegetables, such as
   peas, beans, corn, and carrots
1 tablespoon chopped parsley
1/4 teaspoon thyme
1/4 cup heavy whipping cream
1/4 cup grated Cheddar cheese
Pinch of paprika

1. Preheat broiler.
2. Melt butter in saucepan. Add onion and saute until translucent. Add mushrooms and saute for 1 minute. Sprinkle in flour, blending well. Add stock and bring to a boil, stirring constantly. Add turkey and any available cooked vegetables. Stir well. Add parsley, thyme, and cream.
3. Spoon mixture into buttered baking dish; sprinkle thickly with grated cheese and paprika. Broil until crisp and brown all over. Serve with cooked noodles or boiled rice.

Sliced Turkey in Chestnut Sauce

Serves 4

3 tablespoons butter
2 onions, chopped
1 carrot, chopped
1 1/2 tablespoons flour
2 teaspoons tomato paste
3 cups stock
1/4 cup sherry, optional
1 bay leaf
3 sprigs parsley
1 sprig thyme or 1/4 teaspoon
   dried thyme
Salt and pepper to taste
4 to 5 tablespoons chestnut
   puree
3 to 4 chestnuts, peeled and
   roughly chopped
8 large slices cooked turkey
2 tomatoes, sliced, optional

1. Melt butter in saucepan. Add onions and carrots; saute for 10 minutes. Add flour, blending well. Stir in tomato paste, stock, and, if desired, sherry. Bring to a boil, stirring constantly. Add bay leaf, parsley, thyme, salt, and pepper. Cook, stirring, for 10 to 15 minutes, until sauce thickens. Strain. Add chestnut puree and reheat, stirring, until smooth. Add chopped chestnuts.
2. Preheat oven to 350 degrees.
3. Place turkey slices in ovenproof dish. Add tomatoes, if desired. Cover with sauce and bake for 15 minutes, or until thoroughly heated. Remove from oven, and serve with crisp fried potatoes.

Turkey Noodle Ring

Serves 4

8 ounces egg noodles
5 tablespoons butter
3 onions, 1 chopped, 2 finely
   sliced
1 clove garlic, peeled and
   minced
1 cup heavy whipping cream
1 egg
1/4 cup grated Cheddar cheese
1 tablespoon chopped parsley
Salt and pepper to taste
1 cup sliced mushrooms
2 tablespoons flour
1/2 cup turkey or chicken
   stock
3/4 cup milk
2 cups chopped cooked turkey
1/4 cup cooked peas and corn
2 tablespoons chopped pimento
2 hard-boiled eggs, quartered
Pinch of paprika

1. Preheat oven to 350 degrees.
2. Boil noodles following package directions until almost cooked; drain. Melt 3 tablespoons butter in saucepan. Add chopped onion and garlic; saute until onion is translucent. Add noodles. Beat cream and egg together, then add to noodle mixture. Stir in grated cheese and parsley. Season with salt and pepper, blending well.
3. Spoon noodle mixture into buttered 7-inch ring mold; press in well. Cover with buttered parchment paper or foil and bake for 45 minutes, until set. Remove from oven and turn out on hot serving dish.
4. While noodle ring is cooking, melt 2 tablespoons butter in saucepan. Add 2 sliced onions and saute for 5 to 6 minutes. Add mushrooms and saute for 1 minute more. Sprinkle in flour, blending well. Add stock and milk; bring to a boil, stirring constantly, then simmer for 5 minutes. Remove from heat. Add turkey, peas, corn, pimento, and quartered eggs. Season well and keep warm until noodle ring is ready.
5. To serve, spoon turkey mixture into center of noodle ring and sprinkle with paprika.

Turkey and Ham Patties

Serves 4

1 package frozen puff pastry,
   thawed
1 egg, beaten
3 tablespoons butter
1 onion, finely chopped
3 tablespoons flour
1 cup milk
$^1/_2$ to $^3/_4$ cup chopped cooked
   turkey
$^1/_2$ cup chopped cooked ham
1 tablespoon chopped parsley
Salt and pepper to taste
Pinch of mace

1. Preheat oven to 475 degrees.
2. Roll out pastry to $^1/_4$ inch thick.
Using cutter 2$^1/_2$ inches in diameter,
cut out 8 patties. Using smaller cutter,
about 1$^1/_2$ inches in diameter, make
cut in center of each patty, being
careful not to cut through to bottom.
Brush each patty with egg; do not
allow egg to run over sides of patty or
pastry will not rise.
3. Place patties on dampened baking
sheet and bake for 15 to 20 minutes,
until patties have risen and are golden
brown. Remove from oven, take off
center lids carefully, and reserve.
Scoop out soft pastry inside and
discard. Keep pastry shells warm.
4. To make filling, melt butter in
saucepan. Add onion and saute for 5
minutes. Stir in flour, blending well.
Add milk and bring to a boil, stirring
constantly. Add turkey, ham, parsley,
salt, pepper, and mace. Simmer until
heated thoroughly, then spoon into
patty shells. Place lids on top, and
serve at once.

Turkey Balls

Serves 4

2 cups chopped cooked turkey
$^1/_2$ teaspoon salt
$^1/_4$ teaspoon pepper
$^1/_8$ teaspoon cinnamon
2 tablespoons grated Parmesan
   cheese
1 egg yolk
3 slices bread
2 tablespoons butter

1 teaspoon tomato paste
2 cups turkey stock
1 tablespoon flour

1. Combine turkey with salt, pepper,
cinnamon, cheese, and egg yolk. Soak
bread in water for 5 minutes, then
squeeze dry and add to mixture. Blend
well until mixture is smooth. Roll into
12 balls.
2. Melt 1 tablespoon butter in large
saucepan. Add tomato paste and
stock; cook for 5 minutes. Place turkey
balls in saucepan and simmer for 20
minutes. Remove balls from pan and
place on serving dish.
3. Boil pan liquid rapidly until reduced
by half. Melt remaining tablespoon
butter and blend with flour. Add flour
mixture to pan; cook, stirring
constantly, until sauce thickens. Pour
sauce over turkey balls, and serve.

Deviled Turkey Legs

Serves 4

3 tablespoons butter, melted
Juice of $^1/_2$ onion
Juice of 1 crushed clove garlic
2 tablespoons ketchup
2 tablespoons Worcestershire
   sauce
1 tablespoon Dijon mustard
1 teaspoon sugar
Pinch of cayenne pepper
Salt and pepper to taste
2 large cooked turkey legs, halved
Oil for frying
4 tomatoes, halved

1. Mix melted butter with onion and
garlic juices, ketchup, Worcestershire
sauce, mustard, sugar, cayenne
pepper, salt, and pepper.
2. With sharp knife, cut shallow
gashes in turkey legs. Put turkey
pieces into dish and spoon sauce on
top. Marinate for at least 1 hour,
turning frequently.
3. Preheat broiler.
4. Heat oil in deep skillet until hot. Fry
turkey until brown all over, turning
frequently. Drain.
5. Broil tomato halves until browned.
Serve turkey with boiled rice,
garnished with broiled tomatoes.

Turkey Divan

Serves 4

$^1/_4$ cup butter
$^1/_4$ cup flour
$^1/_4$ teaspoon salt
2 cups chicken stock
$^1/_4$ teaspoon Tabasco sauce
$^1/_4$ cup grated Parmesan
   cheese
$^1/_2$ cup heavy whipping cream
4 ounces rigatoni, cooked
1 (10-ounce) package frozen
   broccoli, thawed
1$^1/_2$ cups diced cooked turkey

1. Preheat oven to 350 degrees.
2. Melt butter in saucepan. Stir in
flour and salt. Gradually add chicken
stock and cook, stirring constantly,
until mixture thickens and boils.
Remove from heat; stir in Tabasco
sauce, cheese, and cream.
3. Put rigatoni in bottom of greased,
2-quart casserole dish. Top with
broccoli and turkey. Pour sauce over
all. Bake for 40 minutes, or until
broccoli is tender. Sprinkle with
additional grated cheese, and serve.

Turkey-
Green Bean Puff

Serves 6

1 (10$^1/_2$-ounce) can condensed
   cream of chicken soup
$^1/_3$ cup milk
2 tablespoons butter, melted
$^1/_2$ teaspoon onion salt
Pinch of cayenne pepper
1 cup diced cooked turkey
2 cups chopped cooked green
   beans
$^1/_2$ cup chopped peanuts
4 eggs, separated
$^1/_4$ cup grated Swiss cheese

1. Preheat oven to 375 degrees.
2. Combine soup, milk, butter, onion
salt, and cayenne pepper in greased,
1$^1/_2$-quart casserole dish. Stir in
turkey, beans, and peanuts. Bake for
10 minutes.
3. While casserole is cooking, beat egg
yolks until foamy. Add cheese. Beat

egg whites until stiff, then fold into yolk-cheese mixture. Pile fluffy egg topping over casserole ingredients after the 10 minutes of baking time is up. Return to oven and continue baking, uncovered, for 30 minutes. Serve at once.

Turkey Casserole

Serves 4

¼ cup butter
½ pound mushrooms, sliced
2 tablespoons flour
1 teaspoon salt
1½ cups milk
1 bouillon cube
¼ teaspoon Tabasco sauce
2 cups diced cooked turkey
2 tablespoons diced pimento
2 cups thin egg noodles, cooked
¼ cup grated Parmesan cheese
1 cup soft, buttered bread crumbs

1. Melt 3 tablespoons butter in saucepan. Add mushrooms and saute for 5 minutes. Stir in flour and salt, blending well. Gradually stir in milk, then add bouillon cube. Cook, stirring constantly, over medium heat until mixture thickens and boils. Remove from heat; stir in Tabasco sauce.
2. Preheat oven to 375 degrees.
3. Place turkey, pimento, and noodles in shallow baking dish. Pour mushroom sauce on top. Sprinkle with cheese and dot with remaining butter. Sprinkle buttered bread crumbs around edge.
4. Bake casserole for 20 minutes, or until browned. Remove from oven, and serve hot.

Turkey Mandarin

Serves 4

2 tablespoons finely chopped scallions
1½ cups diced celery
2 tablespoons oil
2 cups diced cooked turkey

¼ cup coarsely chopped, toasted almonds
Grated rind of ½ lemon
1 tablespoon lemon juice
⅔ cup mayonnaise
Salt and pepper to taste
1 cup crushed potato chips
½ cup grated Cheddar cheese

1. Preheat oven to 375 degrees.
2. Saute scallion and celery in oil for 6 minutes. Combine sauteed scallion and celery with turkey, almonds, lemon rind, and lemon juice in mixing bowl. Add mayonnaise and toss lightly. Season with salt and pepper.
3. Sprinkle bottom of greased, 2-quart casserole dish with potato chips. Spoon turkey mixture into dish. Sprinkle with cheese and scatter remaining potato chips around edges. Bake for 25 minutes, or until cheese begins to bubble. Remove from oven, and serve hot.

Fried Goose with Apple Rings

Serves 4

8 slices cooked breast of goose
Salt and pepper to taste
4 to 5 tablespoons flour
1 to 2 eggs, beaten with 1 teaspoon oil
1 to 1½ cups fresh white bread crumbs
½ cup oil
4 to 5 tablespoons butter
2 cooking apples, peeled, cored, and sliced into rings
1 tablespoon sugar
1 cup beef gravy
1 tablespoon red wine vinegar
2 teaspoons Worcestershire sauce

1. Season goose slices well with salt and pepper. Cover with flour, then dip in egg. Coat with bread crumbs.
2. Heat oil in frying pan, then add butter. When butter is foaming, cook goose slices until golden brown and crisp all over. Remove, drain, and keep warm.
3. Reheat fat remaining in frying pan,

having removed any loose crumbs that may burn. Fry apple rings until golden brown, sprinkling on each side with sugar. Remove apples from pan.
4. Combine gravy, vinegar, and Worcestershire sauce. Heat and season to taste. Arrange goose slices on platter. Surround with apple rings, and serve with gravy.

Chicken Pudding

Serves 6

2 cups finely diced cooked chicken
1 cup cooked whole kernel corn
1 cup cooked peas
2 tablespoons grated onion
2 tablespoons finely minced parsley
1 cup cracker crumbs
1 teaspoon salt
¼ teaspoon pepper
3 eggs, well beaten
¾ cup sour cream.

1. Preheat oven to 350 degrees.
2. Combine all ingredients, blending well. Pour into greased, 2½-quart casserole dish. Bake, uncovered, for 45 minutes, or until set. Remove from oven, and serve hot.

Chicken Dandy

Serves 6 to 8

3 cups diced cooked chicken
2 cups cooked rice
1 cup fresh bread crumbs
¼ cup chopped green pepper
¼ cup chopped sweet red pepper
1 teaspoon salt
½ teaspoon curry powder
⅛ teaspoon pepper
¼ cup finely chopped peanuts
3 cups chicken broth or milk
4 eggs, well beaten

1. Preheat oven to 350 degrees.
2. Combine all ingredients, blending well. Pour into greased, rectangular baking dish about 2 inches deep. Bake for 1 hour, or until set. To serve, cut into squares or oblongs.

Chicken and Macaroni au Gratin

Serves 8

1/4 cup butter
2 tablespoons flour
1 (3-ounce) package cream
   cheese
1 teaspoon salt
Pinch of cayenne pepper
1/4 teaspoon garlic salt
Pinch of nutmeg
1 cup milk
1 cup chicken bouillon
2 tablespoons chopped pimento
1 cup sliced cooked mushrooms
2 1/2 cups diced cooked chicken
2 cups cooked macaroni
1/2 cup grated Swiss cheese

1. Preheat oven to 350 degrees.
2. Melt butter over low heat and blend in flour, cream cheese, salt, cayenne pepper, garlic salt, and nutmeg. Gradually add milk and bouillon, stirring constantly until slightly thickened. Add pimento, mushrooms, chicken, and macaroni.
3. Spoon mixture into greased, 2-quart casserole. Top with cheese and bake for 25 minutes, or until lightly browned on top. Remove from oven, and serve hot.

Savory Chicken Pie

Serves 6

1/4 cup butter
1/4 cup flour
1 teaspoon salt
1 cup chicken broth
1 cup milk
1 tablespoon prepared
   mustard
1/4 teaspoon rosemary
2 cups diced cooked chicken
1 (8-ounce) can whole pearl
   onions, boiled and drained
1 cup cooked peas
1 (3-ounce) can mushrooms,
   drained
1 envelope instant mashed
   potato flakes
Melted butter
Paprika

1. Preheat oven to 350 degrees.
2. Melt butter in saucepan. Stir in flour and salt, blending well. Add chicken broth and milk; cook over low heat, stirring constantly, until smooth and thickened. Blend in mustard and rosemary. Add chicken, onions, peas, and mushrooms.
3. Spoon chicken mixture into 1 1/2-quart casserole dish; bake for 30 minutes.
4. Prepare mashed potatoes following package directions. When casserole is cooked, pipe mashed potatoes around edge. Brush potatoes with melted butter and sprinkle with paprika. Return to oven and continue baking for 15 minutes, or until lightly browned. Serve at once.

Super Chicken Casserole

Serves 4

2 ounces egg noodles
1 tablespoon butter
1 medium onion, chopped
1 (10 1/2-ounce) can condensed
   cream of chicken soup
1/2 cup milk
1 cup diced cooked chicken
1/2 cup cooked lima beans
1/2 cup shredded Cheddar cheese

1. Cook noodles in lightly salted water according to package directions; drain.
2. Preheat oven to 375 degrees.
3. Melt butter in small frying pan; saute onion until golden brown. Combine onion with soup, milk, chicken, beans, and cooked noodles. Pour into 1-quart casserole dish; top with cheese. Bake for 25 minutes, or until hot and bubbling. Remove from oven, and serve.

Giblet Pie

Serves 6

1 1/2 cups thinly sliced potatoes
1 cup thinly sliced onions
1 cup chopped cooked spinach,
   drained
1 1/2 cups chopped cooked chicken
   or turkey giblets
1 cup sauteed sliced mushrooms
1 cup chopped cooked chicken
   or turkey
1 teaspoon salt
1/8 teaspoon pepper
1/8 teaspoon nutmeg
1/8 teaspoon thyme
1 cup stock made from giblets
2 tablespoons butter, melted
1/2 cup sour cream
1 uncooked, 9-inch pastry crust

1. Preheat oven to 350 degrees.
2. Layer bottom of greased, 2-quart casserole with potato slices, then onion slices, spinach, giblets, mushrooms, and turkey; sprinkle each layer with mixed salt, pepper, nutmeg, and thyme. Repeat layers, ending with potatoes.
3. Blend stock with melted butter and sour cream. Pour over casserole. Cover dish with pastry; pinch pastry to edge of casserole and make several slits in top. Bake, uncovered, for 1 1/4 hours, or until browned. Remove from oven and cool slightly before serving.

Chicken with Pineapple and Almonds

Serves 4

2 tablespoons butter
1/2 cup canned pineapple cubes,
   drained
1 1/2 tablespoons cornstarch
1 teaspoon salt
Pinch of cayenne pepper
Pinch of cinnamon
Pinch of ground cloves
1/2 cup pineapple juice
2 tablespoons minced chutney
2 cups chicken stock
2 cups diced cooked chicken
1/2 cup sliced celery
1/2 cup slivered blanched
   almonds

1. Preheat oven to 350 degrees.
2. Melt butter in saucepan. Add pineapple cubes and saute for 5 minutes. Mix cornstarch and seasonings together. Combine with pineapple juice, chutney, and stock. Add to pineapple cubes and stir over low heat until sauce thickens.
3. Place chicken, celery, and 1/4 cup almonds into greased, 1 1/2-quart casserole dish. Pour on sauce, and mix well. Sprinkle with remaining almonds. Bake, uncovered, for 25 minutes. Remove from oven, and serve.

Chicken Potatopies

Serves 8

6 tablespoons butter
1/2 cup flour
4 cups chicken stock
1 cup light cream
3 cups diced cooked chicken
1/2 cup diced cooked ham
1 (6-ounce) can sliced mushrooms, drained
1 cup finely diced celery
1 (12-ounce) package frozen peas, thawed
3 cups mashed potatoes, seasoned with salt and pepper
Melted butter

1. Preheat oven to 400 degrees.
2. Melt butter in saucepan. Stir in flour, blending well. Gradually add stock and simmer, stirring constantly, until slightly thickened. Add cream, chicken, ham, mushrooms, celery, and peas. Simmer for 15 minutes.
3. Grease 8 individual, 12-ounce casserole dishes. Divide chicken mixture evenly among dishes. Pile mashed potatoes in crowns around edges of casseroles. Brush with melted butter. Bake, uncovered, for 25 minutes, or until golden brown.

Cracker-Crush Chicken Pie

Serves 6

2 tablespoons butter
3 tablespoons flour
1 cup milk
1 teaspoon salt
Pinch of cayenne pepper
1 teaspoon curry powder
3 cups coarsely chopped cooked chicken
2 cups light cream
1 tablespoon finely chopped parsley
2 cups coarse cracker crumbs
1/2 pound sliced mushrooms, sauteed

1. Preheat oven to 400 degrees.
2. Melt butter in saucepan. Stir in flour, blending well. Gradually add milk and stir over low heat until thickened. Add seasonings.
3. In separate saucepan, heat chicken in cream over low heat for 5 minutes. Combine chicken-cream mixture with seasoned milk mixture in other saucepan. Add parsley. Spoon into greased, 2 1/2-quart baking dish. Bake, uncovered, for 10 minutes. Remove from oven.
4. Arrange cracker crumbs around edge of casserole. Make series of neat circles of overlapping mushroom slices in center. Return to oven for 5 minutes, then serve.

Hot Buffet Salad

Serves 4 to 6

2 tablespoons butter
2 tablespoons flour
1 1/2 cups milk
1/2 cup pickle relish
1/4 cup mayonnaise
2 tablespoons lemon juice
1 teaspoon salt
1/8 teaspoon pepper
2 cups cooked elbow macaroni
2 cups diced cooked chicken
1 large tart apple, chopped
23 stalks celery, chopped
2 pimentos, chopped
1/2 cup finely chopped pecans

1. Preheat oven to 350 degrees.
2. Melt butter in saucepan over low heat. Blend in flour, then milk, stirring constantly until smooth and thickened. Add all remaining ingredients except pecans. Spoon mixture into greased, 2-quart casserole dish. Sprinkle with pecans. Bake, uncovered, for 30 minutes. Remove from oven, and serve hot.

Chicken and Stuffing Casserole

Serves 6

1/4 cup melted butter
1/3 cup chopped onion
5 cups soft bread cubes
1/2 teaspoon salt
Pepper to taste
1/4 teaspoon sage
2 1/2 tablespoons cornstarch
1/2 cup milk
2 cups chicken broth
1 cup cooked peas
2 cups diced cooked chicken

1. Melt butter in frying pan. Add onion and saute for 5 minutes. Combine bread cubes, salt, pepper, and sage. Add to pan with onion, mixing well.
2. Combine cornstarch with milk in 2-quart saucepan. Add chicken broth. Bring to a boil over medium heat, stirring constantly. Add peas and chicken.
3. Preheat oven to 350 degrees.
4. Place half of bread stuffing mixture on bottom of greased, 8-inch square baking dish. Pour half of chicken mixture on top. Repeat layers. Bake for 30 minutes. Remove from oven, and serve.

Cornwall Duck Pastry

Serves 6

2 cups sifted flour
1 teaspoon salt
1/3 cup cornmeal
2/3 cup shortening
4 to 5 tablespoons cold water
2 cups diced cooked duck
1 cup diced cooked carrots
6 medium onions, sliced and
  sauteed until soft
2 tablespoons chopped parsley
1 (10 1/2-ounce) can cream of
  celery soup
1 cup light cream
1/2 teaspoon salt

1. Mix flour, salt, and cornmeal together. Cut in shortening with 2 knives or pastry blender until mixture resembles coarse meal. Add water, mixing with fork, until dough holds together but is not sticky. Roll out to 1/8-inch thickness and cut into 6 circles.
2. Preheat oven to 425 degrees.
3. Combine remaining ingredients and divide evenly into 6 greased ramekins. Top with pastry. Press to rim of dish with fork. Make several slits in top. Bake for 25 to 30 minutes, or until browned and sauce bubbles through slits.

Spanish Chicken

Serves 4 to 6

3 cups sliced cooked chicken
2 large onions, sliced
1 red sweet pepper, seeded
  and cut into strips
1 green pepper, seeded and
  cut into strips
1/2 cup tomato sauce
1 tablespoon tomato paste
1 (16-ounce) can stewed
  tomatoes
1 teaspoon salt
1/2 teaspoon garlic powder
1/4 teaspoon pepper
10 pitted black olives, sliced
10 pitted green olives, sliced

1. Preheat oven to 350 degrees.
2. Layer chicken, onions, and peppers in greased baking dish.
3. Combine tomato sauce, tomato paste, tomatoes, salt, garlic powder, and pepper in saucepan. Heat to boiling. Pour sauce over layered chicken and vegetables. Cover and bake for 30 minutes. Uncover casserole, sprinkle with olives, and bake for 15 minutes more. Remove from oven, and serve hot.

Chicken Chow Mein

Serves 4

1 green pepper, seeded and sliced
1 red pepper, seeded and sliced
1 cup boiling water
2 1/2 tablespoons butter
1 small onion, chopped
2 stalks celery, sliced
1 tablespoon flour
1 cup chicken broth
2 tablespoons soy sauce
Freshly ground pepper to taste
1 (4-ounce) can sliced mushrooms,
  drained
1/2 pound cooked chicken breast,
  cut into bite-size pieces
6 cups water
Salt
8 ounces egg noodles
Oil for deep-frying
1/2 cup sliced almonds, toasted
  and slightly salted

1. Blanch green and red pepper slices in boiling water for 5 minutes. Remove and drain. Melt 1 1/2 tablespoons butter in saucepan. Add onions and celery; saute until onions are translucent. Sprinkle with flour, blending well. Add chicken broth and bring to a boil, stirring constantly. Simmer for 10 minutes. Season with soy sauce and pepper. Add pepper slices, drained mushrooms, and chicken pieces. Cover and simmer for 15 minutes.

2. Meanwhile, bring 6 cups slightly salted water to a boil. Add noodles and cook for 15 minutes. Drain and rinse with cold water. Set aside 1/3 of noodles. Place remaining noodles in heated bowl. Add 1 tablespoon butter, cover, and keep warm.
3. Heat oil in skillet until very hot. Cut noodles that were set aside into approximately 2-inch-long pieces. Add noodles to hot oil and fry until golden. Drain on paper towels.
4. To serve, spoon chicken mixture over buttered noodles; top with fried noodles and toasted almonds.

Casserole of Turkey Leftovers

Serves 4

2 cups diced cooked turkey
2 cups diced boiled potatoes
1 cup cooked peas
1 large carrot, shredded
3 tablespoons vegetable
  shortening
1 onion, diced
3 tablespoons finely sliced
  celery
1 green pepper, seeded and
  cut into strips
1 cup water

1. Preheat oven to 350 degrees.
2. Place turkey in bottom of casserole dish. Top with potatoes, peas, and shredded carrot.
3. Melt shortening in frying pan. Add onion and saute until browned. Add celery and green pepper; saute for 2 minutes. Spoon onion mixture into center of casserole and stir lightly. Add water to casserole. Cover and bake for 20 minutes. Uncover and bake for 10 to 15 minutes longer, or until lightly browned on top. Remove from oven, and serve.

Texas Turkey Trot

Serves 4

2 tablespoons vegetable oil
1 medium onion, chopped
1 green pepper, seeded and
   chopped
1/2 cup ketchup
1/3 cup pickle relish
Juice and grated rind of
   1 lemon
1 tablespoon prepared mustard
8 generous slices cooked
   turkey

1. Heat oil in frying pan. Add onion and green pepper; saute for 5 minutes. Add ketchup, relish, lemon juice and rind, and mustard. Simmer for 5 minutes.
2. Add turkey to sauce and cook until well heated. Transfer to serving dish, and serve.

Creamed Turkey à la Pasha

Serves 6

1/3 cup butter
1 small onion, chopped
1/3 cup flour
3 cups milk
4 chicken bouillon cubes
1/2 cup blanched slivered
   almonds
1/4 cup seedless raisins
1 whole clove
1 bay leaf
12 slices cooked turkey
6 slices bread, toasted, buttered,
   and cut into 4 triangles

1. Melt butter in saucepan. Add onion and saute until translucent. Stir in flour, blending well. Add milk and bouillon cubes. Cook, stirring constantly, until sauce thickens. Mix in almonds, raisins, clove, and bay leaf. Simmer for 5 minutes, then remove clove and bay leaf.
2. Add turkey to sauce and cook over low heat until turkey is hot. Spoon turkey mixture over toast triangles, and serve at once.

Turkey in-the-Corn Pudding

Serves 6

1 tablespoon grated onion
2 tablespoons butter, melted
1 teaspoon salt
1/4 teaspoon pepper
1/4 teaspoon paprika
3 eggs, well beaten
1 (4 1/4-ounce) can undiluted
   evaporated milk
1 1/2 cups diced cooked turkey
1 cup whole kernel corn

1. Preheat oven to 375 degrees.
2. Combine onion, butter, and seasonings with eggs; blend thoroughly. Mix in remaining ingredients.
3. Pour mixture into greased, 1 1/2-quart casserole dish. Set dish in pan of warm water and bake for 40 minutes, or until knife inserted in center comes out clean. Remove from oven, and serve.

Turkey-Noodle Cocottes

Serves 4

1/2 pound egg noodles
2 tablespoons butter
2 1/2 cups diced cooked turkey
1 (10 1/2-ounce) can condensed
   cream of mushroom soup
1 cup light cream
2 tablespoons capers
1/2 cup grated Cheddar cheese
Paprika for garnish

1. Cook noodles according to package directions; drain and toss with butter.
2. Preheat oven to 325 degrees.
3. Grease 4 individual casserole dishes and line with noodles. Combine turkey, mushroom soup, cream, and capers; spoon over noodles. Sprinkle with grated cheese and paprika. Bake for 25 minutes, or until golden brown on top. Remove from oven, and serve piping hot.

Baked Curried Turkey and Rice

Serves 4

1 cup long-grain rice
1 medium onion, chopped
1/3 cup butter
2 tablespoons curry powder
3 cups diced cooked turkey
2 1/2 cups turkey broth
Salt to taste

1. Preheat oven to 350 degrees.
2. Saute rice and onion in melted butter, stirring often until rice turns pale yellow. Blend in curry powder and saute for 2 minutes longer. Stir in turkey, broth, and salt. Spoon mixture into greased, 2-quart casserole. Bake for 25 minutes, or until liquid is absorbed and rice is fluffy. Remove from oven, and serve.

Chicken Noodle Casserole

Serves 10

1 (8-ounce) package egg
   noodles
1 tablespoon butter
1/2 onion, chopped
2 tablespoons chopped green
   pepper
1 (10-ounce) can cream of
   mushroom soup
2 cups diced cooked chicken
Salt and pepper to taste
1/2 cup grated Cheddar cheese

1. Cook noodles in boiling water until just tender, following package directions; drain.
2. Melt butter in saucepan. Add onion and saute until translucent. Add green pepper and soup, mixing well.
3. Preheat oven to 350 degrees.
4. Grease 2-quart casserole dish. Place half the noodles in bottom of dish, then cover with half the chicken. Season with salt and pepper, then add half the mushroom soup mixture and half the grated cheese. Repeat layers using remaining ingredients. Bake for 45 minutes. Remove from oven, and serve.

Chicken Casserole with Horseradish Mustard

Serves 4

1 bunch fresh broccoli, cut into
   florets, or 1 (10-ounce) package
   frozen broccoli
2 tablespoons butter
2 tablespoons flour
1 cup milk
1 cup grated Cheddar cheese
1/4 cup prepared horseradish
   mustard
Salt and pepper to taste
2 cups diced cooked chicken

1. Cook broccoli in 1 cup boiling water for 2 minutes, or until just tender. If using frozen broccoli, follow package directions, being careful not to overcook. Drain broccoli and set aside.
2. Melt butter in saucepan. Add flour and cook over medium heat, stirring constantly, for 30 seconds. Gradually add milk and bring to a boil, stirring constantly. Add cheese, horseradish mustard, salt, and pepper; stir over low heat until cheese melts. Remove from heat.
3. Preheat oven to 350 degrees.
4. Place chicken in bottom of medium-size casserole dish. Cover with broccoli, then pour sauce on top. Bake for 25 minutes, or until bubbly and thoroughly heated. Remove from oven, and serve.

Roll-Topped Turkey Casserole

Serves 8

1 tablespoon butter
2 cups cooked ham, cut into
   strips
2/3 cup milk
2 (10-ounce) cans condensed
   cream of celery soup
2 cups diced cooked turkey
1 (16-ounce) can pearl onions,
   drained
1 cup cooked peas
2 (8-ounce) packages
   refrigerated crescent rolls
1/2 cup shredded Cheddar
   cheese

1. Melt butter in frying pan. Add ham and saute until browned. Remove from pan and set aside.
2. Preheat oven to 400 degrees.
3. Mix milk and soup together. Add ham, turkey, onions, and peas to soup mixture, mixing well. Place in shallow, rectangular baking dish and bake for 20 minutes.
4. Separate rolls and lay flat. Sprinkle Cheddar cheese in center of each roll; roll up following package directions.
5. Remove casserole from oven and stir. Cover top of casserole with cheese-filled rolls. Bake for 15 to 20 minutes, or until rolls are browned. Remove from oven, and serve.

Turkey François

Serves 4

2 tablespoons butter
1/2 cup sliced onion
1 cup diced celery
2 1/2 tablespoons flour
1/2 teaspoon curry powder
1 chicken bouillon cube
1 1/2 cups milk
2 cups diced cooked turkey

1. Preheat oven to 350 degrees.
2. Melt butter in frying pan. Add onion and celery; saute until celery is just tender. Remove from heat.
3. Combine flour and curry powder in small bowl.
4. In saucepan, dissolve bouillon cube in milk; gradually add flour mixture. Cook over low heat, stirring constantly, until sauce thickens. Add onion, celery, and turkey.
5. Transfer turkey mixture to buttered casserole dish. Bake for 45 minutes. Serve immediately.

Blue Cheese and Chicken Filled Puffs

Serves 4

1/2 cup boiling water
1/4 cup butter
1/2 cup flour
2 eggs
1 cup diced cooked chicken
1/4 cup diced celery
2 tablespoons finely chopped
   green pepper
Salt and pepper to taste
2 teaspoons chopped onion
2 tablespoons mayonnaise
1/2 cup crumbled blue cheese

1. Preheat oven to 375 degrees.
2. Combine boiling water and butter in saucepan; stir until butter melts. Add flour and stir vigorously until batter forms a ball in center of pan. Remove from heat. Beat in eggs one at a time.
3. Place spoonfuls of batter on greased cookie sheet, heaping them up well in center. Bake for 25 to 35 minutes. Make small slit in each puff; cool on cake rack.
4. Combine chicken, celery, green pepper, salt, pepper, onion, mayonnaise, and blue cheese in bowl; mix well.
5. To serve, slice off tops of puffs. Fill each puff with chicken mixture. Replace tops.

MICROWAVE EXPRESS

Tarragon Chicken Breasts

Serves 6

1 cup chicken stock
1 cup apple juice
1 tablespoon chopped fresh tarragon
6 large boneless chicken breasts, skinned
1 teaspoon cornstarch
Apple slices for garnish
Parsley sprigs for garnish

1. Place chicken stock, apple juice, and tarragon in large casserole dish. Microwave on high for 3 minutes, or until mixture boils. Add chicken breasts, cover, and microwave on high for 5 to 6 minutes, turning once after 3 minutes. Remove chicken, cover, and keep warm.
2. Stir cornstarch into cooking liquid. Microwave on high for 1 to 1 1/2 minutes, stirring every 30 seconds.
3. Arrange chicken on 6 warmed dinner plates and spoon a small amount of sauce over each breast. Serve garnished with apple slices and parsley sprigs.

Tangy Chicken Casserole

Serves 4

3 pounds chicken pieces
1/4 cup flour, seasoned with salt and pepper
2 tablespoons safflower oil
1 cup mayonnaise
1 cup orange juice
Paprika to taste

1. Roll chicken pieces in flour seasoned with salt and pepper. Heat browning dish on full power for 4 minutes. Add oil and heat for 2 minutes longer. Add chicken pieces and microwave for 4 to 5 minutes, turning when chicken is golden brown on each side.
2. Combine mayonnaise and orange juice in shallow casserole dish. Add chicken, cover, and microwave on high for 15 minutes. Remove cover and turn chicken. Microwave, uncovered, for 15 minutes. Remove from oven, sprinkle with paprika, and serve.

Crumbed Chicken

Serves 4 to 6

1 1/4 cups cracker crumbs
1/2 teaspoon paprika
Salt and pepper to taste
1 egg, beaten
1 tablespoon milk
8 chicken drumsticks or mixed pieces

1. Mix cracker crumbs, paprika, and seasonings together on flat plate. Combine beaten egg and milk in shallow bowl. Dip chicken into egg mixture, then into crumb mixture. Press coating onto chicken pieces.
2. Arrange chicken pieces on round plate, making sure meatiest sections are toward outside of plate. Microwave, uncovered, on full power for 10 minutes. Turn chicken pieces halfway through cooking to ensure even cooking. Microwave on medium for 8 to 12 minutes longer, depending on thickness of pieces. Remove from microwave, and serve.

Honey-Glazed Chicken

Serves 6

Marinade

1/2 cup soy sauce
2 tablespoons finely chopped onion
2 cloves garlic, peeled and chopped
1 tablespoon oil
1/2 teaspoon freshly grated ginger

Chicken

1 (2 1/2- to 3-pound) chicken
1/4 cup honey
2 tablespoons soy sauce

1. To make marinade, combine soy sauce, onion, garlic, oil, and ginger. Place chicken in plastic bag and set in bowl. Pour marinade over chicken and close bag. Refrigerate for 4 hours, or overnight, turning chicken 2 or 3 times.
2. Drain chicken well; discard marinade. Fold wings under, and tie legs securely to tail. Place chicken, breast side up, in deep casserole dish. Microwave on full power, turning chicken every 6 minutes. Cook chicken for 10 to 12 minutes per pound.
3. Combine honey and soy sauce. Baste chicken frequently with this mixture during first 6 minutes of roasting time. Let chicken stand for 10 minutes, loosely covered, before carving. Place chicken slices on platter, and serve.

Turkey Duchesse

Serves 4

¹/₂ pound ground turkey
¹/₂ pound turkey sausage
1 onion chopped
1 tablespoon chopped parsley
1 (10¹/₂-ounce) can celery soup
S   and pepper to taste
2 hard-boiled eggs, sliced
4 potatoes, cooked and mashed
2 tomatoes, sliced
Parsley sprigs for garnish

1. Line loaf pan with wax or parchment paper. Combine turkey, sausage, onion, parsley, soup, and seasonings in large bowl. Pack half of mixture into loaf pan. Arrange hard-boiled eggs down length of pan, then cover with remaining mixture. Pack down firmly.
2. Cover with plastic wrap and cut 2 slits in plastic. Microwave on full power for 5 minutes; turn dish halfway and cook on high for 8 more minutes. Remove from oven and let stand for 5 minutes. Uncover and invert onto serving platter.
3. Cover top of loaf with piped rosettes of mashed potatoes. Press tomato slices onto sides of loaf. Microwave, uncovered, on full power for 2 minutes. Garnish with parsley sprigs, and serve.

Appled Chicken Breasts

Serves 4

4 boneless chicken breasts
2 tablespoons flour
Salt and pepper to taste
2 tablespoons butter
1 onion, chopped
1 cup apple cider
1 clove garlic, peeled and crushed
¹/₂ teaspoon fresh rosemary or ¹/₈ teaspoon dried rosemary
1 tablespoon Dijon mustard
1 Granny Smith apple, cored and sliced
Paprika

1. Place chicken breasts between 2 layers of wax paper and flatten slightly with mallet. Sprinkle chicken with flour and seasonings. Heat browning dish on full power for 4 minutes. Place butter in dish, add chicken, and microwave for 2 minutes on each side.
2. Transfer chicken to shallow casserole dish. Add onion to browning dish and toss in butter. Microwave for 1 minute. Stir in remaining flour. Add apple cider, garlic, rosemary, and mustard, stirring until combined. Pour mixture over chicken, cover, and microwave on full power for 8 minutes. Stir, then microwave on high for 10 minutes.
3. Add sliced apple to casserole dish and microwave on high for 2 minutes. Sprinkle with paprika before serving.

Chicken Broccoli Bake

Serves 4

3 pounds chicken pieces
¹/₄ cup flour
Salt and pepper to taste
3 tablespoons safflower oil
1 (10¹/₂-ounce) can cream of chicken soup
2 teaspoons turmeric
³/₄ cup milk
³/₄ cup light cream
1 pound fresh broccoli
3 tablespoons water
1 (14-ounce) can corn, drained
1 cup grated Cheddar cheese
1 tablespoon chopped parsley

1. Roll chicken pieces in flour seasoned with salt and pepper. Heat browning dish on full power for 5 minutes. Add oil and chicken to dish. Microwave on full power for 2 minutes on each side. Place lightly browned chicken pieces in shallow casserole dish.

2. Sprinkle remaining flour over chicken. Combine soup, turmeric, milk, and cream, and pour over chicken. Cover and microwave on high for 15 minutes.
3. Place broccoli and water in dish. Cover and microwave on full power for 6 minutes. Drain, then arrange broccoli in single layer in casserole dish. Add corn and ¹/₂ cup Cheddar cheese to chicken liquid; spoon mixture over broccoli and arrange chicken pieces on top of broccoli. Sprinkle remaining cheese on top. Cover and microwave on high for 10 minutes. Sprinkle with chopped parsley, and serve.

Glazed Chickens

Serves 6

2 (2-pound) broilers

Stuffing

4 slices bread, crumbed
¹/₂ cup chopped pecans
¹/₃ cup seedless raisins
Grated rind and juice of ¹/₂ orange
¹/₂ teaspoon chicken bouillon powder
3 tablespoons chopped onion
¹/₂ teaspoon chopped fresh sage
2 tablespoons butter, melted
Salt and pepper to taste

Glaze

¹/₂ cup apricot jam
2 tablespoons orange juice
2 tablespoons brown sugar

1. Rinse chickens and pat dry with paper towels. To make stuffing, combine all stuffing ingredients; stuff chickens with this mixture. Fold wings under and tie legs securely with string. Shield wing tips and ends of legs with foil and place chickens in casserole dish.
2. To make glaze, combine all ingredients in small bowl. Microwave on full power for 1¹/₂ to 2 minutes. Remove from oven and mix well.

3. Cover chickens and microwave on full power for 8 minutes. Remove foil and brush with glaze. Microwave, covered, for 8 minutes, brushing frequently with glaze. Remove from oven, coat evenly with glaze, then cover and microwave for 4 minutes more. Remove from oven and let stand 10 minutes. To serve, split chickens in half and serve with stuffing.

Savory Chicken Casserole

Serves 4

3 pounds chicken pieces
1/4 cup flour
Salt and pepper to taste
1/4 teaspoon paprika
1 tablespoon butter
1 onion, chopped
1/2 cup chopped celery
1 cup chicken stock
1/4 cup dry white wine
5 teaspoons tomato paste
1/2 cup sliced mushrooms

1. Roll chicken pieces in flour seasoned with salt, pepper, and paprika. Heat browning dish on full power for 4 minutes. Place butter in dish, add chicken, and microwave on full power for 5 minutes. Turn chicken halfway through cooking time. Transfer chicken to casserole dish.
2. Microwave onion and celery in browning dish for 2 minutes. Stir in stock, wine, and tomato paste. Add any remaining flour, whisking until well blended. Pour sauce over chicken. Cover and microwave on full power for 15 minutes. Add mushrooms, stirring well. Microwave on full power for 3 minutes, and serve.

Chicken with Barbecue Sauce

Serves 4

1 (3-pound) chicken, cut into serving pieces
1/2 cup ketchup
2 tablespoons chili sauce
1 teaspoon honey
1 teaspoon mustard
1 tablespoon Worcestershire sauce or meat sauce
1 clove garlic, peeled and finely chopped

1. Place chicken in 10-inch glass baking dish. Place breasts in center of dish. Combine ketchup, chili sauce, honey, mustard, Worcestershire or meat sauce, and garlic. Brush chicken with mixture. Microwave, uncovered, on roast setting for 30 minutes.
2. Turn chicken pieces over after 15 minutes. Brush with remaining barbecue sauce; rotate dish 1/4 of a turn. Remove chicken from microwave, and serve.

Chicken Royal

Serves 4 to 6

2 1/2 cups fresh bread crumbs
1 1/4 cups milk
1 large egg, beaten
2 medium-size mushrooms, chopped
1/4 pound ground veal
1/4 pound ground pork
1/2 teaspoon salt
1/4 teaspoon pepper
1 (4 1/2-pound) chicken
2 strips bacon
1 clove garlic, peeled and crushed
1 tablespoon oil
2 cups chicken bouillon
1 tablespoon cornstarch
2 tablespoons cold water

1 (8-ounce) can mushrooms, drained
1 (3-ounce) jar artichoke hearts, drained
1 large orange, cut into wedges

1. Put bread crumbs and milk in bowl. Cover and let stand for 30 minutes. Add egg, mushrooms, veal, and pork. Season well with salt and pepper. Mix to form firm stuffing.
2. Pat chicken dry with paper towels. Season inside with salt and pepper. Put bacon and garlic inside chicken; fill with stuffing mixture. Truss chicken and place, breast side down, on roasting rack or on an inverted saucer set in glass baking dish. Brush skin with oil.
3. Cook for 16 minutes on high. Turn chicken breast side up; rotate pan 1/4 of a turn. Cook on roast setting for 16 minutes more, basting frequently with 1 tablespoon oil or pan drippings. Transfer chicken to serving dish and let rest for 15 minutes before carving.
4. Strain off all but 2 tablespoons fat from roasting pan. Add chicken bouillon. Stir cornstarch with cold water to form paste; stir into pan juices. Bring to boil on high. Microwave for 2 minutes on high, stirring once after 1 minute.
5. In separate glass bowls, heat mushrooms and artichoke hearts in juice from containers. Cook for 2 minutes, or until warm. Drain. Place chicken on platter and garnish with artichoke hearts, mushrooms, and orange wedges.

Chicken Breasts with Lemon and White Vermouth

Serves 4

8 boneless chicken breasts, skinned
1/4 cup butter
4 scallions, finely chopped
Grated rind and juice of 1 lemon
1/2 teaspoon tarragon or marjoram
1/3 cup white vermouth
Salt and pepper to taste

Sauce

1/2 cup heavy whipping cream
1 tablespoon cornstarch
2 tablespoons cold water
Salt and pepper to taste
2 tablespoons finely chopped parsley

1. Arrange chicken breasts in 10-inch glass baking dish. Dot with butter and add all remaining ingredients except salt and pepper. Cover with wax paper. Cook on roast setting for 15 minutes.
2. After 7 minutes, rearrange chicken, placing center pieces at edge of dish. Rotate dish 1/4 of a turn. Season with salt and pepper immediately after chicken breasts are cooked.
3. Remove chicken from baking dish. Arrange on bed of steaming hot rice and keep hot while preparing sauce.
4. Pour cream into baking dish with cooking juices, and microwave on high for 1 minute. Mix cornstarch with cold water to form paste; add to baking dish, stirring until well mixed. Microwave for 1 minute. Stir well, season with salt and pepper, and pour sauce over chicken breasts. Garnish with parsley, and serve.

Curried Chicken

Serves 4

1 (2 1/2- to 3-pound) chicken, cut into serving pieces
1/4 teaspoon powdered ginger
1 teaspoon seasoned salt
3 tablespoon flour
2 tablespoon olive oil
1 medium onion, chopped
2 cloves garlic, peeled and minced
1 teaspoon curry powder
1 tablespoon peanut butter
Chicken broth
1/2 cup coconut milk
1/4 teaspoon ground cardamom
1/4 teaspoon ground cloves
1/2 teaspoon cinnamon
2 tablespoons lemon juice

1. Rub chicken with ginger and salt. Shake 1 tablespoon flour inside microwavable oven-roasting bag. Add chicken pieces; close bag tightly. Make several 1/2-inch slits in bag. Place in baking dish. Microwave on high for 15 to 18 minutes, or until chicken is cooked thoroughly. Let stand for 10 minutes. Drain juices from bag; reserve. Remove chicken from bag and arrange in casserole dish. Set aside.
2. Place oil in 1-quart casserole dish. Add onion and garlic, stirring well. Microwave on high for 2 minutes. Add curry powder, peanut butter and 2 tablespoons flour; mix well. Microwave on high for 1 minute.
3. Add enough chicken broth to reserved juices to make 1 1/2 cups liquid; combine with coconut milk and curry mixture. Stir well with wire whisk. Microwave on high for 3 minutes, stirring once each minute. Add remaining ingredients, mixing well. Pour sauce over chicken, cover, and microwave on high for 3 to 4 minutes, until hot. Remove from microwave, and serve.

Chicken with Rice

Serves 4

2 tablespoons butter
1 onion, finely chopped
3 stalks celery, chopped
2 egg yolks
1 (10 1/2-ounce) can cream of chicken soup
1/4 teaspoon marjoram
1/4 teaspoon thyme
1/2 teaspoon salt
2 cups cooked rice

1. Microwave butter in covered shallow baking dish on medium for 2 minutes, until melted. Add onion and celery to butter. Cover and microwave on high for 3 minutes. Stir.
2. Combine egg yolks and chicken soup; beat well. Stir mixture and seasonings into cooked vegetables. Cover and microwave on high for 1 minutes. Remove from oven; stir with whisk to distribute egg yolks evenly throughout sauce.
3. In separate dish, microwave chicken on high for 2 minutes. Add chicken to sauce. Cover and microwave on high for 3 minutes. Let stand, covered, for 5 minutes before serving.
4. Pile cooked rice onto platter. Cover with chicken, and serve.

Salami-Stuffed Chicken Legs

Serves 5

4 ounces salami, finely chopped
1 large onion, finely chopped
2 tablespoons parsley
10 chicken legs
1 cup flour
1/4 teaspoon pepper
1 teaspoon salt
2 eggs
1/4 cup milk
2 cups bread crumbs

1. Mix salami, onion, and parsley together in bowl. Gently loosen skin around chicken legs, starting at thick end of leg, being careful not to cut or tear skin. Carefully pack salami mixture evenly under skin of each leg.

2. Combine flour and seasonings; pour into shallow bowl. Beat eggs and milk together; pour into shallow bowl. Pour bread crumbs into shallow bowl.

3. Roll chicken in seasoned flour. Dip in eggs, then cover with bread crumbs. Brown legs on stovetop in hot oil. Drain on paper towels. Arrange on microwave roasting rack with bone side to center and flesh end out. Microwave on high for 10 minutes. Rearrange chicken on roasting rack by moving center legs to outside and moving outside legs to center. Microwave chicken on high for 5 minutes. Let stand 5 minutes. Check for doneness by inserting microwave thermometer into fleshy part of center leg, following instructions that come with thermometer. Microwave for 5 minutes longer if needed. Remove to platter, and serve.

Spatchcock Turkey

Serves 4

2 teaspoons poultry seasoning
1 teaspoon salt
2 turkey legs and thighs, cut at joint into serving pieces
2 lemons, thinly sliced
1/4 cup chutney
1 tablespoon ketchup
Juice of 1 lemon
1/4 cup soft brown sugar
4 fresh tomatoes, sliced
4 baked potatoes

1. Rub poultry seasoning and salt into turkey. Cover each with lemon slices. In small glass bowl or casserole,

combine chutney, ketchup, lemon juice, and sugar. Microwave on low for 1 or 2 minutes, until bubbling. Spoon over turkey and microwave, uncovered, on roast setting for 20 minutes.

2. Serve with tomato slices and baked potatoes.

Turkey Tourangelle

Serves 4

1/4 cup butter
1/2 cup finely chopped onions
1 cup sliced mushrooms
1 teaspoon salt
1/4 teaspoon white pepper
1/4 cup dry white wine
1 (10 1/2-ounce) can cream of mushroom soup
1/2 cup sour cream
2 cups sliced, cooked white turkey meat

1. Place butter in covered shallow glass baking dish; microwave on medium for 2 minutes to melt butter. Add onions; microwave on high for 2 minutes. Stir. Add mushrooms and seasonings. Cover and microwave on high for 3 minutes.

2. Add wine to mushroom soup; beat until well mixed. Add to sauteed vegetables; microwave, covered, on high for 4 minutes. Add sour cream. Gently stir to mix sauce ingredients. Remove from microwave.

3. Place turkey on shallow tray; microwave on high for 3 to 4 minutes, or until heated thoroughly. Arrange turkey on serving platter; cover with sauce, and serve.

Chicken Chasseur

Serves 4

1 (3-pound) chicken, cut into serving pieces
1/4 cup flour, seasoned with salt, pepper, and paprika
1 tablespoon vegetable oil
1 tablespoon butter
8 link sausages
1 onion, chopped
1/2 cup chopped celery
1 cup chicken stock
1/4 cup dry white wine
5 teaspoons tomato paste
Bouquet Garni (3 sprigs parsley or chervil, 1/2 bay leaf, and 2 sprigs thyme, tied in a bunch)
4 ounces mushrooms, sliced

1. Roll chicken pieces in seasoned flour. Heat browning dish on high for 4 minutes. Place oil and butter in dish, add chicken, and microwave on high for 5 minutes. Turn chicken halfway through cooking time. Transfer chicken to casserole dish.

2. Arrange sausages in browning dish. Microwave on high for 4 minutes, turning after 2 minutes. Remove sausages and set aside.

3. Microwave onion and celery in browning dish for 2 minutes. Add any remaining flour, stirring until well blended. Then add chicken stock, wine, and tomato paste, stirring well. Pour over chicken and add bouquet garni. Cover and microwave on high for 15 minutes. Add mushrooms and sausages, stirring well. Microwave on high for 3 minutes. Remove bouquet garni, and serve.

Chicken and Mushroom Crêpes

Serves 6

Crepes

1 cup flour
¼ teaspoon salt
1¼ cups milk
¼ cup water
3 eggs
2 tablespoons butter, melted
Vegetable oil

Filling

¼ cup butter or margarine
½ pound fresh mushrooms, sliced
½ small onion, finely chopped
¼ cup flour
2 cups milk
2 chicken bouillon cubes
Pepper to taste
1 teaspoon tarragon
½ cup sour cream
3 tablespoons dry sherry
2 cups diced cooked chicken
2 tablespoons finely chopped parsley

1. To make batter, place flour, salt, eggs, milk, and water in blender or food processor; blend for 30 seconds. Add butter and blend for a few seconds more. The batter should be the consistency of milk. Refrigerate batter for 1 or 2 hours before cooking.
2. Brush pan with thin layer of oil; heat over medium heat until slight haze forms. Add about 2 tablespoons batter to pan, enough to thinly cover pan bottom; tilt pan so that batter is spread evenly. Cook over medium heat until crepe is lightly brown underneath and shakes loose from bottom of pan. Turn crepe over with spatula and cook for about 30 seconds more, or until crepe is lightly browned. Lift out of pan and place on sheet of waxed paper until ready to use.
3. To make filling, place butter in a deep casserole dish and microwave on high for 45 seconds. Add mushrooms and onion, stirring until coated with butter. Microwave, covered, for 2 to 2½ minutes.

4. Blend in flour and microwave for 30 seconds. Stir, then microwave for 45 more seconds. Stir again, then gradually stir in milk. Add bouillon cubes, pepper, and tarragon. Cover and microwave on high for 3 minutes, stirring after each minute. Stir in sour cream and sherry. Set aside 1 cup of sauce.
5. Add chicken and 1 tablespoon chopped parsley to remaining sauce, mixing well. Spoon small amount of chicken mixture onto each crepe. Roll crepes up and arrange in 2 casserole dishes. Spoon remaining sauce over crepes, cover, and microwave each dish on medium for 5 to 6 minutes, until heated thoroughly. Sprinkle with remaining parsley, and serve.

Boned Stuffed Chicken

Serves 6

2 tablespoons vegetable oil
1 small onion, chopped
1 chicken liver, chopped
½ pound bulk sausage
1 cup bread crumbs
2 tablespoons chopped parsley
1 (16-ounce) can apricots, drained and chopped
¼ cup seedless raisins, chopped
1 (3½- to 5-pound) chicken, boned
Salt and pepper to taste

Stock

4 cups boiling water
1 onion, cut into pieces
1 carrot, cut into pieces
1 stalk celery, cut into pieces
Salt to taste

1 teaspoon chicken bouillon powder
3 black peppercorns
1 bay leaf

1. Pour oil into large bowl and microwave on high for 2 minutes. Add onion and chicken liver, tossing until coated with oil. Microwave on high for 2 to 3 minutes. Add sausage, bread crumbs, parsley, apricots, and raisins; mix well.
2. Lay boned chicken flat and season with salt and pepper. Place stuffing in center and roll up chicken. Sew up with string. Cover with cheesecloth and tie ends with string.
3. Combine all stock ingredients in large, deep casserole dish. Microwave on high for 5 minutes. Carefully add chicken roll, cover, and microwave on high for 25 minutes. Remove chicken roll from stock and cool. Remove cheesecloth and thinly slice chicken. Arrange chicken slices on platter, and serve.

Caramel Duck

Serves 4

1 (4-pound) duck
Salt and pepper to taste
1 onion
1 apple, peeled, cored, and quartered
3 tablespoons butter
¼ teaspoon ginger
3 tablespoons honey
3 tablespoons brown sugar
3 tablespoons orange liqueur
2 oranges

Sauce

2 teaspoons cornstarch
2 teaspoons gravy powder
⅔ cup stock made from duck giblets or chicken stock
½ cup orange juice
1 tablespoon orange liqueur

1. Season duck with salt and pepper. Place onion and apple in cavity. Tie duck into shape with string and shield wings with small strips of foil. Secure neck skin with wooden toothpick. Place duck, breast side down, on

roasting rack or in cooking bag. Allow 14 to 15 minutes cooking time per pound. Microwave on high for 10 minutes. Drain off excess fat.

2. Combine 1 tablespoon butter and ginger; spread mixture over breast and thighs. Return duck to rack, breast side down. Microwave on high for half the remaining cooking time. Drain off excess fat and turn duck over. Microwave on high for 5 minutes.

3. Combine honey, brown sugar, and orange liqueur. Spread over duck and microwave on high for remaining time, basting with glaze once or twice. Remove duck from microwave; discard string and toothpick. Let duck stand for 10 to 15 minutes. Strain cooking liquid and measure out ½ cup; set aside to use for sauce.

4. Peel oranges and slice into ¼-inch slices. Microwave 2 tablespoons butter in shallow casserole dish on high for 1 minute. Add orange slices, turn slices over immediately, and microwave on high for 2 to 3 minutes. Remove from oven and keep warm.

5. To make sauce, combine cornstarch, gravy powder, stock, and orange juice in bowl. Add reserved cooking liquid and liqueur, stirring until well mixed. Microwave on high for 5 minutes, stirring every minute.

6. To serve, arrange orange slices along duck breast, and spoon small amount of sauce on top. Serve remaining sauce separately.

Chicken Strata

Serves 6

8 slices bread
Butter, to spread
2 cups diced cooked chicken
1 small onion, finely chopped
1 stalk celery, finely chopped
½ green pepper, seeded and chopped
¾ cup mayonnaise
Salt and pepper to taste
½ teaspoon tarragon
¼ teaspoon grated fresh ginger or ⅛ teaspoon powdered ginger

2 medium eggs, lightly beaten
1½ cups milk
1 (10½-ounce) can mushroom soup
1 cup grated sharp Cheddar cheese

1. Lightly butter 3 slices of bread, cut into ½-inch cubes, and set aside. Cut remaining bread into ½-inch cubes as well. Place half of unbuttered bread cubes in deep, lightly greased, 9-inch casserole dish.

2. Combine chicken, onion, celery, green pepper, mayonnaise, salt, pepper, tarragon, and ginger; spread over bread cubes. Top with remaining unbuttered bread cubes. Beat eggs and milk together and pour over bread. Cover and refrigerate for at least 1 hour, or up to 12 hours.

3. Spread soup on top of chicken mixture; cover with buttered bread cubes. Cover and microwave on high for 16 to 18 minutes. Uncover, sprinkle with cheese, and microwave on high for 3 to 4 minutes, until cheese melts. Remove from oven and let stand for 8 minutes, then serve.

Crispy Crumbed Chicken

Serves 4

1 cup crushed barbecue potato chips
1 tablespoon poppy seeds
1 (3-pound) chicken, cut into serving pieces
3 tablespoons butter, melted

1. Combine potato chips and poppy seeds on plate. Dip chicken pieces into melted butter, then coat with potato chip mixture. Press coating onto chicken pieces.

2. Arrange chicken pieces on bacon rack or round plate, making sure meatiest sections are toward the outside. Microwave, uncovered, on high for 10 minutes. Turn chicken pieces to ensure even cooking. Microwave on medium for 8 to 12 minutes longer, depending on thickness of pieces. Remove from heat, and serve.

Chicken Liver Stroganoff

Serves 4 to 6

2 tablespoons cornstarch
2 cups milk
1 chicken bouillon cube
¼ teaspoon salt
⅛ teaspoon pepper
⅛ teaspoon nutmeg
2 tablespoons butter
2 tablespoons vegetable oil
2 onions, sliced
1 pound chicken livers, halved
1 tablespoon vinegar
½ cup sour cream
Paprika to taste
Parsley sprigs for garnish

1. Mix cornstarch with 1 cup milk and set aside. Add bouillon cube to remaining milk and microwave on high for 2 to 3 minutes, stirring occasionally. Add salt, pepper, nutmeg, and butter, stirring until butter has melted. Stir in cornstarch mixture, mixing well. Microwave on high for 3 to 4 minutes, stirring every minute, until mixture thickens. Remove from microwave.

2. Place 1 tablespoon oil in casserole dish; add sliced onions and microwave on high for 5 minutes, stirring twice. Add onions to sauce and keep warm.

3. Pour remaining oil into casserole dish and add chicken livers. Microwave on high for 3 minutes, stirring after each minute. Add vinegar to chicken livers, stir well, and microwave for 3 minutes longer. Remove from heat, pour sauce over livers, and toss to coat. Finally, stir in sour cream; do not reheat. Garnish with paprika and parsley, and serve.

INDEX